The Best American
Spiritual Writing 2004

The Best American Spiritual Writing 2004

EDITED BY *Philip Zaleski*

INTRODUCTION BY *Jack Miles*

HOUGHTON MIFFLIN COMPANY
BOSTON • NEW YORK   2004

ISSN is available.
ISBN 0-618-44302-9
ISBN 0-618-44303-7 (pbk.)

Printed in the United States of America

VB 10 9 8 7 6 5 4 3 2 1

"A Texas Childhood" by Rick Bass. First published in *Doubletake,* Spring 2003. Copyright © 2003 by Rick Bass. Reprinted by permission of the author.

"Parable" by Dan Bellm. First published in *Image,* Spring 2003. Copyright © 2003 by Dan Bellm. Reprinted by permission of the author.

"Hidden City" by Scott Cairns. First published in *Spiritus,* Fall 2003. Copyright © 2003 by Scott Cairns. Reprinted by permission of the author.

"Miss Ivory Broom" by Robin Cody. First published in *Portland Magazine,* Spring 2003. Copyright © 2003 by Robin Cody. Reprinted by permission of the author.

"Here and Now We Are Walking Together" by Robert Coles. First published in *Notre Dame Magazine,* Summer 2003. Copyright © 2003 by Robert Coles. Reprinted by permission of the author.

"Parable of the Moth" by Robert Cording. First published in *Image,* Summer 2003. Copyright © 2003 by Robert Cording. Reprinted by permission of the author.

"The Water Will Hold You" by Lindsey Crittenden. First published in *Image,* Winter 2003. Copyright © 2003 by Lindsey Crittenden. Reprinted by permission of the author.

"Fire to Fire" by Mark Doty. First published in *Shenandoah,* Fall 2003. Copyright © 2003 by Mark Doty. Reprinted by permission of Burnes & Clegg.

"Earth Music" by David James Duncan. First published in *Portland Magazine,* Fall 2003. Copyright © 2003 by David James Duncan. Reprinted by permission of the author.

"The Green-Eyed Monster" by Joseph Epstein. First published in the *Washington*

Contents

Contents

ix

Foreword

LATELY I HAVE been reading from the Book of Proverbs, the Bible's capacious collection of pithy sayings to guide one safely through the perils of life. Gathering maxims — or at least repeating them to others — can be a risky occupation, as Dr. Thomas Fuller (1654–1734), author of *Gnomologia: Adages and Proverbs* (1732), reminds us: "Constant popping off of proverbs," he observed, "will make thee a byword thyself." However, the Bible's apothegms, mostly attributed to Solomon but more probably the fruit of many minds, shine with wisdom and bear rereading and repeating. Crack them open and one finds good practical advice ("He who corrects a scoffer gets himself abuse"), humor ("As a door turns on its hinges, so does a sluggard on his bed"), profundity ("Hatred stirs up strife, but love covers all offenses"), and even the occasional left hook ("A gracious woman gets honor, and violent men get riches"). But this was the saying that stopped me in my tracks: *"Death and life are in the power of the tongue."*

I cannot think of a better expression of the immense potency of words. Words can create, quicken, heal; words can destroy, maim, kill. Spells, charms, prayers, damnations, curses, salutations, manifestoes, laudations, admonitions, invitations, encouragements, prophecies: words of power haunt us from birth to death. Can we wonder at Jesus' warning that "on the day of judgment men will render account for every careless word they utter; for by your words you will be justified, and by your words you will be condemned"? If this be true of casual speech, how much truer of the written text, whose influence can last millennia. The perception is not exclusively biblical. Emily Dickinson writes of a man who consumed "the precious Words" and then "danced along the dingy Days," and Wittgenstein more expansively suggests that "if we spoke a different language, we would perceive a somewhat different world." "Words," Kipling says, "are the most powerful drug used by mankind."

This power of tongue and pen to dispense life or death descends with special force upon the spiritual writer, for he or she deals in the most important things of life. The twenty-four essays and ten poems in this collection address the eternal oppositions of good and evil, virtue and vice, creation and destruction; the sorrows and exaltations of heart, mind, and soul; the ceaseless quest for God. Writers who trade in subjects like these bear a grave responsibility, for every word they write leaves its mark upon their soul and upon the souls of all who read their work. Their words may become sacraments, visible signs of an invisible grace, or they may turn to poison and ashes, signifying the abyss — or nothing at all. The following, from the London *Sunday Express* of January 25, 1959, exemplifies the saving force of words. It describes the actions of three soldiers, marooned on the Greenland ice cap during World War II, who sought solace through prayer:

> They knelt in the sunshine, praying continually. There was only one prayer they all knew, and they chanted it together unceasingly, as children recite a memorized lesson, uncomprehendingly. "Our Father, which art in heaven . . ." they chanted right through to the end, and then straightway back to the beginning again, hundreds of times, as though rescue depended absolutely on their maintaining an unbroken stream of prayer.

This ceaseless devotion buoyed their spirits, steeled their wills, and seemed to have played a key role in their ability to survive until help arrived. Contrast this with the avalanche of violence, hatred, and terror that assaults us daily through television, movies, newspapers, magazines, and the bestseller lists. What effect does this poisonous lectionary have upon our faculties of perception and cognition, and in turn upon our ability to meet the world with faith, hope, and charity? Words have consequences; writing is a moral act. To recognize this pays a triple dividend, for it inoculates us against the three deadly literary vices of pandering to popular taste, creative laziness, and didacticism. The last item may surprise those who fear that any talk of moral writing will unleash an army of bluenoses ready to censor at will or of apparatchiks who will demand a political subtext to every sentence. But such worries stem from misunderstanding the obligations placed upon us by the moral nature of the craft. To write ugly prose, or to cripple one's language to meet the standards of the day, or to warp one's creation into a political placard — all this is to write immorally. The task of the spiritual writer is to uphold truth and beauty at whatever cost, in whatever way his art demands.

Words save or damn. This means that the work of the spiritual writer must inevitably encompass the spiritual transformation (or *metanoia,* in the very helpful biblical term) of himself, others, and the world. This, too, needn't carry fearsome connotations of Mrs. Grundy, much less Torquemada. A better model might be Dickens, whose *A Christmas Carol* presents with consummate artistry the archetype of spiritual rebirth, or even Kenneth Grahame, whose chapter "The Piper at the Gates of Dawn" from *The Wind in the Willows* presents an unforgettable portrait of the created world, epitomized in the persons of Mole and Rat, submitting to the fearsome glory of the divine in the person of the Great God Pan. One finds the same basic pattern, in an endless variety of shading and coloration, reappearing throughout the classics of spiritual literature — works as disparate as Augustine's *Confessions,* Rumi's *Mathnawi,* or the *Bhagavad-Gita.* All of these works speak of self-transformation, of the indefatigable quest to find and sustain a harmony between God's divine speech — revealed in scripture, the natural world, and the order of events that fill our lives — and our own mortal speech of mouth, heart, and soul. That quest is not always an easy, long walk across smooth green fields; there will be ditches and barricades, mountains and crevasses, as often as not of our own making, that we will need to climb or circumnavigate or blunder through. We needn't hesitate for fear of failure, however. To make the attempt is already to succeed, for no effort made under the sign of heaven is in vain. Here we have not only the world's religious scriptures but the laws of the art of writing as assurance. Good spiritual literature — and, I would suggest, all good literature — finds its voice in struggle, in the interlocked battles that each of us fights between truth and illusion, hope and despair, love of other and love of self. Even those writers most closely associated with decadence or depravity — for example, Baudelaire or Huysmans — succeed insofar as they chronicle the conflict between good and evil; de Sade, who felt no such struggle, is a very boring writer.

I am often asked by readers of this annual series what makes a good spiritual writer. If the interlocutor has personal aspirations in mind, he or she often frames it thus: how can I become a good spiritual writer? The answer, as the reflections above will suggest, call for revolution on two fronts. One must strive constantly against mediocrity in one's work, aiming always for lucidity of thought and beauty of expression; so much might be recommended to any writer in any genre. In addition, however, one must contend against mediocrity in one's self, working always to become more, better, truer, clearer, more open than one was, to "increase and abound in love to one another," in Paul's memorable formulation. This two-fold front sets spiritual writers apart from all other literary practitioners. Novelists, poets, essayists outside the guild need not take their spiritual temperature every time they raise their pens; but with the spiritual writer it is different. The additional burden this imposes, while palpable, may be less than supposed. The relationship of art to character is enormously complex and clearly resists reduction to a convenient formula, but one senses the possibility of symbiosis between the two. In some mysterious way, as the classics of spiritual writing repeatedly testify, art can be part of inner work, and this work will imprint itself upon one's art. This process can be seen, for example, in the *Confessions,* where Augustine's prose becomes a form of prayer, a way of worship, a path towards sanctity. What spiritual writer does not long for a similar consummation, the creation of literature worthy not only of his high artistic calling but of his stature as a creature created in the image and likeness of God?

Many people helped in the production of this volume. My thanks to Anton Mueller, Erica Avery, and the entire team at Houghton Mifflin; to Kim Witherspoon, David Forrer, and all at Witherspoon Associates; to Jack Miles; to everyone who contributed in ways large and small; and, of course, to my beloved Carol, John, and Andy.

PHILIP ZALESKI

Introduction

"Who is the greatest in the kingdom of heaven?" And calling to him a child, he put him in the midst of them, and said, "Truly I say to you, unless you turn and become like children, you will never enter the kingdom of heaven. Whoever humbles himself like this child, he is the greatest in the kingdom of heaven."

— Matthew 18:2–4

BY NOW the word *spirituality* ought not embarrass me, but like the word *mommy*, it still does. *Mommy* has its place and, especially, its time; but we cringe a bit, don't we, when we hear an adult unselfconsciously say, "Mommy phoned this morning." The word is out of place, or past its time. Adults don't talk that way. Or shouldn't.

Or so we think. Perhaps adults sufficiently serene in their adulthood do not blush at *mommy*. But because *spirituality* is a word that I first heard in a little world that shaped me as powerfully as a second family, a world that I left behind only after a struggle, this word carries for me some of the same baggage as *mommy*. The contributions to this year's *Best Spiritual Writing* are varied, authentic, engaging, and repeatedly surprising, yet for me, I confess, they summon up the memory of a time when spirituality and adulthood seemed antithetical.

I was introduced to spirituality at the age of fourteen as a brother in the devotional fraternity called the *sodality* (from the Latin *sodalis*, companion) that was a part of life at all Jesuit secondary schools. Starting in freshman year, we *sodalists* were introduced to the school of spirituality called *Ignatian* — techniques of prayer and meditation developed by Ignatius Loyola, the founder of the Society of Jesus (the Jesuits). Back in 1956, our initiation into *men-*

tal prayer, as the beginner's exercise in Ignatian spirituality was then called, began in much the same way an introduction to Pilates training might now — that is, in a group and under the direction of a trainer.

The first step, once we had gathered in the chapel at the appointed hour, was the recitation of one of the Roman Catholic prayers that we all knew by heart. This in itself created a mild sense of fraternity, relocated us, and brought us to a kind of preliminary focus. The second step was a minute or two of silence. The third step was the instruction "Place yourself in the presence of God," about which more below. The fourth step was another interlude of silence — still brief, but a little longer than the first one. The fifth step was the leader's presentation in a five-minute talk of a subject suitable for meditation. A typical subject would be Christ's prayer during his agony in the Garden of Gethsemane: "Father, if it be possible, let this cup pass from me, but not my will but thine be done." The priest — the leader was always a priest on the faculty of the school — might evoke darkness, the chill of the night, the danger, and so forth, and direct our attention to Christ's honesty and his courage. Then would begin the sixth step in the exercise, the central period of silence or mental prayer proper. Rather than asking God for something, mental prayer was simply thinking about something in the presence of God and awaiting what might ensue within the mind. After the lapse of nearly fifty years, I cannot recall the exit formula — there was one — that was spoken after perhaps fifteen minutes to signal the end of the central exercise. Coming out of mental prayer felt a bit like awakening from hypnosis. Returned to ourselves, we recited a concluding prayer in unison and tramped out of the chapel for the rest of the school day.

What transpires in the minds of fourteen-year-old boys instructed to place themselves in the presence of God? Twenty years later, a friend's son told us of a study allegedly proving that sixteen-year-olds experience a sex-related thought every thirty seconds. My friend was surprised. I was not. And to me, the chapel at St. Ignatius High School was, in memory, the place where I seemed most aware of the intervals. Yet I testify that the command "Place yourself in the presence of God" produced a shift of consciousness that the succession of tumescence and detumescence did not undermine.

Did we even believe in God? At one point in John Updike's first novel, *The Centaur,* an inspired high school teacher is preaching — no other verb will quite do — the grand sweep of evolution from the Big Bang to the rise of human consciousness. The novelist directs our attention to a boy in a back seat whose gross sex-preoccupation seems to undercut the nobility of the lecture. But behind the character in the novel, there broods the novelist himself. Updike is a Christian inspired in spite of himself by this godless vision. Were he an atheist, he would be inspired in spite of himself by the Christian vision. The text of belief and unbelief seems so often to read like a giant palindrome.

Rather than by the Christian vision per se, I myself was entranced by the *esprit de corps* of the Jesuit order. Over a ten-year period beginning with my eighteenth year, the Jesuits turned me into an intellectual of sorts, but they first turned me into a fellow Jesuit through two full years of an intense initiation into Ignatian spirituality. This was an experience that, as I would later conclude, reversed my normal movement from adolescence to adulthood and turned me, powerfully albeit temporarily, from an adolescent back into a child. And though I was, to say the least, confused and embarrassed by the reversal, I return to it in memory with a kind of longing.

A month after entering the order, I was led through the Spiritual Exercises of St. Ignatius — a month of silence interrupted by only a few hours of conversation every six or seven days. For the remainder of that two-year novitiate, I rose at five every morning and meditated in silence for an hour at a desk provided with a kneeler before walking silently to the chapel for Mass and then from the chapel to the refectory for a silent breakfast. My life included no television, no radio, no newspapers or magazines, and no reading material other than books on, what else, spirituality. All my needs — food, shelter, clothing, health care, recreation, and companionship — were provided for. In all those regards, I had, as never since early childhood, literally nothing to worry about; and for long minutes — in the chapel, for example, after the morning's meditation had ended but before daily Mass began — nothing to think about, either. And I began to like it that way. Against the predictions of some, I began to like having nothing on my mind.

Besides practicing Ignatian meditation every morning, a novice attended more general lectures on Christian spirituality. One learned about the history of monasticism and about the various schools of spirituality. One read classics in the related literature. One learned of the *via purgativa,* the *via contemplativa,* and, for the sainted few, the *via unitiva.* As beginners, we were on the *via purgativa.* Purgative asceticism — fasting, mild (and closely controlled) self-flagellation, and the use of the "discipline," a kind of barbed bracelet worn for an hour or two around the thigh — would help us get started.

Did it take? It is easy to answer that it did not. By divers paths, most of those who started out with me to become Jesuits are now ex-Jesuits. But, yes, something did take, though not in the way I once thought it did. Novitiate life, often silent and solemn, was not always so; and this matters more in retrospect than it did at the time. A Jesuit of the generation before mine entitled his memoir of Jesuit training *I'll Die Laughing.* I have never, before or since, laughed with such abandon as I did during those two years. Nor have I ever lived so physical a life, a life of sports played to such joyous exhaustion. Never before or since have I lived a life in which so many hours were spent exuberantly out-of-doors or in which I seemed to feel the passing of the seasons in every pore of my skin.

As for sex, though I know now that others have other tales to tell, my experience during those first two years consisted entirely in noctural emissions: never a dalliance with another boy, never an act of masturbation. We were given three rules to follow: *tactus* (Latin for "touch"), the rule forbidding us to touch one another (tagging in tag football or collisions in basketball or handball were exceptions to the rule); "particular friendship," a rule that, in effect, meant that we were to strive to treat all the brethren with equal affection; and "custody of the eyes" — that is, no "meaningful" gazing. These three rules, which at my novitiate seemed to be strictly observed, preserved chastity pretty effectively. But in effect they made us act as if we had yet to enter puberty; and in saying this, I return to the troubling question with which I began. Must one become a child to enter the kingdom of heaven?

At Harvard in the turmoil of the late 1960s, still a Jesuit but now a Harvard graduate student as well, I awoke one morning to an oddly frightening thought: I could not recall when I had last had a wet dream. *Why should this matter?* I asked myself. After all, I had taken a vow of celibacy. The answer that came — not instantaneously but quickly enough — was that I had not authentically renounced sex but only, somehow, indefinitely postponed it. When vowing celibacy, I had unconsciously made (to use a phrase from Jesuit casuistry) a mental reservation. But I had pronounced my vows all of eight years earlier. Time was fleeting! Though I was only twenty-seven, the physical change I had noticed was enough to send a simple but chilling message: I would not be forever young. And from that morning on, something began to unravel.

Ignatius Loyola built his spiritual exercises around the transformation that he had brought about in himself while recovering from a crippling war injury. But at the time of this transformation, the charismatic Basque had behind him years of life as a courtier and as a soldier. He had fathered a child. A novice in the spiritual life, he was anything but a sexual novice. But could the regimen that turned this sexually experienced if not, in fact, somewhat debauched courtier into a monk be imposed on virginal Irish-American boys to the same transformative effect? What was there to transform?

In the 1960s, younger American Jesuits had already begun to object that traditional Jesuit training infantilized them. But for the sexual sharpening of that point and its linkage to Ignatius himself, I am indebted not to them but to a Jewish classmate at Harvard. Jeremy (as I will call him) was one of surprisingly few Jews who brought no rabbinical training and no Jewish religious commitment with them into Harvard's Hebrew Bible program. His path to the Tanakh had led not from any yeshiva but rather from an undergraduate love affair with Israeli Hebrew as a rapidly evolving literary language. Jeremy read the dense Hebrew prose of S. Y. Agnon for pleasure and, to universal amazement, without a dictionary. His prickly manner with the religious Jews in our classes presaged a battle that he would join only later, but it is always easier to see another's humpback. When it came to Catholicism, Jeremy had an unforced, intuitive, sympathetic, and in the end quite correct understanding of what was eating at his Jesuit classmates.

Jeremy was a good friend, and I remember him fondly. All the same, I blushed hot when he made his historical/sociological observation. He was gentle, he was wry, but I was mortified anyway.

One way to state the human condition, I submit, is to assert that for our species meaningless sex is impossible. However *mere* we would like mere sex to be, some sort of meaning always crowds in on it. Sex can represent strength, youth, beauty, health, love, safety, consolation, wealth, power, transcendence, oblivion, escape — a list that any reader of this sentence can lengthen. For me, at that time in my life, it represented adulthood. I could not begin to be an adult, I thought, until I ceased to be a virgin. It was sexual experience that separated the men from the boys, and I was still, in a painfully unbecoming sense of the phrase, just one of the boys.

As this *transitus* got under way, the Society of Jesus and everything I had learned about spirituality in my specifically Jesuit training came to seem part of an embarrassingly prolonged boyhood. It mattered not a little that in the 1960s the word *spirituality*, ubiquitous in Roman Catholic piety, was still rare in Protestant, Jewish, and secular discourse. The difference of dialect mattered because at just this time, in the wake of the Second Vatican Council and of the election of John F. Kennedy, American Catholics as a population were emerging self-consciously and awkwardly from their socioreligious ghetto and looking to take their natural place in the larger American society. To use the word *spirituality* was, for me, to ring the leper's bell: Catholic! Catholic! Worse, it was to hint at an appalling defect of masculinity: spirituality as the chaste seminarian's substitute for physicality. I felt like Hester Prynne wearing a V for Virgin instead of an A for Adulteress.

When I wrote my Jesuit superior in Chicago (though studying at Harvard, I belonged to the Chicago "province" of the order), he wrote back asking if I had discussed with my spiritual director a request for dismissal from the Society. (A Jesuit who wanted to depart on good terms did not just quit or walk out; he requested dismissal.) The man's question was perfectly honorable and reasonable within the assumptions of the order, and I recognized it as such. Yet *spiritual director* prompted the same sort of wince that *spirituality* prompted. What would people think — the people I wanted to meet, the people I wanted to think me one of them — if they knew I had something called a spiritual director? At some emotional level, it was as if a young man, planning to go abroad, were to notify his father tersely of his intentions and hear back solicitously, "But have you talked this over with Mommy?"

Yet consultation with a spiritual director was a step that I felt con-science-bound to take. If this was to be a divorce, and that seemed pretty likely, I wanted it to be an amicable divorce. Giving spiritual direction a chance constituted good faith in the secular sense of the phrase. To my good fortune, I found my way to a brilliant and rather worldly Jesuit philosopher, then a scholar in residence at a posh psychiatric clinic in the Berkshires. An afternoon with him, as the snow deepened outside, effectively became my exit interview from the order. In memory, the soundtrack for the long drive back to Boston is James Taylor's "Sweet Baby James," a song mysteriously about adulthood and rock-a-bye infancy, not to speak of the Berkshires, Boston, snowy December, and an unfinished journey to an unknown destination.

Adulthood is a meaning that sexual experience can bear at most only briefly and once. As a transition to adulthood, losing one's vir-ginity is rather like disembarking from a ship. Once one is ashore, even if one is the last to disembark, one is ashore for good. The thing is done. But in my case, as it happens, other meanings fol-lowed on apace.

Not long after leaving the order and the church as well, I began to read a good deal about Buddhist meditation. I attended a num-ber of lectures and began to meditate regularly. I found appealing, even consoling, the doctrine of *anatta*, according to which the self is an illusion, a transitory event "co-dependently originated" from multiple starting points. I found plausible the claim that the illu-sion of self is preserved only in normal consciousness, wherein arises normal desire, the origin of all pain, and that liberation is accomplished by "the slaying of the mind," vividly pictured as a hyperactive monkey hopping from branch to branch. Unlike Jes-uit meditation, Buddhist meditation is not an attempt to think seriously and at length *about* something such as Jesus' agony in Gethsemane but rather an attempt to kill the monkey — to halt ordinary thinking altogether and subside into a protracted pre-cognitional or extra-cognitional state. The Buddhist-inspired exer-cises that I undertook at this time produced an effect that seemed different from but experientially just as real as the more familiar Je-suit effect of placing myself in the presence of God. But what I found most arresting was the fact that the brief periods (only some minutes in duration) during which I seemed to achieve what was referred to as mindfulness resembled nothing so much as the sense of mental emptiness that I had by then experienced during peak moments in sexual intercourse.

It was only years later that I learned of vajrayana Buddhism and the cosmology behind ego-obliterating tantric sex. The Los Angeles County Museum of Art is home to the Heeramoneck collection of Tibetan art, including a stunning array of esoteric mandalas portraying ecstatic divine copulation in a way that is intended to erase not just the distinction between gods and men but also that between self and world and, ultimately, between order and chaos. Had I happened into such an experience of ego-erasure at the time when I surrendered within the same brief period my virginity and the Jesuit cosmos that had engulfed me from puberty on? I wondered: perhaps so. But by the time the idea occurred to me, I had turned the page in a dozen ways. I can only say that during my earlier "Buddhist period," though I was willing to take it on faith that true enlightenment is only arduously achieved, I could not deny a certain sense of *déja vu* when taking instruction. If, to quote a well-known Buddhist saying, the Buddha at the moment of enlightenment was like a deer in the deer park, if that state of mind — a state of animal rather than human consciousness — is the goal of Buddhist meditation, then Buddhism may be respectfully and uninvidiously characterized as an attempt to exit the normal adult spiritual condition. But this seemed an exit that I had by then experienced, however fleetingly, in two quite different settings.

Or so I thought. We give human children little stuffed animals to play with because, in a way, children *are* little animals. Their consciousness has not yet matured to the adult human state. Their little minds are not yet jumping from branch to branch with adult human agility. Buddhism has always seemed to me an attempt not merely to return to a childlike state of consciousness — call it the stuffed-animal state — but boldly to progress or descend past that state to something even more devoid of human ideation. I honor that effort, and yet I would add that descending only as far as the stuffed-animal state takes some doing; and this is the experience that I seem to recall in the luminosity of my first Jesuit years.

I begin with the observation that though we were not mistaken as Jesuits in our late twenties to object that our training had juvenilized us, juvenilization has more than one meaning. Yes, we had been excused from adult responsibility in a way that left us superficially and temporarily ill equipped to assume such responsibility later. But that same deprivation — joined during a period of two full years with strict sexual abstinence and with a deprivation from all else that might have given our incipiently adult minds whereon to think — ushered us back through the gates of puberty into a kind of induced second latency. And that second latency, however artificial, remains in memory a distinct, vivid, and deeply attractive spiritual state. We were not like deer in the deer park, no, but we were, after all, in surprisingly close approximation to the spiritual condition of prepubescent children. Everyone saw this about us. Everyone, even elderly retired Jesuits who had been through the experience themselves years earlier, shook their heads and laughed when they saw it in us. But there it was. Think of it, if you will, as standing on your head. Headstanding may be crazy, but it is certainly possible, and its effect upon the brain, whether you call the effect beneficial or not, is unlike that of any other exercise you can perform. At the time, I liked it rather well.

All this was, you will understand, a long time ago. I now have a daughter at Berkeley. Next year, my wife and I will celebrate the silver anniversary of our wedding. But when I am asked to address myself to "spiritual writing," much of this tangled process crowds its way back in. There was a time not too long ago when I would have tried to talk about it without using the word *spirituality*. But by a roundabout path, I have come to a point where I can speak some of the old words without the old fear of being somehow tainted, disqualified from competing in the larger world, or, worse, dragged all the way back in.

The memory of spiritual intensity in childhood has been for one writer after another the touchstone for all spiritual experience worthy of the name. Jesus was far from the only one. I spoke above of sports played to joyous exhaustion and of the seasons of the year felt in every pore of the skin. Whom does that bring to your mind? It brings the poet Dylan Thomas to mine. Who has spoken better of that state of heightened but joyfully unreckoning sensitivity? "In the sun born over and over," he wrote, "I ran my heedless ways."

The novitiate stood on a bluff overlooking a river. Leaving the park-like grounds, we would hike through woods cut by cold creeks

to a farmhouse the novitiate owned, situated on a remote hilltop.
Remembering these hikes and the larky feeling of boys on a holiday, I think of Wordsworth in a dozen passages like:

> The sounding cataract
> Haunted me like a passion; the tall rock,
> The mountain, and the deep and gloomy wood,
> Their colors and their forms, were then to me
> An appetite; a feeling and a love,
> That had no need of a remoter charm,
> By thoughts supplied, nor any interest
> Unborrowed from the eye.

Many from all backgrounds cherish some such memory from
childhood. But granting that the intensity of childhood experience
is a recognizable state, even a familiar one, one must still ask: Is it
also a state to which the adult can return after the natural moment
for it has come and gone? Is it possible to create a spiritual discipline to turn the man, even the sexually ardent young man, back
into a boy? *That* is the question — the question of whether an intense but transitory personal experience can ever be replicated
and then built into an ongoing adult life.

Never completely, I would answer, but perhaps partially. As Jesuit
novices, it seems to me that we tried our best. And we had a warrant
for our attempt in the Gospel passage that I have placed as an epi-
graph to this essay. Many of those who are revered as spiritual leaders radiate a youthfulness that age cannot touch, a maturity beyond
mere adulthood. As Jeremy suggested, it may be a mistake to attempt this step beyond adulthood before reaching adulthood in
the simpler sense. Hinduism with its rich and rooted acknowledgment of the stages of life may be wiser here than Catholic Christianity. But if one does try to be, so to speak, young before one's time,
well, you may count on it: something will happen. Racing ahead
that way is, perhaps, a bit like reading a great classic before you are
old enough to appreciate it. I read *King Lear* for the first time when
I was fifteen. It means incomparably more to me now than it did
then, but it meant something to me even then. This is what I meant
when I said above that "something took" in the Jesuit novitiate.

The fact that I grew accustomed to hearing "formed" Jesuits,
caught up in the swirl of their later lives as teachers, administrators,

lab supervisors, drama coaches, and what have you, speak of the novitiate as a lost world suggests to me that the spiritual effect of which I speak was a secondary, largely unconscious effect. Primarily and consciously, we were learning and practicing the rationalized Ignatian spirituality of mental prayer. Perhaps at the peak moments of that spirituality, such as the nature meditation that comes at the conclusion of the Spiritual Exercises, the two did seem briefly to work in tandem. But more often, they did not; and the more powerful experience was the one less attended to, the one that lingers as an indelible memory, however transitory it may have been as a spiritual condition.

As I said above, it was the *esprit de corps* of the Society of Jesus that made me, at the age of seventeen, want to enlist. How powerfully, as adolescents leave their families behind, they yearn to belong to something else! And how painful it can be not to make the team, not to be admitted to the fraternity, not to be chosen for the cast. At such a moment, a boy or girl feels not so much rejected as orphaned. The hoped-for replacement family has turned one out. Adults, too, often have a desire to belong to something larger than themselves, but theirs is a tamed and domesticated version of the awful adolescent craving. The developed adult appetite (*capacity* might be a better word) for group identity doesn't eat at the achieved adult but feeds him. The earlier, more rampant appetite — for those who are lucky enough to make the team or the fraternity or the cast — can easily go beyond nurture to intoxication. It certainly did for me.

Years after leaving the Jesuits, I learned with a faint jolt of recognition that the motto of the French Foreign Legion is *Legio patria mea:* "The legion is my fatherland." The legion and not, as one might expect, France. This brought a shock of recognition because my own earlier motto could so easily have been *Societas ecclesia mea:* "The Society is my church." "The Society" is what Jesuits call the order among themselves. That it is "of Jesus" goes without saying. But as with young legionnaires, so with young Jesuits: in the end, first things must come first. If you have your doubts about France, you don't belong in the Legion, however exciting you may have found it. And if you have your doubts about the Church of Rome, you don't belong in the Society of Jesus, either.

Ten years after leaving the Jesuits, I ratified a process already well under way by marrying in the Episcopal Church. I had concluded by then both that I could not avail myself of the spiritual resources of Buddhism as well as I could those of Christianity and, more basically, that agnostic disaffiliation, the default option for my generation, was an intellectually unwarranted impoverishment of life. Spiritual life in the Episcopal Church has been, for me, like life lived in a ramshackle but still surprisingly functional old manse. As an Episcopalian, I am accommodated as the adult I must ever be, yet given repeated, fleeting but pungent occasions to be, without shame, a spiritual child again.

I know that the Episcopal Church is not for everyone, but then what is? This seems a flippant question, but I mean to ask it seriously with reference to this anthology of spiritual writing. Of its contributors, one may know, guess, or suspect that several, at least, are committed to developed traditions or disciplines that, for their adherents or practitioners, have historically been answers rather than questions, intended for the many rather than for the few. But in the main, what the contributors choose to write of here is, as I might put it, the vestibule rather than the sanctuary. One detects a pluralistically chastened awareness that comparable experiences, as they come to be preserved and implemented, may lead to incomparable, incompatible rationalizations. These, too, can be shared, but never quickly, never easily, and often at some risk of offense.

The most powerful statement collectively made by this anthology is thus less an assertion of some such tradition or discipline than it is a negation of the mentioned default position in American spiritual life. Again and again in these pages, we find an American man or woman experientially interrupted in and then dislocated from the stultifying routine of normal American materialism. Taken together, the collection thus bespeaks a poignant readiness to take leave of the consumer society whose cosmology may be Big Bang–awesome but whose ideology rarely gets much past "When the going gets tough, the tough go shopping." Just after World War II, Americans believed that science had won the war and saved the world from tyranny and that the material plenty bestowed by science ("Better Living Through Chemistry" was an advertising slogan of the day) was an innocent blessing, especially for folks who had known such tough times so recently. That belief is the spiritual home, the default *Weltanschauung*, for most Americans over forty. But in the first decade of the twenty-first century, science seems increasingly the unwitting destroyer of the world, while the innocence of American plenty has morphed into obese glut for the few and dire want for the many. It may be time, then, to leave the default position, to leave home.

American spiritual writing at its best is, in sum, a pluriform, multifarious acknowledgment of discomfiture and an opening of exits into a wider world. These acknowledgments and openings, some of which involve a doubling back to childhood, are not the consummation of spirituality, but in their candor and unguarded openness they are the beginning. The reader is led to this volume, I imagine, by the question: *There must be something more. Where can I find it?* The contributors to this volume answer, in effect: *You will find it when it finds you.* Refuse to deny what you know but consent to how little that will always be, and, when the moment comes, the sky will open and the liberating intrusion will descend upon you.

JACK MILES

RICK BASS

A Texas Childhood

FROM *Doubletake*

IT'S LATE JANUARY, and I'm sitting on the porch of my parents' farm in south Texas watching our daughters, ages nine and
six, playing out in the middle of a pasture, surrounded by balmy
breezes and birdsong — a week's respite from the Montana winter.
After long-winter's accruing numbness, this premature burst of
song and of warmth rests exquisitely upon all our skin.

Watching the girls play so far from the Montana wilderness, I
find myself wondering, What from their childhood will inform
them as adults? What images of nature and what relationships last?
The physical memories of the world, surely, and yet also the fabric
of stories. Both must make a child and then an adult.

It seems a paradox to me that the more deeply the physical sensations are felt or otherwise engaged, the more deeply the mind
can be stirred; as if these things that remind me of my own childhood in Texas — birdsong, breeze-stir, sunlight in winter, distant
dog-bark — are but story themselves, occurring again and again.
In that manner they are as strong — once the echo or observation
or even memory of them gets into your mind — as they ever were
to the original physical touch or sensation.

As a culture we have been presented with the idea that a thing
must be either/or. But isn't it a valid possibility that deeply felt
physical experiences act not as a tradeoff for the more interior
world of emotion or story, but instead as a gate or path into a
deeper interior world? For a long time I thought the two were
oppositional: the physical senses versus the life of the mind, as if
the two were engaged eternally in some giant tag-team match of

winner-take-all. Like so many others, I fell into the trap of thinking we were separate from nature — that we had not been birthed from dust, and that because of the size and complexity of our brains, we were the exception to any rule we desired.

Where we live now — the girls and my wife, Elizabeth, and I — is deep in the Montana forest on the edge of Canada. I wonder how my daughters' lives and interiors will be shaped — not formed, but shaped — by their seeing, in all the days of their childhood, these mountains and their storms, these moose and wolves and eagles and bears; shaped by helping me hunt and take and then give thanks for, and then clean and prepare, our own meals from the forest — deer and elk and fish and mushrooms and berries. How will it all add up for them — the day the wolf was in the yard, the day the mountain lion followed us while skiing, the day the golden eagle caught the goose in the marsh? What world, what fabric of values, will we protect for our daughters, and what inspirations and understandings will come from the fabric of the elements we have chosen to make available to them? What is the sum of this daily appreciating, becoming accustomed to these things — not taking them for granted but being so accustomed to them that their presence in your life fits you like your own skin?

In such a life of woodsy immersion, where children learn not through any specific instruction but from the general comings-and-goings of the days — the behavioral differences of black bears and grizzlies, the seasonal migrations of birds, and the differences in all the animals' tracks — do the occasional childhood upwellings of grace (characterized chiefly by a sudden sense of profound belongingness and the witnessing of extreme beauty) manifest themselves differently for woods-children than for children of the suburbs and the inner cities?

I believe, as do others, that there are these lightning-spark transformative moments in our lives, epiphanies, in which the milieu of all of one's previous experience is illuminated into an Event, an experience more profound somehow than even memory itself, so that the Event seems to have somehow always been within you, waiting only to occur, predestined, miraculous, and splendidly unique, and yet, in retrospect, completely unavoidable.

But I also want to believe deeply that the general background dailiness of one's life is as important, in the long run, as any of those handful of defining moments that occasionally come upwelling from the reservoir of one's life to provide that sudden jolt of deeper awareness or even of understanding.

I don't know. Maybe a slow and steady braid of daily beauty is every bit as durable and powerful, perhaps even more so, as any tiny cluster or bouquet of crucible-forged revelations. Perhaps in the end it's all the same and there's little difference, in this regard, between a Houston suburb, a city park, and a Montana wilderness.

I don't believe that, however. I believe that the epiphanies of the natural world's beauty are more a testament to the incredible strength and purity of the hearts of children, that those epiphanies can and will come almost anywhere, at any time, rising un-summoned, as if from below. I think also that such a phenomenon makes the presence of wilderness all the more important, not less.

If semi-urban or domesticated nature can carry such profound change and power upon our daily lives, then what mystery must reside and flourish in the seething woods and swamps and mountains that lie beyond the reach of our roads? If such glimpses of grace and revelation can be seen by children in even the narrowest, vanishing wedges of semi-domesticated nature, then what store of tenderness must lie at its source or headwaters, available in such a free and undiluted state as to be readily observed and deeply felt by even the jaded eyes and hardening hearts of adults?

"Of what avail are forty freedoms," wrote American ecologist Aldo Leopold, "without a blank spot on the map? I am glad I shall never be young without young country in which to be young." It was nearly sixty years ago, and if he were still alive, I wonder at which he would marvel more: the fact that so much wild country has been lost — even as he noted the rampant pace and breadth of its leave-taking, three generations ago; or at the speed of time's passage, as if ultimately surprised not at the quantity of loss, but by the brute and simple law of how damned fast time passes.

I grew up in the suburbs of Houston, at the edge of the suburbs, at the edge of the Katy prairie, in the ribbon of hardwood forest that laced the edges of Buffalo Bayou. There was a farthermost place I could get to by riding my bike down sandy trails for a mile or so, beyond the last road, beyond the last house, and then by traveling

farther on foot, through greenbriar and cane and willow and dew-
berry, along the game trails that followed the high cutbank bluffs
of the serpentine bayou — several miles of bayou-bend oxbow in
order to traverse a single mile on the map. It was a style of physical
discourse or engagement that perhaps impressed itself upon my
way of thinking, even my way of sentence-making, and is still where
I am most comfortable.

There was always something to see, and I didn't want to miss anything: leopard frogs leaping from bluffs out into the muddy current below; giant soft-shelled turtles floating camouflaged in sun-
dappled patches of the bayou, their dinosaur-necks seeming as
long as those of snakes; primitive alligator gars longer than I was
tall and as thick around as my waist, cruising on the surface like
mysterious submarines; armadillos more beautiful than any bronze
or golden jewelry, scurrying across the trail, alarmed by my approach; box turtles wandering through the forest; and flying squirrels, fox squirrels, gray squirrels, raccoons, and opossums scurrying up the trees. Nine-lined skinks scampered across and beneath
the dry leaves of oak and hickory, sounding like the first few fault
drops of rain upon those same leaves.

Sometimes there were even deer on the edge of the bayou (what
a shock it was to encounter an animal larger than myself!) and often while I was running down one of those trails, running for the
joy of being alive and with the wind in my face, I would sometimes
surprise any deer coming down those same trails. In their fright,
they would crash through the brush and hurtle down those steep
banks and dive out into the bayou and begin swimming for the
other side.

There was a lake back in those woods — a deep swamp, really, already in the first stages of eutrophication, and all the richer for it. I
called it Hidden Lake for the fact that I never encountered anyone
else there, or a sign of anyone's presence — no stumps, no litter,
not even any footprints — as well as for the manner in which one
came to the lake: passing through an old-growth forest of pine and
hardwoods, with no indication that the lake lay before you until
you stumbled right upon it.

The many gray-spar rotting hulks of dead trees surrounded its
blackwater reflection, forming roots for an aviary that was nothing
less than astounding. Great blue herons as large as pterodactyls
would croak their ancient cries and leap into the sky (sometimes in

their haste the old rotten limbs they'd been perching on would fall into the lake with large splashes), and wood ducks, which back then had been hunted almost to extinction, would leap from those same black waters in a spray and blur, squeaking their whistley alarm cries. Best of all were the snowy and cattle egrets: ghostly birds rising and flying through the forest, as brilliant white as the water beneath them was black — then: slow, graceful departure mirrored perfectly in the still waters beneath them.

I went there almost every day after I got home from school — now over thirty years ago — until the roads began creeping into the forest. Bulldozers and chainsaws and concrete trucks arrived, and fluttering ribbons were tied to trees that I knew individually. And just like that, over the course of only a season or two, the woods were filled with noise, and then they vanished.

I was moving into adolescence by that time and probably had my attention diverted anyway for a while. In that regard I never really grieved the loss, as I had begun to supplant it, even as the forest was being leveled, the swamp being drained. It could have been a lot more painful than it was.

It is clear to me only now, in the writing of this memory, that what was most valuable in those sojourns, beyond the direct exposure to wildlife in its native habitat, was the complete absence of awareness that that habitat would not last forever, that in fact it was doomed even as I was running through those woods, in total lack of what Wendell Berry has called "the forethought of grief."

And perhaps an even larger blessing was my failure to realize, for a long time, that I was part and parcel of that taking: that my weight-upon-the-earth, which was and is more or less the equal to any of us in this country, was part of the very thing that was flushing those copperheads and box turtles from hiding and sending those deer crashing into the bayou, swimming for the other side, to the brief safety of the wilder country beyond.

Those days, I believe, were for me the braid rather than the epiphany: the slow accruing weave that helped form a medium out of which future lightning-bolt moments could occur once struck, once ignited. These were days in which I became more fluent in the language spoken to me, that had been speaking to me and would speak to me again and again.

I don't think, though, that any sort of woods-fluency is a prerequisite for illuminating or defining moments to occur. I think these illuminations or epiphanies of beauty are a far more universal phenomenon, one in which the beauty of the natural world and the grace of our inclusion in it are shown to us as if drapes or curtains have been peeled back, or blinders lifted from our eyes.

Instead of our requiring any sort of earned woods-fluency, I suspect that there are periods in our lives when we are susceptible or sufficiently undistracted to refocus upon the world and see deeper into its beauty. And whether such moments result from some cellular activity within us, some maturation, some shifting hormonal processes, some new-forming variance in the profile of our blood-chemistry, or whether these moments — these shining moments — are dispensed to us from above, dispensed to us every few years as if from some great and largely impersonal cog-and-gear revolution of stars and time and chance and fate, I have no idea: only that they exist.

But why? Almost anything can be explained through the lens of natural selection. Even love can be diced and parsed into terms of scientific advantage. But not these shining moments. Are they flaws, or at least crevices, in the system? What possible reason can there be for these occasions in which we are shown — as if through a rent in the clouds, or a slot-crevice in the cliffs, or even a tear in the curtain — such fuller magnitude of the beauty in which we are immersed?

Growing up in the suburbs, I milked whatever wildness I could from the faint patterings of creatures beneath the leaves and from the high-above brayings of the great migrating flocks of geese. (Migration is always synonymous with weather changes, and from little more than those rare north winds, most of the petrochemical haze that hung over the city like a glowing dome would clear out.) I milked wildness as much from the ghosts of wildness gone by, or from the imagination, as from any remnant essence of the thing.

Perhaps instinctively, I often looked north in those years, five hours north and west, to the place where my family had gone deer hunting each year since the 1930s. The place we called "the deer pasture" was up in the hill country. It seemed infinitely wilder than did the prairie around Houston, which was being devoured by the swelling population, in the boom of which I was but one, and de-

voured by the first breezy ticklings of nonstop run-and-gun afflu-
ence.

Hunted for all the decades previous by my grandfather and father, uncle and cousins, the deer pasture was for me a hard-scrab-
ble land of granite domes and prickly pear, scorpions and rattle-
snakes. Ghosts even seemed less distant: fragments of arrowheads
could be found, as could the remains of homesteaders' cabins, far
back in the clutches of the encroaching juniper, at the edges of
vanishing seeps and springs. It was a place steeped in story and
even myth — a place where these two things converged with a biological richness.

Living just across the upthrown side of the Balcones Escarpment,
a geological uplift that separates ecotones as distinctly as did the
parting of any sea (square in the midst of a buckled igneous zone
that geologists call the Central Texas Mineral Uplift), the deer pasture was home not just to deer and turkeys, but to foxes, bobcats,
coyotes, and even the rumors of mountain lions.

Our family went there to camp, to see the flowers in spring, and
to picnic in summer. Because it was such a long drive from Houston — even longer in those days of rougher roads — we usually arrived late at night, not having left until my father got off work on a
Friday evening.

Awakening as we crossed the cattle guard and drove in on the
caliche road, I would look out the windshield to see jackrabbits and
cottontails racing down the shining white ribbon of road in front of
us, eyes red-ablaze in the headlights' illumination, raising puffs of
white dust with each acrobatic leap. Getting out to open the gate, I
would always be struck, almost overwhelmed, by the brightness of
the stars, by the cleaner scent of the woods around me, by the silence, and by the sounds that helped define or bound the silence:
the frogs and crickets, owls and coyotes. The big sweet nothing.
Even then it aroused in me a feeling of great calm, great peace, and
even now, after having seen far greater wilderness, it still does.

It was at the deer pasture where one of the deepest lightning-
strike moments occurred; rather, one of the first and most lasting
images of nature filled me. I was probably nine or ten years old,
and it was New Year's Eve. We were staying in the hunting camp's
ramshackle old shed. There'd been an ice storm that day, and the
hills and woods were glazed — the whole world seemingly encased

in a sheet of ice — and the adults, my uncle and father and grandfather, were inside playing dominoes by gas lamp, and they sent me
down to the creek with a flashlight to get a bucket of water.

The night was filled with rune-fog, especially down along the
creek. It seemed to me that ice-fog was the steam rising from the
earth's back; that the earth was living, and the night was living,
and that I was fully in it. There were flocks of geese passing or circling overhead, looking for a place to land but perhaps unable to
descend through such dense fog. I think they were circling our
cabin's lone lantern, which must have been the only light they
could see below, and which must have appeared as only a dull glow.

The little creek was frozen; I was going to have to break through
the ice with a rock to gather water. Before I did, though, I noticed
that I could see fish underneath the ice — pale little bluegills,
bloodless-looking, caught in the beam of the flashlight, finning in
place. The flashlight's beam passed right through them.

Everything was the same color, everything was transparent or
translucent — ice, water, fish, flashlight beam — and I lay there on
my belly watching those fish through the ice, and I had never seen
before how complex but also ordered is the stacking of the world:
of all the layers and levels of the world, and all the worlds-beneath-
worlds.

Somewhere above me it was a clear night with stars, and the
geese were up in that world, circling and looking; and then below
that, there was a skin of fog wrapped around the earth; and on that
frozen earth was a small boy with a flashlight; and with the probe of
that flashlight's beam traveling through and then beneath the skin
of the ice there was creek water running beneath; and in that cold
water there were those little fish, their tails ruddering them in
place, fish hanging suspended in that one probe of light, as if the
light was the ice, and they were captured, their world revealed. And
behind me, up on the hill, the world of men and manhood, my uncle and father and grandfather were playing dominoes, safe and
warm in the cabin of yellow window square light, while I was out in
the cold, alone for the moment but also not alone, listening to and
seeing all these different worlds at once and knowing that some
were calling to me louder than others, and that I could choose, or
be chosen by, any one of them. . . .

It was those fish that gave me comfort — knowing that they

could live and survive beneath that ice, just as I sometimes felt that it was as if I too lived beneath a sheet of ice, somehow beneath or separated from the rest of the world.

I think I had been led to believe before that that there was only one world, and that you were either in it or out of it; that the world was like a kind of a club or membership. It was such a relief to me, such an awakening, to see instead that there was a latticed structure of many worlds, and that some of us live only at slightly different levels from each other — the animals included — and that those levels can change at any time and in any season. It is all alive and all moving, like those geese above, circling, looking for a place to come down through the fog.

I prefer the slow and enduring form of sculpting — a geological sort of pace that allows for rises and falls, mistakes and redemptions both, but with absolution and success in the end; a pace in which any and all clumsiness yields finally to grace, as if that clumsiness has finally metamorphosed, transformed by time running across and around it, like a river running across a boulder and polishing it to some elegant and fitted shape.

It doesn't matter, does it, whether you get your hundred volts one day at a time, a volt each day, or all at once? So keenly felt is even a single volt of world's beauty, world's wonder, that often even a single volt feels to me like a hundred. I am drawn more toward the daily, understated devotional of staring out at a marsh for long moments at a time or at a forested mountainside than toward any search for high-intensity moments of illumination. I'm not sure the husk of my body could hold up to the rigors of any amped-up intensities, so sweet and total are the pleasures of even those single volts.

My girls are far flashier in the world — far more fitted to it, already: bright and beautiful and certainly deeply loved. What will their moments be? Which will influence them more strongly — the slow daily braid, the continuum of nature, or the curtain-parting moments of supreme revelation?

It can't be controlled, of course, or perhaps even observed, not even by them. Of my own defining moments in nature, only rarely do I ever remember being aware of thoughts such as: I surely will never forget this! or, Wow, this is a revelation! Even those highly illuminated moments sank deep, as if into the river of my life, and it was only after I had gone some distance that I understood in retrospect what had happened: that those were foundational images, mid-river boulders that changed somehow the patterns of all the subsequent flow downstream. A different braiding, then, as the divided currents merged.

The moments cannot be set up in advance. Magic comes when it comes. Perhaps this is another reason I tend toward, or am more comfortable with, the accumulated daily sweetness over the exalted once- or twice- or thrice-in-a-lifetime euphorias. I can help provide for, or lead the girls to, those quieter places. No one can do magic, but any of us can show up for work each day, can lead children to the raw materials which, once braided, conduct that magic. Like apprentice workers pushing a wheelbarrow full of various quarry stones to the place where a master stonemason is working, we can gather and select and then ferry those individual days. Beyond that, nothing — only magic. The laborers can only show up for work.

Maybe I am seeing what I want to see; maybe we have the ability, or the good fortune, to almost always find what we are looking for, even when it is not there. But the other day I had not been thinking of these things — the illuminating moments of childhood — when one seemed to pass before my youngest daughter, Lowry, and me, upwelling neither from the buried humus of centuries below us, nor from the braid-and-twine of the blood within us, but instead passing before us like fog, like a single layer of cloud whose slow-drifting path intersected that day with our own curious wanderings.

It was a rainy day in January, cold and raw, ragged and dark. The old fallen snow was the only light in the world, and even that was dull. The moss hanging from the trees was sodden, and it was one of those days when dusk seemed determined to arrive two hours early.

The girls were home from school and were hanging out on the couch, eating slices of apples and slices of cheese, watching some video — *The Princess Diaries* or something like that. My older daughter, Mary Katherine, discovered she had some homework undone, and Lowry and I ended up going outside to ski for a while. I have to confess, though, that I kind of forced the issue — something about the comfort with which they were ensconced alarmed me, the fact that they had not been outside all day, and that dusk was coming on. There might have been a little of my own winter-craziness, stir-craziness, at play, too, for I ended up issuing a mandate, a proclamation, acknowledging to Lowry that yes, I understood she didn't want to go outside, didn't want to ski, but that it was going to be a requirement on this rainy day, even if only fifty yards up the driveway. It was for our health, to break the braid, the pattern, of the couch.

I don't know why I felt we had to get out that afternoon. Certainly, other winter days have passed — rainy, foggy, drizzly days — in which none of us venture outside. But this nearing-dusk day I was agitated. It didn't seem that I was asking too much. "Fifty yards," I told her. "I know that you don't want to go outside today. We'll come right back in. But we have to go fifty yards up the driveway. We just have to get out for a minute or two. We don't even have to have fun," I said. "Think of it as work — like emptying the cat litter or something."

Maybe this was shaping up to be a train wreck. Cat litter equals the great outdoors? What surer way to dull a child's innate curiosity and even enthusiasm for the natural world? Had I snapped from the seasonal deprivation of light and turned into one of those awful eco-fascist parents? How was this dictum any different, really, to a six-year-old, than forced wind sprints or a hundred push-ups?

There were a few tears as Lowry got up and turned the movie off and then pulled on her snow pants and laced up her cross-country ski boots. "Why do we have to go fifty yards?" she asked. A valid question, to which I answered, "We just do."

Lowry stamped outside. She can be more obstinate than a mule, more obstinate than me. "Why?" she asked again, and now that I had her outside in this nasty, foggy day, now that we had broken the cycle of the couch — where she had also spent the previous afternoon, I now recall — I had achieved what I wanted, and I was able to negotiate downward: "Okay, you don't have to ski fifty yards. I'll pull you in the sled for fifty yards."

She dug in further, sulked deeper. She's not one to negotiate. Give her any weakness and she moves away from it, not toward it. Was I going to have to physically lift her in the sled? "Oh, wall," I said, "please, Daddy, don't pull me around in the sled, please don't make princess ride in the sleigh, oh, wan." For a moment she started to giggle — it was enough for me to lift her in — but then she folded her arms and the Great Lip came back out.

"I don't want to go," she growled, and I felt like I had gone too far. Yet I had made too much of the importance of getting outside for a breath of fresh air, even if only for a minute, to back down. The child-rearing books, I knew, would have all sorts of lucid and correct advice, but that didn't do me any good, for Lowry was already in the sled.

We started up the driveway, into the gloom. I pointed out the fifty-yard mark ahead. She pouted and griped the whole way, milking her full fifty yards' worth. My God, I thought, how I hope she ends up on our side. How formidable an adversary she would be against us.

At the fifty-yard mark, I turned around, true to my word. I began running down the steep hill, and finally that broke the shell, the plaster cast of displeasure. As she laughed and then asked me to do it again, I felt like an alchemist or magician. It was the most amazing feeling, as if I had been holding her unhappiness cupped in both of my hands, had done some trick, then rolled it around for a moment, as if mixing dust-and-water to make clay, and when I opened my hands again, there was happiness, where previously had existed only unhappiness.

It wasn't me, of course. It was the woods and the earth — the slope of the hill, the laws of gravity — and the condition of childhood, which seeks joy so earnestly, so relentlessly.

I pulled her a few more times, and then, truth be told (raging hypocrite!), I began to long for the warmth of the woodstove, the winter cabin light of hearth and home. Lowry was all bundled up, but I had neither coat nor gloves, certain that we would travel only fifty yards.

Each time I suggested that we head back inside, she coaxed me into one more run. But then, finally, when we truly had made the last run (the one-more after the one-more after the one-more after the one-more), rather than going inside to warm up (hot chocolate, I urged her, and Harry Potter), she became absorbed by the myriad of deer tracks stippling the snow, made by the herd of half a dozen that wanders down the driveway at various times of the day.

There were tracks everywhere, traveling in all directions — days and days of tracks. And Lowry, with her typical singularity of focus, seized upon one track among all the hundreds of others and then began following it, hunched over like Inspector Clouseau.

As best as I could tell, she stayed with it, too, parsing out for a little while that one deer's tracks among so many others, identifying it by size and shape, and smoking-gun freshness, the blue-glaze sheen of that one set of tracks among dozens possessing a slightly brighter glow. But soon enough, she was tracking in a wandering maze of tight little circles with me behind her, a kaleidoscope of trailing, so that seen from above, our path would resemble those swirling teacup-bumper-rides in amusement parks.

It was nearly full dusk now, and farther into the woods, darker still. And again, now that my mission, my goal, was accomplished, I kept wanting to quit and to go back to the house and warm up — even as Lowry was growing more and more engaged with following those tracks.

I followed behind her and was careful not to comment or correct her, letting her believe instead that she was hot on the trail of that deer, stalking it, inch by inch and foot by foot, and that we might come upon it at any moment. So lost was she in following the one set of tracks through the maze — traveling in slowly widening circles — that I felt certain she had lost track of time and was so completely into the tracking that in her mind we had traveled miles, rather than continuing to circle back to more or less the same starting point.

Eventually, however, the circles widened enough so that we found ourselves coming nearer the marsh. And then, as if believing she was following the same deer (and perhaps, at any given moment, she was), Lowry left off her circling-style of tracking and began following the tracks on a line, like a hunter eagerly closing in, having solved both the riddle and the challenge: according to Lowry, the deer — still only one among dozens or hundreds — traveled down toward my writing cabin, where he circled before heading off farther into the woods.

Do I know for certain that Lowry was betranced — illuminated — during this strange trailing, this impromptu, wander-some exploration? Not at all. And even during the traveling, the thought had not yet occurred to me. It was only when we heard the eerie whooping dusk cry of a pileated woodpecker, and she took my hand and led me to a clump of winter-bare alder and hunkered down into a hiding position, that I began to consider that she was deeply in another world — or rather, deeply in this one.

"If we hide," she said, crouching behind a slender tree, "maybe he won't see us. Maybe he'll come closer."

The woodpecker called again from high above and not very far away, and Lowry pressed herself in closer against the spindly little alder, and motioned for me to hide myself better. We watched intently, waiting for the woodpecker to show itself. I could feel Lowry's focus, patient and keen, and I marveled at the purity of her desire. She didn't want to trap or hunt the bird, or even sneak up on it. She just wanted to see it and to watch it, unobserved.

There was no way we could hide sufficiently behind that bare little alder, but Lowry didn't know that, or didn't believe it; and we waited longer, watching and listening. It was only when we finally heard the bird call again from much farther away and noted a deeper dimness — almost, but not quite yet, true dark — that we rose from our crouch and began walking back up the trail toward the house, with Lowry leading the way, excited and fulfilled. So strange was the turnaround in her mood and demeanor that I wondered if the woods-euphoria hadn't somehow been set up by the chemistry of the tears, allowing her to feel the day more sharply.

Goofy thoughts, I know. But she seemed so self-assured, both curious and confident, that I couldn't help but wonder if the images of the day weren't etching themselves indelibly upon her, like light coming through a brief lens opening to expose itself to the waiting film within. There's no way to tell, other than to one day ask her about it, far into the future — to see if that memory has withstood the test of time. It may be that she won't remember at all, that the moment was not for her the vertical illumination of light that I imagined I was witnessing, but instead simply more of the daily braid of her life.

And again, perhaps it is this simple: how powerful, natural, and necessary it is to our imaginations that that wild and rare bird had a place to fly off to. It just vanished from sight and sound when it flew off deeper into the woods. But it didn't vanish. It — with our imagination in tow — kept going, drawn farther and gracefully into the wilds.

Maybe this is what I'm getting at: wilderness is not necessary to develop a love of nature in children. I'm convinced we're born with a reverence for the natural world, and that such an affinity can then be strengthened, maintained, corroded, or buried — like anything else in the world.

The joy, the illumination, the realization, or remembrance of that love can be stimulated by one ant, one sparrow, one seashell held to one's ear. And surely there will almost always be ants, geraniums, deer tracks, and birdcalls for children to ponder over and be smitten and captivated by. But they should retain the choice of being able to decide whether to travel even further, then, with that love and that imagining. Without wilderness, we ultimately compromise our ability to imagine further. Without wilderness, we ultimately become less human. Whether we like it or hate it or are indifferent is beside the point; we need it.

Meanwhile, back at the ranch, the wild Montana girls are sitting in lawn chairs out in the cow pasture, feet propped up, wearing their sunglasses and swimsuits, beach towels over their shoulders, books in hand. The only things more surreal in this image than the scraggly bonsai-reach of the thorny limbs of the weesatche and gnarled mesquite trees around them are the endless anthill-like mounds of manure, the scattered horse pods and cow pies.

But there's space, a comfortable amount of space, and there's also the exquisite luxury to our Pacific Northwest psyches of sunlight in the winter. A physical model, perhaps — that yellow light pouring down upon us — for how it is in our interiors, in those unmappable but deeply recognizable moments when that larger grace and the hint of a larger understanding, or at least a larger acknowledging, pours down upon us.

Will these vacation days spent in another, more pastoral landscape become some of the illuminating moments? If so, how might that affect who these girls become? Or will these soft vacation days be folded into the braid, the daily and nightly river mixing in with mountain lion and bull elk and simply continue on, helping to form the horizontal platform or foundation, rather than any highly visible vertical structure?

Traditions and rituals, then — secure, predictable, and repeating — can be their own kind of vertical structure upon the landscape of who-we-are and who-we-become. The repetitions or constancy

of traditions can be like those currents influencing boulders em-
placed midstream, allowing for growth and complexity and creativity and movement downstream. It sounds at first like a paradox:
how can something identified by its quality of sameness, of un-
changingness, bring forth the fruit of change and spur the imagination? And perhaps, in this regard, tradition in the out-of-doors is
a strange hybrid between rare illumination and the more common,
even daily, accrual of habit.

To know or believe that there are places in the natural world that
are not likely to change too dramatically in a lifetime — or even
two or three or four lifetimes — might serve as a refuge against the
world's dynamic essence.

So tradition can be a landscape (be like a wilderness, even, secure forever, unerodable), and story, or memory, can be like another of the physical senses, as deeply felt as any touch or odor or
taste or sight, as deeply felt as any intuition or song.

Imagine, then, please, the sweetness I encounter on those occasions when I am able to bring my Montana girls out of the wilderness and down to the same Texas landscapes I inhabited at their
age: the pastoral farm with its muddy stock tanks to fish, and the
deer pasture — both were the one-time, ultimate arbiter of wildness to a young boy, but now a quantum step down in wildness to
these girls. Imagine the wonderful disorientation I feel as we arrive
there at night, with jackrabbits bounding in front of the beam of
our headlights, zigging and zagging in all directions as Mary Katherine gets out to open the gate.

The same scents, the same sounds, and even the same stories,
there at the camp-house that night. We build a bonfire of cedar in
the same firepit, and sit outside looking up at the same stars, and
despite the fact that the lions and bears and wolves and jaguars are
gone, it is still its own kind of wildness to me, if not to these girls.
Though I can also say truthfully that if the farther horizons of
Montana's wildernesses no longer existed, this place, too, and even
its stories and traditions, would lose some of its wildness — wildness finally seeping out of this place and all the other ones like it, in
the manner of blood trickling from a wound that will not heal.

The sameness of these things allows and encourages us to
change, to grow, to reach and stretch, to dive deep and travel far,
dream, and imagine. To go away and to return again, becoming

as shaped in our travels as any of the other enduring shapes in the world: the mountain that looks like the profile of a sleeping woman, the tree that looks like the silhouette of an old man with his arms outstretched. The child standing next to a creek in the fog with a flashlight, peering down through the ice at a school of translucent, suspended fish is little different, thirty years later, from the young girls stalking along that same creek, trying to sneak up on, with their own flashlights, the night frogs and crawdads.

A clamant wildness — irrepressible, running beneath the surface, across the surface, and just above the surface. A clamant wildness in the heart of the farthest roadless area; a clamant wildness in the sight of a single butterfly in a suburban backyard. A clamant wildness in a single story, told or dreamed or remembered, and a clamant wildness in the touch of a single rough stone, gripped in the palm of one's hand.

We need it all, and our children deserve the possibility of it all: the wild and the pastoral both, the swamps and mountains and forests, all the different types of forests, and all the different types of deserts, and coastlines, and grasslands. Whatever the wild or natural world has, it is part of us, part of who we are, and always have been, as well as who we are becoming. As we lose those landscapes, these experiences, one by one, we run the risk of becoming evermore brittle, until one day our imaginations and even our spirits may become as barren as a wash or gully in a dry land, through which water once murmured and alongside which cool shade-trees grew, but no more.

We do not have to go looking any farther or further for wildness, but we need to know, or at least be able to imagine, that it exists. We need to be able to at least hear the echo of where we came from, even if a long time ago, even if barely or dimly remembered now. We need the dream of such a past and need to have the promise, or at least the opportunity, of such a future. Wildness and green pastoral meadows sculpt us even now, as do the last few blank spots on the map.

DAN BELLM

Parable

FROM *Image*

I lit the candles of the Sabbath and covered my eyes,
terrified in the mind as I was and waiting for rest.
And the evening passed. And as they reached their end
the one became turbulent, sputtering, loud,
the left one on the table, the one facing my heart,

the heart, of it burning out impurely and rough,
a red with tarry shadows, spitting death at me,
the other placid as prayer, clear light and patient
in the copper hourglass bowl, steadfast as the soul
of the one I love, soothing me, being also alive,

and this one I knew would last and burn long tonight,
the other flail down like madness and hard living
of every sort, the darkness that is touched and felt.
And I sighed for the love, and sighed the poor candle out.
Then I could rest, having yielded half the light.

Bo, Exodus 10:1–13:16
Yitro, Exodus 18:1–20:23

SCOTT CAIRNS

Hidden City

FROM *Spiritus*

> . . . that you might approach the Jerusalem of the heart . . .
> — Isaac the Least

And now I think Jerusalem abides untouched,
the temple yet intact, its every cornerstone
in place, its vault replete with vivid scent, its ark

alight with vigil lamps whose oil is never spent.
In psalm the pilgrim asks forgiveness, pleads that God
return the Spirit to the heart, and look, the Ghost

had never left, had never for an instant drawn
away, had only watched His presence made obscure
by soul's own intermittent darkening. Just so,

the three companions of the Lord had blindly walked
the lesser part of three dim years before their eyes
beheld the Light that bathed the Son eternally.

Just so, the Light of Tabor spools extending past
the vision of the multitude, if nonetheless
apparent to the meek, the poor, the pure in heart.

Just so, the Holy City bides within the heart,
awaits the day the pilgrim will arrive, will quit
the road, turn in to greet his City's boundless sweep, and see.

ROBIN CODY

Miss Ivory Broom

FROM *Portland Magazine*

I AM IN LOVE with a six-year-old. She is in the first grade and rides in a wheelchair on my school bus to a special education class at Sitton Elementary School, far north in St. Johns, near the University. She is the first child I pick up each morning. We have some quality time together.

First a little background on the human neural tube. In embryonic development, the neural tube begins as a flat plate of cells that folds down the center. The two edges loop to form a tube. The tube then develops into the brain and spinal cord.

Unless it doesn't. Something goes haywire in the unfolding of genetic instructions about how to make and run a human being. If the upper end of the neural tube (near the brain) stays open, it's fatal. If the lower end of the neural tube stays open, it isn't fatal, and surgeons can repair this condition soon after birth, but what you get is an incomplete child. You get spina bifida. You get Miss Ivory Broom. Only her top half works.

Knowing this, I was a nervous wreck before I even got to Ivory's house the first day of school. I'd practiced the hydraulic lift and tie-downs on a spare wheelchair at the bus yard, but you never know how a fragile child will fit securely. What if I have to brake suddenly? What if some idiot runs a stop sign and hits us broadside?

Anyway, here she came, that first day, wheeled out from a low green house by a young mother in purple bath thongs. Ivory herself was not at all the pathetic broken creature I'd prepared myself for. She was fair-skinned with freckles and big fearless blue eyes and light brown hair that her mom had fixed into a complex French braid. No bigger than a large chinook salmon, Ivory came rolling toward the bus strapped tightly into her wheelchair and wearing an eager lopsided grin like this was a yellow amusement park ride and she was the luckiest girl in the world to get on it. Ivory waved her little fingers at me as the lift took us up, and I thought, *Uh-oh, she lacks arm control, too.* But no. She was showing me — so proud — her two-tone manicure.

I had focused so hard on what's wrong with Ivory that she just floored me with what's right! Her tiny fingers. Her pretty hair. Her spirit. Turns out this kid has huge spirit.

She also has the lungs and brass voice of a squad sergeant. Although her brain works slowly, Ivory has language. She bellows it out one syllable at a time. Like the other day I told her she was lucky to have a mom who loves her so much, and she said, "YOU . . . GOT . . . THAT . . . RIGHT."

I told Ivory I love my own daughter, and my daughter's name is Heidi.

She thought that was very funny. Ivory thinks almost everything is funny. When she was through laughing — one har at a time — she said, "BUS . . . DRI . . . VER . . . YOU . . . ARE . . . A . . . CHAR-AC . . . TER."

Well, I guess that's not exceptional, now that I write it. Maybe you had to be there. You had to hear the life-loving relish with which she belts it out. Or just the other morning we were almost to school. I had a full load of six broken kids on the bus and Ivory back there said, "OOOH . . . GROSS!!!"

What's gross, Ivory?

Never, on this run, is everyone's attention beamed in one direction. But here she'd nailed all of us. We waited. The dramatic tension was exquisite.

"MY . . . SNOT," she said.

Because, you see, when Ivory has the sniffles but fumbles her tissue onto the floor, she cannot pick it up. She was just letting me know so I could stop the bus and let Jacoby get up to assist her. Oh, that's the other thing. Jacoby. Jacoby Hagens is (or was, at the start of the school year) a tough sullen fifth grader who got kicked out of his neighborhood school for defiance and for not trying. Self-pitying, resentful for having to ride this short bus "with the retards" to his own special ed program, Jacoby can poison the air inside my bus just sitting there if he chooses to. At first, he chose to. Or maybe, I think now, he was just scared. Lost. But anyway, Ivory's

daily greeting — "JA . . . CO-BY. . . . I . . . AM . . . HAP-PY . . . TO . . .
SEE . . . YOU" — began to coax a smile out of him.

Soon Jacoby began sitting opposite Ivory's wheelchair and talking to her.

And just the other day — this really got me — I saw in the mirror
they were holding hands across the aisle back there. Jacoby now has
a spring in his step to the bus each morning. He is teaching Ivory
her numbers. He also helps Ashley (brain-squashed, from the car
wreck that killed her mother) and Anthony (developmentally delayed) fasten their seatbelts, which they cannot do themselves. His
teacher tells me Jacoby is doing his schoolwork. (!) The little ones
recently elected him President of the Bus.

So you see, Ivory would not let Jacoby brood. What we have here
is a busload of children who have every reason to feel sorry for
themselves. But despair? Ivory Broom won't have it.

So anyway. You've seen schoolbuses. Mine is a short one, a special ed bus with never more than half a dozen kids aboard. You get
to know them. This bus has five seats and two wheelchair spaces.
The lift folds outward from the right rear. What I do is I drive these
birth-damaged or world-beaten children to schools often far from
where they live. I make several runs and put ninety miles on the bus
each day. It's not all candy and balloons like on the Ivory Broom
run. Some kids are "special" because their behavior was too disrup-
tive where they were. I glimpse some home lives that reek of desperation. Every day I see despair. I hear it in the children's voices.

"My daddy's in jail."

"We're not having Christmas this year. Dad says we can't afford
it."

"Mom didn't come home last night."

When I asked one girl her plans for the weekend, she said,
"We're canning." *That's nice,* I thought. *Putting up preserves.* But it
became clear she meant scavenging the trash for aluminum cans.

Some unimaginable sadness. Some things I never would have
thought of. One middle schooler was so increasingly hyper on the
ride home I called his mother out to the bus. She was too zonked to
make sense of me. Later, the boy's teacher explained to me it's not
unheard of for a parent to take a kid's medications, to be downing
the meds herself.

Not that I could say for sure that's what happened. But boy . . .

Despair is when you're Devon and you're twelve and you have a slow brain and bad teeth and the wrong clothes and got kicked in the nuts by those girls on the playground and told you are dirty because you are black, and YOU got in trouble because you fought back. The teacher wrote it up — fighting with girls — and now your dad will fly into a rage when you get home. You're the last rider on this demeaning short bus. You rock in your seat and your eyes are wild with fear and your shoulders begin shaking. Your eyes meet those of the bus driver in the overhead mirror, and it all comes gushing out.

"My dad won't believe me," Devon sobs. "I'm always in trouble. I'm stupid. I'm ugly. It's not fair," Devon wails, and this is the rock-bottom truth. It's just not fair. He hopes nobody will be at his home, and I will have to deliver him to Children's Club. Try to imagine. How would you like to be terrorized at school and afraid to go home? Devon is not a bad boy.

Suck it up, Devon. I'll talk to your dad when we get there.

But hey. You have kids? Hug your children. We can beat back despair on my Ivory Broom run because those children come from loving families. They get a kiss good-bye from Mom or Dad, and smiles when I deliver them home. It just goes to show you. What a difference to the damaged ones a warm family makes.

Now here comes Samantha, a late addition to my Ivory Broom run. Another wheelchair girl. Samantha is twelve, with breasts and makeup. Belligerent, self-absorbed, foul-mouthed, she came wheeling out that first day from a squalid house by an unwashed uncle with mean dull eyes. Right away Samantha informed me, "I have an attitude."

Please, Samantha. Not on my bus, you don't. Consider these sweet other children.

Ivory, of course, adored Samantha from the start. You know how little girls look up to big girls. Only more so: Samantha's wheelchair is motorized.

One morning before loading, Samantha threw a feeble punch at her uncle and kicked off a wheelchair footrest and — with Ivory watching, wide-eyed — screamed obscenities skyward. I closed the lift and drove off and left her on the sidewalk. And because she would much rather go to school than stay home, her behavior improved in succeeding days. But then another morning Samantha told me, as I was lifting her, that she was tired of living. She didn't want to go on living. Think of this. Your heart goes out to a young person so desperate, so despairing. And so in the privacy of the lift I whispered to Samantha that if she comes out with the F-word one more time — just once — I am going to wring her neck.

Not really. I didn't say that. You can't threaten a student. There are school psychologists for this sort of situation.

But what I was saying was I took this bus-driving job just hoping for routine. Routine, I'd thought, might kill dread. And it's true, there is something to be said for scheduledness. But the real deal is story. You've got all these little characters, and each of them is a story. You can't help thinking who, or how much, they are.

Story, it turns out, is the assassin of despair.

This began to dawn on me on a different run. I had a busload of five sad little autistic K-1 boys who had no words in common except "Uh-oh" and "No." There was a brief, one-block descent on that run where I turned from Southeast Sacramento Street and dropped off the Alameda ridge on 60th. The bus nosed down and Eddy Lavares said "Uh-oh" and all the boys screamed bloody murder until I wheeled left onto Thompson and announced, "We made it!"

This is a very short story, but it is. The boys never tired of it. Day after day. "Uh-oh." Screams. "We made it!"

What I'm saying here is these boys didn't have words, but they had story. We were our own story. This story brought them great joy. Still, I didn't quite realize what we had there until the children on my Ivory Broom run — with more complexity because three of them are what you might call verbal — came up with the same story. Yes.

We were cruising west on Lombard in the pre-dawn dark. Light rain. Mushy leaves lined the street.

"Bus Driver!" said Ashley, in high alarm. "Car behind us!"

They all, except Ivory, turned to look. Ivory cannot turn. "WHAT!?" she said.

"Car behind us!"

Well, on Lombard there is always a car behind us. But now Hurricane Lee, as rear gunner, aimed over the back seat and made machine gun sounds. The others (who could) formed pistols of their fists and forefingers and blasted away at the offending vehicle. I don't encourage guns on the bus, but what the hell. It's 'a story. We were one step ahead of the Federales, my little desperadoes and me.

"Ditch them," Jacoby said.

I have to stay on my route, always, but coming up was a turn off Lombard onto Charleston Street. And there — sure enough — as I wheeled to the right, the Federales sailed on down Lombard and away.

We ditched them. *We made it!*

One morning I was messing with their heads. *OK, kids. No school today. We're going to Dairy Queen.*

Now this was not automatically a welcome idea. These kids love school, they really do, and they want to go there. Ivory looked at me as if I were developmentally delayed. But we loaded Samantha, the last passenger, and I "phoned in" to Dairy Queen our orders — seven Oreo Blizzards, six cokes, and a senior coffee — on the intercom. Yes, I have an intercom. It echoes inside the bus like the voice of God.

"He's kidding," Samantha reassured Ivory. "See, we're going to school."

I stopped the bus at Pier Park and opened the door and "took in" our orders plus napkins from the woods. Jacoby distributed the goods, and we had a good lip-smacking time of it. Story is powerful to these kids. Anthony got so happy he wet his pants. Continuing on to school, I scolded Hurricane Lee for eating too fast and warned Ashley not to spill any. By the time I got them to school, Hurricane Lee was retching and two others rolled off the bus with tummy aches.

Ivory tolerates, but does not relish, such foolishness.

What Ivory likes are the classics. Snow White is her favorite character. Ivory asks for that story when the other kids have been dropped off, when only she and I are bound homeward. But "Snow White" does get tiresome and has too many characters if you ask me, and so I also tell her "Snow White and the Beanstalk." "Snow White and the Three Bears." Ivory really gets into that one. I tell the story slow enough that she can repeat the best lines. Pretty soon she is only listening, rapt. I get to the part where *Somebody has been sleeping in* my *bed,* and Ivory goes, "OH-MY . . . (deep breath) . . . GAAAWD!!!"

Explain this to me. I've taught *King Lear.* I taught *Sometimes a Great Notion* to sharp sophomores. Yet I don't recall any classroom experience more satisfying than when Ivory Broom breaks into "Snow White and the Three Bears" with "OH-MY . . . GAAAWD!!!"

I get the willies, you know? The good willies.

Now this Hurricane Lee whom I have mentioned once or twice is a turbocharged seven-year-old in flashy athletic gear who sprints across the lawn and leaps onto the bus each morning while still getting dressed, swinging his backpack, papers flying in his wake. I thought at first the Hurricane spoke a squeaky language all his own. In fact he just talks unintelligibly fast. He has a smile that can light up all of February, but the boy cannot sit still. Ivory keeps an eye on him for me. "BUS . . . DRI . . . VER . . . LOOK . . . WHAT . . . HUR-RI . . . CANE . . . LEE . . . IS . . . DO-ING!!"

On the ride home, the Hurricane sleeps.

One afternoon my nerves were shot. While loading the kids at school, I suggested that Hurricane Lee drive the bus today, and I would go in the back and sleep.

Ivory, stern as royalty, said. "NO!!! *YOU* . . . DRIVE . . . THE . . . BUS."

So it's not exactly true, what I said before, that Ivory thinks everything is funny. In the story that is our bus ride, nonsense is not funny. We each have our roles to play, and Ivory keeps us straight.

Oh, Ivory, I was just pulling your leg.

Now that, to her, is funny. Hilarious.

"PULL-ING . . . MY . . . LEG!!!"

Ivory loves the words. She takes the full flavor of new ones and makes them her own. She doesn't miss much unless the words go too fast for her. She does struggle with words that come over the two-way radio, and will ask me for clarification. But she never complains. That's the thing. Her flamboyant lack of self-pity. Can you imagine?

I pick her up at 6:53 A.M., and we don't get to school until nearly 8:00. She is six, and she can't move on the bus. At school she takes nourishment through a tube straight to her stomach. She is only

now learning to eat. On the way home Ivory is often exhausted.
"I . . . AM . . . *NOT* . . . TIRED." But then her eyes don't track, and
her little hands won't work right. Even then, she will not complain.
    Are you comfortable back there, Darlin?
    "TEN-FOUR. THANKS."

See, I try to explain this and my eyes get watery just on their own.
This is Ivory Broom's story, but it is my story, too. I can't wait to get
up and get going each day. Fire up the bus. Hear what Ivory has to
say.
    I told you how Ivory loves "Snow White and the Three Bears"?
Well, there's a problem with the ending to that story, and Ivory
knows it. I didn't know it until she kept giving me that puzzled no-
reaction, a baffled silence, whenever I finished. Like, Is that all?
Snow White just ran out of there and fled through the woods? Because if you think about it, Snow White should never have gone
into the three bears' house in the first place.
    So then what? I asked Ivory. *What happened to Snow White?*
    Ivory thought it over. "AND . . . THEN," she said, "SNOW . . .
WHITE . . . SAW . . . A . . . BLUE . . . BUT-TER . . . FLY."
    So you see: now we have a satisfactory ending to that story.

ROBERT COLES

Here and Now We Are
Walking Together

FROM *Notre Dame Magazine*

WE ALL DREADED getting Miss Avery for the fifth grade — those of us in the fourth grade, awaiting the next year's classroom assignment. "She's tough," one of us remarked; "real bad tough," affirmed another.

At the edge of change, we were mulling over our future. In so doing, we were dealing in our own way with larger matters that confront all of us human beings: luck, both good and bad, chance and circumstance, as they befall us, help shape our destiny.

So it went — American youngsters in the late 1930s, a terrible world war around the corner, a stern, demanding teacher who raised her voice and reportedly raised a stick, too (the blackboard pointer, which rumor had her using aggressively, punitively against those who earned her disfavor or worse). "You cross her, and she'll come at you," we'd heard.

I was assigned to "room five," where she supposedly reigned supreme, if not tyrannically. To this day I see us all sitting in that classroom, headed by Bernicia Avery, a Vermont lady, heavyset, with white hair and alert blue eyes that darted everywhere and sometimes concentrated mightily, unrelievedly on the one of us who had gotten her ire up. To this day, also, I can hear the words that came my way one school morning: "Bobby! I've called your name twice before." Lifting my eyes, I realized how closely I was being watched by my fellow students, who knew well the dramatic possibilities immediately ahead: "This is a school," she bellowed. "You are not at home, alone in your bedroom or study room, reading a book on your own. You are here, with others, and we all deserve your attention as much as that book, valuable as it is!"

Our eyes met, stayed fixed on one another for a second or two — and then my head lowered. I stared at the book, then the floor beyond it. She had been sitting behind her big teacher's desk, but now she got herself up. Ominously, she had a ruler in her right hand — not the notorious blackboard pointer, thank God, but a 12-inch ruler. *Bang*. That ruler went crashing on the desk of Sally Davis, sitting on the first desk's seat, four or five ahead of mine (we tall boys got put farther back, a measure of "God's grace," to use an expression Miss Avery herself summoned every once in a while, when she wanted to explain the apparently inexplicable — a merciful turn of events that happened for no apparent reason).

As she began her walk, she spoke: "We are entitled to travel on our own paths, but here and now we are walking together." I finally lifted my eyes to acknowledge the speaker, the ruler of us seated young ones who had all attention focused on her magical (malevolent, some in the room thought) right arm, held a bit high. Suddenly she waved the ruler briefly and then *crash* on Doris Newman's desk, whose occupant memorably flinched, we all sure enough noticed.

Then, this terse finale, which six decades later holds fast to my head's awareness. "We should pay attention to others, as well as ourselves." A pause, while we took in the admonition. "We spend time looking at ourselves and looking out for ourselves, but please, let us look to our right and to our left, to our front and to what's going on to our back. Please, let us be mindful of others, as we hope they will be of us!"

Then, to our considerable surprise, she was at the blackboard, not in pursuit of that famously feared pointer but with chalk in her right hand. Word for word she scratched the message out for us, now to notice hard and long. When she was through with the chalk, she asked us all to read out loud, in unison, those words: a classroom's chorus to a written moral aria.

Needless to say, we obliged, even as we noticed our teacher giving her spoken best to the words she had dispatched in our direction. When we'd all finished, she suggested that we salute the American flag. Puzzled, surprised, at a loss, we nevertheless went along — a relief, maybe, to be going through ethical rote, rather than the reflection that had been prompted in us.

Back home that day's afternoon, I told my mother of the instruction offered us. We'd all been told to write down what our teacher had called for us to witness and consider — and there it was, now mine, in my hand, for my mom to contemplate. She read my words quietly, then read them out loud — not to me, but to herself. I can see her looking out the window, often her wont, then her eyes directed at me, and then her words: "If more people lived up to those words, the world would be a better place to live." Yes, I sure agreed in my thinking — my mother now had linked arms with my teacher, and I was very much a link between them.

Soon enough, we were on to other matters, tasks — my mom cooking and I readying myself, with some milk and cinnamon buns, for strenuous playing outdoors. As I left I noticed my mother still looking at my scribble — and then her decision to pin it on the bulletin board she kept for herself in the pantry. She saw me seeing and said: "We've got to look out for other people, as well as for ourselves." She'd repeated what we'd heard said in school, but her voice told her son, perched between home and the street, that this maternal declaration was deeply felt and so ought to be kept in mind for the future days to follow in such abundance.

Here I am, in another lifetime, so to speak, remembering Miss Avery and her times of tough insistence: a teacher who wanted us to learn our letters and numbers, yes, but a teacher who also wanted to keep us a bit free of the self-preoccupation that tempts us often, a bit free to turn outside ourselves so we might be fellow citizens to others. A big freedom, indeed — to be pushed now and then from the mind's inevitable self-consciousness in the direction of our fellow wayfarers and citizens; human inwardness given the outward life of human connection — an expressive and introspective freedom that both defines our humanity and gives it the sovereignty of enactment in the everydayness of our time spent here living with others as well as ourselves.

ROBERT CORDING

Parable of the Moth

FROM *Image*

Consider this: a moth flies into a man's ear
One ordinary evening of unnoticed pleasures.
When the moth beats its wings, all the winds
Of earth gather in his ear, roar like nothing
He has ever heard. He shakes and shakes
His head, has his wife dig deep into his ear
With a Q-tip, but the roar will not cease.

It seems as if all the doors and windows
Of his house have blown away at once —
The strange play of circumstances over which
He never had control, but which he could ignore
Until the evening disappeared as if he had
Never lived it. His body no longer
Seems his own; he screams in pain to drown
Out the wind inside his ear, and curses God,
Who, hours ago, was a benign generalization
In a world going along well enough.

On the way to the hospital, his wife stops
The car, tells her husband to get out,
To sit in the grass. There are no car lights,
No streetlights, no moon. She takes
A flashlight from the glove compartment
And holds it beside his ear and, unbelievably,
The moth flies towards the light. His eyes

Are wet. He feels as if he's suddenly a pilgrim
On the shore of an unexpected world.
When he lies back in the grass, he is a boy
Again. His wife is shining the flashlight
Into the sky and there is only the silence
He has never heard, and the small road
Of light going somewhere he has never been.

LINDSEY CRITTENDEN

The Water Will Hold You:
A Daughter at Prayer

FROM *Image*

I KNEW NOTHING OF PRAYER when, as a child, I watched my mother disappear. Sitting next to me on a wooden pew in St. Stephen's Episcopal Church, she leaned forward to pull down the prayer bench, slip onto her knees, press her palms together, and bow her head. Her wool dress and stockings, her black patent-leather purse upright and open next to her in case she needed to reach for a pressed handkerchief, her shoes and hair and arms all remained recognizably *Mommy,* but with her face hidden — she didn't rest her head against her hands as much as *in* them, to shut out everything else — she became other. No longer mother or wife or Sunday school teacher, but her *self,* gone somewhere else, somewhere that — it seemed — had nothing to do with me.

She went there again, years later, when she was upset and I tried to comfort her. Weeping in a deck chair, she pushed my arms away and clutched her hands to her chest when I bent to hug her. She and my father had argued, I recall; I don't remember the specifics, but their disagreement would have played the recurring tape loop I'd heard my whole life — she was oversensitive and he was callous, she was a spoiled little girl and he an unfeeling boor. She wanted, now, to be alone. "Leave me be," she said, and hunched further into herself.

She went there, too, the summer she was dying, as we both stood in the shallow end of my parents' swimming pool and she mentioned how, sick with tuberculosis at age nineteen, she'd been sent to a chiropractor by my grandmother. "My God," I said. "Why?"

"Oh, I've told you that before," she replied, splashing water with her hands.

"No, Mom, you haven't. And whenever you say you've told me something before, it's something you never have."

"Oh." She leaned back on the steps and kicked her legs. "Aren't you funny."

She distrusted hovering concern, loathed wringing hands. The worst word, I learned early on, wasn't a four-letter curse or the taking of the Lord's name in vain (whatever that meant). No, the word that our household, under her domain, did not allow, was *pity*. My mother didn't want any, and — she'd announce, in case you had any doubt — she wouldn't be handing any out, either.

I remember my confusion: did pity differ so from sympathy, from kindness, from letting me stay home (as I craved) to hide out from fourth grade? On days I was sick with a sore throat or a tummyache, she made me cinnamon toast and dealt Double Solitaire on top of the bedcovers and rubbed my back. But on days I was nervous about having to Steal the Bacon in P.E. or face down the fifth-grade toughs who'd been teasing me the day before, her message consisted of "No one ever said life was easy. Off you go." From her big-boned hands, capable of wiping spills, soothing tears, and dealing with spiders in the bathtub (a swoop of her hand, a crunch of paper towel, and *There:* the bug was dead), to her exclamatory voice and effusive enthusiasms, my mother was indomitable, her strength a force of nature that shaped my world.

From a young age, I wrote stories and drew pictures, and my mother would go through my *Wizard of Oz* garbage can to find out — she told me years later — what I was thinking.

"Why didn't you just ask me?"

"I don't like to pry," she said.

An adult by then, I didn't remember throwing my creations away — but I did remember the impulse, even at age four or five, to keep things to myself, to hide from my mother my inner world.

She had no boundaries with the people she loved. "My mother," I once told a friend, "could take the weather personally." When she saw signs in me of vulnerability or insecurity or anger, she couldn't let me linger there. And she often turned my enthusiasms into her own property, as I learned when, high on painkillers after having my wisdom teeth pulled, I showed her my yearbook and the photo of my longterm crush, only to listen the next day as she told a friend over the phone, "Some boy named Chris who looks like he never combs his hair."

"I can't handle this upheaval," she announced one Thanksgiving after I admitted I didn't want to see my brother — he'd been lying, stealing, doing drugs — because I wasn't sure I could sit across the table from him without throwing something breakable. "I have a turkey to worry about."

After being voted "prettiest hair" in her high school yearbook and getting an A in Mark Schorer's English 1B at U.C. Berkeley, my mother had to cut her social life and college education short when she was diagnosed with TB. She survived the TB and nine months of hospitalization and several years of follow-up treatment by not feeling sorry for herself, not getting depressed — by hardy German strength and will, by suppressing her vulnerability. There were places she didn't want to go — and if on occasion she had to, she went alone.

The first time you dive into a swimming pool, you're told the water will hold you — but *still.* You stand on the edge, toes curled, unconvinced. The object of your hesitation and longing lies before you, discrete and intact. And then you're in. You slip right through, feeling the water slide against your skin. You can't grab hold, but maybe you don't need to. It holds you.

Each day, as I sit down to pray, I negotiate that scrim between my morning — coffee cup, unmade bed, weather outside — and the deep inner space offered by prayer, by listening. Prayer is a dive, yes — but it is also an excavation. It is bold impulse, pure throw of yourself into the unknown, and premeditated, intentional methodology. We divide space into a grid and begin, carefully, in one corner, to dig and turn over, to examine and consider. We pick up the prayerbook, hold the rosary, determine what it is we want to ask or thank God for on this day. And yet, for all our planning, we still have to leap.

Open my lips, O Lord, and my mouth shall proclaim your praise. Closing my eyes, I see a void shot through with dots and dashes of light, untempered by time or space, as if the universe had turned itself inside out through my mouth. "I had a pit inside me," a friend said, "and then I saw it was a galaxy." *Create in me a clean heart, O God, and renew a right spirit within me.*

At St. Stephen's Episcopal Church, on Christmas Eve and Easter and every Sunday until our priest went through a divorce in which my parents sided with his wife, I swung my legs and put my quarter in the collection plate and watched my brother squirm and my father take him outside and my mother disappear into her hands. Prayer, like dress-up, held mystique and allure — as well as the notion that I'd figure it out some day. In the meantime, I blew bubbles with my saliva, secure at least that *that* wasn't it.

Then, when I was ten, my cat was hit by a car, and I discovered that prayer is born out of desperation. I clutched my pillow every night for a week and promised God that if He let her live, I'd do whatever He wanted. God kept His end of the deal, returning my cat with a rattling purr and one cloudy dead eye but otherwise the same. I felt grateful, but had no idea how to pay Him back.

When I turned to prayer as an adult, at age thirty-five, I was desperate again — but much less spontaneous. I woke every morning at three or four to lie awake for hours. I tried warm milk, I tried melatonin and Tylenol PM. I tried turning on the light and reading. I tried turning it off and imagining myself on a tropical beach. I got up at dawn to dry heaves and diarrhea. I had trouble concentrating. I rarely smiled, and when I did, my cheek muscles ached. Those things I'd kept to myself for so long — my enthusiasms and my doubts, my fear of exposure, the adult writer's equivalent of the fourth-grader's dread of P.E. class — began to clamor. I wanted to speak them. I wanted to be heard. I wanted pity.

Prayer, I figured, couldn't hurt. But I didn't know how to begin. "Our father" and "Now I lay me down to sleep" — the extent of my formal repertory — didn't name what I needed. Without believing myself heard, though, I'd been saying *Help* and *I hurt*, pleas that, like toads and worms in a children's fairy tale, had needed to escape. A priest I spoke with said those were a good start, and steered me to a few more — "You are here, I am here," "Have mercy on me," and the Daily Offices of the Book of Common Prayer. I started praying in bed, at the gym, in the car, and as I grew used to the words and the way they stretched my mouth, I realized that the words didn't matter as much as the saying of them. Words, like kneeling or sweeping hands over candles, provide a miner's lamp lighting the path, a voice for the ineffable. A way in.

My mother wasn't particularly interested in the details of how I found my way back into the Episcopal fold. She reminded me how, at age four, I had responded to her description of the Easter resurrection by saying, "Maybe someone in our family will do that." Now she asked, as if I'd been not to 10 A.M. mass but to a cocktail party, "Meet anyone interesting?" When I recounted to her my first foot washing as part of Maundy Thursday services, she shuddered: "Touching my feet — I wouldn't like that one bit."

But that, to me, was the whole point. Maundy Thursday, as my high church parish celebrated it, had moved me so much I wept. I wanted to explain to her the experience of intimacy I felt I'd shared with God and my priest as my priest had sponged and toweled my bare feet. I started to describe the tradition that Jesus had begun with his disciples. "Well," she sniffed. "I certainly don't have all that background. I don't remember that from Sunday school."

In that way, she silenced me. And how often I wished to silence her! When she repeated the tale of my brother climbing out of his crib at nine months; when she turned potentially confrontational topics into commentary on flower arrangements; when she told me once again that life wasn't easy. And yet my mother, who deftly deflected so much, pondered deeply. She and I didn't always meet in our distinctions of what merited further consideration: "What a silly thing to wonder about," she'd say, or "You think too much." I felt the chill of her disinterest, the hurt in those replies.

And yet she loved to tell how she'd overheard me tell a playmate, after disagreeing about whether babies came out of the tummy or out of down there (I argued the latter), "My mommy never lies." (She set us both straight; Sera's mother had had a caesarean.) She repeated with pleasure and pride how she once responded to a friend's announcement that "I'm so lucky, my children believe everything I tell them" with "I'm so lucky, mine don't believe a thing I tell them." My mother fostered independent thinking, contrariety, good solid rebuttals — and any anecdote that planted her in the camp of open-mindedness. "My daughter, the family Democrat," she used to refer to me — frequently, I suspected, to shock her more conservative friends. "For your eighteenth birthday," she announced excitedly in the car one day, "let's get high!" And, one night when I defended France's record in feeding its people and tilling its fields during the 1920s to my father's comment disparaging the Maginot Line, "Good for you!" If I learned anything at the dinner table and in the station wagon of my youth, I learned to ar-

gue, to wonder — and, when my mother looked hurt or disapprov-
ing, to pull back.

My mother liked to say that she had little respect for organized
religion — she'd known too many hypocrites, cared nothing for
the trappings of power — and found God in nature and art and
books. She'd converted from Presbyterianism to Episcopalianism
to marry my father, whose mother cared a lot about such distinctions, but used to say, "It's all one God, whatever you call it." She
didn't care about incense and stained-glass and sermons, as I would
when I joined a high church parish at age thirty-five, but stopped
speechless with her hand on her heart at the sight of Monet's water
lilies when we visited the Jeu de Paume galleries in 1982 and repeated with wonder her hairdresser's tale of tripping on acid and
watching a rose open in 1969. And yet she taught me to dress
(skirt, pressed blouse, leather shoes, purse) for church, for lunches
downtown, and for airplane travel ("After all," she'd say, "you'll be
arriving somewhere"). Today, when I remove my wristwatch in the
evenings, whether or not I'm going out, I hear her voice telling me,
with only a touch of amused irony, "Ladies don't need to know the
hour after sundown." She cared about appearances, but dismissed
what other people thought. Unless she loved them, and then they
could wound her to the quick.

My depression wounded her. Unlike my father, who was able to
recognize my symptoms — listlessness, humorlessness, heaviness of
tread and affect — and listen to me without feeling threatened, my
mother couldn't take my depression any way but personally. "How
do you think that makes *me* feel?" she cried out after I'd told her I
felt so bad sometimes I thought about suicide. I'd been co-opted,
my despair having to make room for worry about her. Feeling un-
met, as flat as my voice sounded, I told her, "Don't worry, Mom. I
won't do anything." "I just don't know what's bothering you so
much," she said, as though I were making it all up.

I hurt, I hurt, I hurt. This phrase resonated throughout my day,
from earliest waking consciousness through footsteps, ringing
phones, and lifting a fork to my mouth. Food lost its taste, books
their pleasure. I'd been to college, I'd been in therapy. I knew how
to think, to reflect, to articulate. I spoke to friends, I wrote in a
journal. I couldn't shut my mind up. I stopped trying to talk to my
mother about how I felt. *This is,* I told her, *not about you.*

Instead of retreating inward for safety, I became trapped there and didn't feel safe at all. When my own thoughts became too circular, I found myself thinking, *Maybe I should pray.* And so I would. I whispered in the produce aisle, yelled in the car, screamed underwater in the swimming pool. I learned the prayer in silence, in breathing, in saying "Okay okay" as steadily as a metronome. A woman at church introduced me to the Anglican rosary, and I strung my own, repeating certain phrases — the Twenty-third Psalm, the morning Daily Devotion from the Book of Common Prayer, images from a haiku I wrote — as I fingered the blue glass beads. I carried the rosary with me, the touch of which through the fabric of my pocket seemed in some moments prayer enough. I would always be a ponderer, but I found ways to quiet the voices, to loosen the tight skein of anxiety. I did not feel instantly better. But I did, over time, believe that I was met by a presence larger than myself, a presence that told me I wasn't alone. I found security in prayer, in returning to a space that wasn't about isolation or retreat from my strong, effusive, passionate, judgmental, exasperating, generous mother, but that offered a way to hold onto myself and to my growing experience of God.

When, in November 1998, my mother was diagnosed with endometrial cancer, I did what I do when I'm scared. I tucked in. I worried. And then I started reaching out by phone and e-mail. Prayers were offered, even by friends who would not describe themselves as devout. "I'll be thinking of her," they told me. "And of you." My mother had a radical hysterectomy, and the pathology report came back negative. She was walking in three days and home in five. But even before the good news that they'd caught it all and it had not spread, I felt one morning gratitude and love so strong that I knew myself carried. Prayer had become palpable.

Just as it had a few weeks later when, overwhelmed and lonely, I went for a run. I came home as taut and tense as when I'd set out, and then I flopped onto a yoga mat to stretch. I began, "The Lord is my shepherd," and before I hit the word *want,* I felt release. The tight box I had been in collapsed — not suddenly and jerkily and violently, but smoothly and almost sensuously, like melting chocolate. The walls were down, and I was surrounded by light and air, by love.

Seventeen months later, driving down Ashbury Street on my way to my parents' house, I remembered that sensation of spaciousness and support and I asked, as blatantly as I could, for God to hold us all in it again: "We're really going to need you now." I'd just hung up from talking to my mother, who'd phoned to tell me the lump on her neck was cancer — this time lung cancer, metastasized to her lymph nodes, liver, and (we would find out, in the weeks and months to come) bones and brain.

Prayer didn't save my mother the way I'd believed, when I was ten, that it had saved my cat. But it did something else. Praying is nothing if not paying attention, for without attention, the dive becomes sloppy, the dig a waste of time. Without attention, prayer becomes rote and meaningless. During my mother's illness, I paid a lot of attention — to every word the doctor said, to every movement of his face as he felt her tumor each week, to how her skin tightened and her rings loosened on her fingers and her ankles swelled and her lips chapped and her smile took up ever more of her increasingly gaunt face. By giving me a place to fall apart — to scream and weep and plead and, yes, to disappear — prayer gave me strength.

"You're my strength," she told me in August, when there were only two months left. "I have to lean on you."

"Of course, Momma. Of course."

Since the diagnosis, in April, I'd felt focus and purpose. Anxiety and uncertainty, second-guessing and wondering, all blew away in the gale force of caring for my mother, helping to watch over my nephew, relieving my dad. Life cinched in tighter — and with more meaning — in the last months. Everything outside of love and care, friendship and prayer and intimacy, felt extraneous. I became more forthright and independent, more blunt and direct. You're not a grownup until you lose a parent, the cliché goes, and I found it true. "What's wrong with me?" I asked my therapist. "I actually feel good."

"You are doing something for your mother," he said. "You are doing something with enormous meaning."

"My mother is dying," I said.

"Exactly."

Even in the beginning, when she told me I wasn't needed, I went with her to her oncology appointments and took copious notes, asked questions that made her sigh in irritation. When I had to miss an appointment, I phoned the doctor to ask what he thought, even though she'd told me not to bother him, he was a busy man. When he kept us waiting almost forty minutes for an appointment, she fussed about my being late to work until I told her I wasn't worried so she shouldn't worry for me. When he told me, one Saturday when I called him on his cell phone, that she might not live past the end of the year, I told him that he needed to tell her that. And when, two weeks into the third chemo cocktail, she found a new lump on her chest, she handed me the phone: "Call Dr. Smith," she told me. "That's not good news," he said, and I hung up and told her that. At the very end, as she lay dying on a hospital bed in our dining room, I phoned him and told him he needed to come tell her that she'd fought the good fight and could let go. "She needs to hear it from you," I said. I would never have believed I could have done these things, until I had no choice and did them.

I sat next to her when the doctor slid the first drip of Taxol and carboplatinum into a vein on the back of her hand, and I shaved her head and giggled with her about how she needed a black leather jacket to complete the look. I wiped urine from the back of her legs and rubbed ointment onto her slack buttocks to prevent bed sores. I watched the radiation oncology technicians draw crop marks on her abdomen, and I stared at the thickness of the door as they shut it and left her inside. I lifted her from bed to wheelchair to commode and in and out of deep armchairs when she had no lower-body strength, when she suddenly could not raise her foot. "Lindsey," she'd say to my father or the nurse, "let Lindsey do it," and she'd lift her arms to me. "Don't worry, Momma," I'd say, bracing my feet and bending my knees the way the PT had shown me, "I've got you."

We bickered over which nurse had night duty, and whether or not she'd taken her four o'clock meds. When she frowned and spoke about Janet's doctor putting a button in the drawer *over there* — and lifted her shaking and slightly yellow hand to point *over there* and then, exhausted by effort and frustration, dropped it on the third clean sheet that day — I said, "Okay, Mom." I had no idea what she was talking about, and she knew it. She narrowed her eyes and pulled her hand out of mine and whispered, as loudly as she could with a tumor pressing on her voice box, "No!" My mother dying was more than ever my mother — and knew when she was being lied to, or pitied.

After the hospice nurse told her (she'd asked him, as soon as she felt the stethoscope on her chest) that she had only a day or two left, I told her we knew what was happening.

"It's awful," I said. My face was close to hers, but she was still a blur through my tears. "I don't know what we'll do, but I don't want you to worry. We'll be okay. We'll be okay, Mommy."

"Thank you," she whispered, and pressed my face against her neck, against the smooth flesh and musky smell that had been my earliest experience of another and without which I couldn't imagine the world. I smoothed her brow and gripped her hand. She gripped back, and we sat like that for a long time. Even after she was too weak to speak or move, her hand never let go. Her strength — and with it her vulnerability, the flip side of the same coin, no longer something to hide or tuck away or be alone with — passed into me. The boundaries blurred completely, grief and loss having opened up the essence of love. When I look at my hands now, moving on the keys, I know it grips me still.

When the task of choosing the readings for her memorial service fell to me, I selected Paul's first letter to the Corinthians, chapter thirteen. My mother had little patience for clanging gongs or clashing cymbals, and — as I'd seen through her fight with cancer and our loss of my brother, six years earlier — infinite love and hope, so the passage seemed right. Also, as my nephew said, "It's easy to understand." From the lectern in Grace Cathedral, I read the words I'd practiced the night before. I made it through without breaking down. I knew I could: I was doing it for her. It wasn't until a few days later, writing in the journal I'd been keeping since her diagnosis, that I realized what I'd really done for her.

My mother, you see, had one story in particular among those she liked to tell. One *über*-story, if you will, of wonder and aliveness. She told it many times, the last of which I recall as a summer day on the deck at my parents' house in Sonoma. I probably gave a sigh, steeled myself for yet another recounting of something I'd heard a zillion times before: Mom and her friend Jackie in high school on "the river," where they'd hold their hands overhead to tan and lean out of windows at night to hear boys sing to them from the driveway. This story, though, took place when she was ten or so, lying awake on a sleeping porch and looking at the night sky scattered with stars. *Who am I?* she thought, and *How do I fit into all that?* She described her experience in a voice throbbing with intensity and openness, her face rapt with mystery and the divulgence of self. Her directness and passion embarrassed me, and I responded as I had many times before — as though I wasn't really listening. *Mm,* I said, and reached for another tomato. I knew what she was talking about but didn't want to hear about it, any more than she'd wanted to hear about my experience of Maundy Thursday. What, out of self-protection, had we kept from one another? What, if she hadn't gotten sick, would we still be keeping from one another?

I knew, as I wrote in my journal, that I'd chosen a passage that addressed what my mother had been talking about on the deck that day: the limitation of human sight, the knowledge in part. "For now we see through a glass, darkly," Paul wrote, speaking of the mystery she'd glimpsed that night in 1940 on the Russian River. On the other side of that dark glass now, she saw face to face. My choosing I Corinthians 13 didn't just speak to those of us left behind. *Mommy,* it said, *I was listening all along.*

Underwater, we see how the sky looks from beneath a wavering scrim, feel how it is to be held by something we can't hold onto. Underwater, we're the same composition of matter and mind, cells and neurons — but we move in ways not possible on dry land. In the pool at the health club, when I've finished my round of businesslike, adult laps, if I have the lane to myself, I float on my back the way I did when I was a child, my face an inch or two beneath the surface, to look up through the squiggles of light and water that always mesmerize.

Each time we dive, we stretch our bodies, suspended for the briefest of instances between dry land and water. When we pray, we float between who we are to the world and who we are to God. It may look, in both, like we're disappearing. And in a sense, we are. When I finish praying and emerge to the surface of morning and bed and desk and work, I know I've been somewhere else. I blink to hold onto the internal spaciousness, the glimpse of transcendence, the wonder of love. That's where she went, that night on the Russian River when she was ten, and — I like to think — all those years later, sitting next to me in St. Stephen's Episcopal Church, and at the very end, gripping my hand. And in going there, made me long to follow.

MARK DOTY

Fire to Fire

FROM *Shenandoah*

All smolder and oxblood,
these flowerheads,
flames of August:

fierce bronze,
or murky rose,
petals concluded in gold —

And as if fire called its double down

the paired goldfinches
come swerving quick
on the branching towers,

so the blooms
sway with the heft
of hungers

indistinguishable, now,
from the blossoms.
*
Tannic yellow, or rust,

a single brassy streak
at each mid-petal
colluding in a bull's-eye ring,

copper circle
around the seed-horde
flashing like a solar flare.

You can't finish looking:
they rear and wave
in pentecostal variety.
You might as well be tracing flames.
*

Maybe nothing gold
can stay separate —
not feather flower fire.
My work's to say
what signals here,
but Lord I cannot
see a single thing.
*

If I were a sunflower I would be
the branching kind,
my many faces held out
in all directions, all attention,
awake to any golden
incident descending;
drinking in the world
with my myriads of heads,
I'd be my looking.
*

*Painters have painted their swarming groups and
the center-figure of all,
From the head of the center-figure spreading a nimbus
of gold-color'd light,
But I paint myriads of heads, but paint no head without
its nimbus of gold-color'd light. . . .*
*

Their rattling August clothes,
faces a swirl of hours,

                              coil in the seed
unwound at last to these
shag faces bent
over the ruining garden:

Warm evening,
                    vertical

and gold,
stalk of the body,
little glistening hairs
radiating out from the curled

& lifted leaves

paired along the stalk, pattern
plunging toward the center
like the line of the thighs. . . .
*
Paul said when the neighbor's puppy
ran across the street, into traffic,
because it wanted to see our dogs,
it looked like "a little flame."
*
Nothing gold can stand
apart from any other, and so

the sunflowers are trafficked
by birds, open to bees and twilight,
implicated, alert: the fire

longs to meet itself
flaring, the longing wants
a multiplicity of faces,

branching and always branching out,

heads and mouths and eyes
wishing always to
fuse with their own heat.

Which is why the void can make nothing lasting:

the life resides in the yellow candling up, signaling,
and the concomitant yellow hurrying down to meet it,

and nothing that is fixed can call
its double down from heaven;

                              in the arc and rub,
the gold calls to the gold, always,
calls to itself in the other, which is why

the corona'd seedhead flashes the finches down.

DAVID JAMES DUNCAN

Earth Music

FROM *Portland Magazine*

I HOLD THE THING we call "nature" to be the divine manuscript. I hold the infinite wilds to be the only unbowdlerized book we possess of the Authorship that gives and sustains life. Human industry is shredding this book like an Enron document. Some call this shredding "economics" and "freedom." It's not quite a lie. But the freedom to shred the divine manuscript is not an economics any lover of neighbor, self, or Earth wishes to practice.

A spiritual hero told me when I was young that "true happiness lies in making others happy." Having found no happiness seeking it for myself, I tried seeking the happiness of others, and found this unlikely statement to be true. The formula was not without side-effects, however, once self-giving starts to give you joy, you grow bewildered by the spectre of selfishness, fall out of the nationalist/capitalist loop, and limp about in search of healthier hopes. A new source of hope for me: the growing reverence for nature and its mysteries among scientists.

Though science itself never caged us, until recently the sciences were committed to mechanistic paradigms and an obsession with the physically measurable that made reverence possible only by disconnecting spirituality and scientific thought. The so-called "Enlightenment" and its empirical thinking led, sans spirit, to the effective naming of things, cataloguing of things, dissecting, extracting, and reconstruction of things, to create the modern world as we know it. By the late twentieth century, the same divorce between spirituality and science had led to genetically warping even the most sacred living things, filing corporate copyrights on ancient living things, and raping, monoculturizing, extincting, and abstracting ourselves from living things as if we were not living things ourselves.

I see two chief causes for the countering outburst of reverence in science — one famous, the other infamous. The infamous cause: suffering. How many biologists, botanists, ethnologists, anthropologists, have been forced to renounce their fields in mid-career because their living objects of study have died out before their eyes? How many more have been so dismayed by the world's barrios, biological dead or disease zones, slave job and oil war zones, that they've abandoned their disciplines to become peace activists or humanitarians?

The famous cause of the new reverence among scientists: the new physics. Quantum mechanics have changed the way we see the universe. The old proton/neutron/electron atom, for instance, is as unfit for describing matter as we now understand it as a Model T Ford is unfit for negotiating a contemporary freeway. Atomic particles are now said to derive from "immaterial wave packets"; space is now said to have had ten original dimensions that collapsed, at the beginning of time, to form the "superstrings" of which subatomic particles consist. Field theory. Morphogenesis. It's hard to keep up with all the ways that physics is telling us that Space, Time, and Matter derive from something infinitely subtler and greater than all three.

One upshot of all this has been a sea-change in the kind of thinking that we can now call scientific. Reason, though still a crucial tool, is no longer Science's despot king. Intuition, imagination, poetry, humility, and reverence now also play their roles, leading to the possibility of scientific statements such as these:

> WILLIGIS JAGER: "There aren't two kinds of laws: matter and mind. Rather, there is a single continuous law for both matter and mind. Matter is the domain of space in which the field is extremely dense."
>
> ALBERT EINSTEIN: "In the new physics, there is no place for both field and matter, because field is the only reality."
>
> TEILHARD DE CHARDIN:"Concretely speaking, there is no matter and spirit. There exists only matter that is becoming spirit."
>
> FREDERICK SOMMER: "Spirit is the behavior of matter. Perception does not take spiritedness into a state of affairs that does not already have it."

*

My daily work is reflection, imagination, and story-telling. The recent sea-change in science has returned the modifier "scientific" to a place of honor in this work. When, for example, I first read in my teens of medieval cosmologists referring to a "music of the spheres," my reason howled in protest because its "education in science" had trained it to do so. Despite reason's howling, though, my heart at the time told me: *You have heard such music.* The science of today adds that if "field is the only reality" and "there exists only matter that is becoming spirit," it is scientific not only to ask my heart where I heard spheric music, but to try to hear it again.

Exploring my heart, I recalled that, years ago, I read the *Upanisadic* description of a state in which "the soul perceives infinite hugeness and infinite smallness as one and the same," and felt a strong intuitive resonation. Then, years later, I found in the Koran the statement, "All Creation in the hands of the Merciful One is smaller than a mustard seed," and felt the same resonation. Then last year I learned of a mathematician, Georg Cantor, who proved in demonstrable mathematical fashion that infinities come in an infinite range of sizes, and that any Infinity, being a unity and hence complete within itself, must include itself, and be a member of itself, "and thus can only be known through a flash of mystical vision." And then one morning last spring, while cleaning my study, I opened a dusty *National Geographic* and found a Hubble Space photo of 150,000 galaxies swirling in a jot of universe "the size of a grain of sand held at arm's length," and tears rose because, in an instant, the entire preceding series of scriptual and mathematical images swept through me, filling me with the *profundo* hum of an indescribable music.

That night, after watching the movie *Captain Corelli's Mandolin*, I dreamed that I was shot dead by a hundred machine guns, shot so many times that a dark bullet-driven wind blew my soul irrevocably away from even my dead body and I was invisible and afraid and had neither breath nor voice with which to call out to my God. I called out in bodiless desire anyway, and a spheric point pierced the wall of the grim gray world in which I drifted, the point expanded, tore that world's wall apart like so much wet kleenex, a light poured through, and I saw my Beloved's cheek and brilliant eye peeking at me through the hole, just that much of Him, yet there was such love in that eye, such *What-a-trick-I've-pulled!* glee, that a posthumous existence without need of this body felt not just possible but certain, and I woke with a jolt of joy, hearing the same kind of music. So when, the next day, I read Annie Dillard writing, "There is no less holiness at this time — as you are reading this — than there was the day the Red Sea parted . . . There is no whit less might in heaven or on earth than there was the day Jesus said, 'Maid, arise' to the centurion's daughter, or the day Peter walked on water, or the night Mohammed flew to heaven on a horse. . . . In any instant you may avail yourself of the power to love your enemies; to accept failure, slander, or the grief of loss; or to endure torture . . . 'Each and every day the Divine Voice issues from Sinai,' says the Talmud. Of eternal fulfillment, Tillich said, 'If it is not seen in the present, it cannot be seen at all.'" I felt an urge to shout: *Hallelujah, Annie! You're singin' the morpho-genetic gospel now!*

If field is the only reality and all matter is becoming spirit, I daresay this shout can be called scientific.

The sensations of field, of palpable presence, of *hum,* still come over me walking the mountains or cities, wading the traffic or trout streams. I don't seek such sensations. They just unfold, unlooked for, in the course of what comes. A spring aspen leaf might brush my face, and I'll close my eyes and find myself feeling the tiny, self-contained universe that is a spring-green aspen cell suddenly making two of itself, and growing, *because it loves to.* I'll witness "fruitful multiplication" in our Montana-winter-blighted fruit trees or the year's brood of Bantam chicks, the creek's insects or the river bottoms' whitetail fawns, the newborn wood-ducks, the kingfishers, the killdeers, and wonder comes upon me in the form of music as the densities, unions, and divisions of love are made palpable. I'll stand by the ocean, see the slight curve of horizon, feel the ocean's hum, and see: *the very seas are a single spherical note.* I'll have the sense, standing in running water, that I've been not just close to the molecules flowing round me but *inside* them: that I've experienced, in the womb or aeons earlier, the coming together and breaking apart of spheric particles of H and of O. I'll witness the aging, sickness, and deaths of plants, animals, family, friends, self, the migrations to new climes, transmigrations into unknowns, jolts into new awareness or bodies, slow breakdowns by organic or industrial attrition, transformations of earth, water, matter, energy, clouds, leaves, souls — and a vast pulsing harmony and an anguish of joy will fill the bit of me left unabsorbed.

It's time I stopped building sentences now and stepped down to the creek, as I've done half my life come evening. This time of year I'll look for the rainbows that migrate up from the bigger rivers to spawn. And I'll find a pair, if this spring is like the last eight, in a tiny side channel a quarter mile downstream. As I approach them on my belly I'll be crawling across spheroid grains of white granitic sand. I'll then lie like a Muslim, watching a female trout an arm's length from my eyes beat her body against gold-colored pebbles, build a stone nest, and fill it with a thousand lit-from-within orange spheres. I'll watch the male ease over like one of the gray-black snow clouds above. And when the milt pours down, each nested sphere will suddenly love to divide and divide till it's a sphere no longer but a tiny, sphere-eyed trout. I'll encounter the same trout over the slow course of summer, drifting down toward the rivers, growing by dividing, defeating time; I'll catch them now and then, release most, eat a few, and the survivors will return in twelve or sixteen seasons, bearing the milt clouds, glowing spheres, and hidden fields that carry the genius of trout toward my children's children's world. There's not much more to discuss here. Either fields beyond matter exist or they don't, the kingdom of heaven is within us or it isn't, and each and every day the Divine Voice issues from Sinai, every inch of Creation is pierced by Its song, and every point, cell, particle, field is so moved by the Music that it loves to sing, swell, shrink, leap, divide, and bear all fruit and all life and all death and all regeneration in response, or It doesn't.

But my honest experience is: *It does, it does!*

I have no rational idea "what it means" when consciousness revs up and perceives mystery or field amid mind, amid life, amid matter, but oh do I have perceptions of what it means. And if I am ever to rise to the Beauty that is Truth, I must describe these *perceptions* as consciousness Truly perceives them. I therefore confess lifelong love for a wilderness found outside myself, till once in a while I encounter it within — a wilderness entered, it seems, through agenda-less alertness at work, rest, or play in the presence of language, rivers, mountains, music, plants, creatures, rocks, moon, sun, dust, pollen grains, dots, spheres, galaxies, grains of sand, stars, every sort of athletic ball, cells, DNA, molecules, atomic particles, and immaterial forces, till it suddenly "inside-outs" me, leading to the perception and adoration of synergies and harmonies that leave my mind wondrous happy but far, far behind my heart. It's a wilderness my dog, Reason, will never succeed in sniffing out, chomping up, or rationally defining, yet a wilderness I've been so often and gratefully assailed by that I've lost all but comic interest in my good dog's sniffing and suspect that even the dog begins to enjoy itself when we get flipped into wilderness's heart.

I believe — based on hydrogen clouds giving birth to stars, exploded stars to planets, spring stormclouds to snow, snowbanks to rivers, orange orbs to trout; I believe based on lives collapsing into ashes and dust, and dust bursting back to life; I believe based on spheric shapes singing, dividing, creating cells, plants, creatures, creating my children, sunflowers, sun, self, universe, by constantly sacrificing all that they are in order to be reconfigured and reborn forever and ever — that when we feel Love's density, see its colors, feel its pulse, it's time to quit worrying about reason and words and cry: *"My God! Thanks!"*

If I stake my life on one field, one wild force, one sentence issuing from Sinai, it is this one: *There is no goal beyond love.*

JOSEPH EPSTEIN

The Green-Eyed Monster:
Envy Is Nothing to Be Jealous Of

FROM *Washington Monthly*

OF THE SEVEN DEADLY SINS, only envy is no fun at all. Sloth may not seem that enjoyable, nor anger either, but giving way to deep laziness has its pleasures, and the expression of anger entails a release that is not without its small delights. In recompense, envy may be the subtlest — perhaps I should say the most insidious — of the seven deadly sins. Surely it is the one that people are least likely to want to own up to, for to do so is to admit that one is probably ungenerous, mean, small-hearted. It may also be the most endemic. Apart from Socrates, Jesus, Marcus Aurelius, Saint Francis, Mother Teresa, and only a few others, at one time or another, we have all felt flashes of envy, even if in varying intensities, from its minor pricks to its deep, soul-destroying, lacerating stabs. So widespread is it — a word for envy, I have read, exists in all known languages — that one is ready to believe it is the sin for which the best argument can be made that it is part of human nature.

In politics, envy, or at any rate the hope of eliminating it, is said to be the reigning principle of socialism, as greed is said to be that of capitalism (though modern capitalist advertising is about few things more than the regular stimulation of envy). On the international scene, many if not most wars have been fought because of one nation's envy of another's territory and all they derive from it, or out of jealously guarded riches that a nation feels are endangered by those less rich who are likely to be envious of their superior position. In this connection, it is difficult not to feel that, at least in part, much of the anti-American feeling that arose after September 11, 2001, had envy, some of it fairly rancorous, at its heart. In the magazine *Granta,* the Indian writer Ramachandra Guha wrote that "historically, anti-Americanism in India was shaped by an aesthetic distaste for America's greatest gift — the making of money." But can "aesthetic distaste" here be any more than a not-very-well-disguised code word for envy?

Is envy a "feeling," an "emotion," a "sin," a "temperamental disposition," or a "worldview"? Might it also be a Rorschach test: tell what you envy, and you reveal a great deal about yourself. It can be all of these things — and more. No one would doubt that, whatever else it is, envy is certainly a charged, indeed a supercharged, word: one of the few words left in the English language that retains the power to scandalize. Most of us could still sleep decently if accused of any of the other six deadly sins; but to be accused of envy would be seriously distressing, so clearly does such an accusation go directly to character. The other deadly sins, though all have the disapproval of religion, do not so thoroughly, so deeply demean, diminish, and disqualify a person. Not the least of its stigmata is the pettiness implicit in envy.

The *Webster's* definition of the word won't quite do: "(1) Obs. malice; (2) painful or resentful awareness of the advantage enjoyed by another joined with a desire to possess the same advantage." The *Oxford English Dictionary* is rather better: it defines envy first as "malignant or hostile feeling; ill-will, malice, enmity," and then as "active evil, harm, mischief," both definitions accounted Obscure. But the great *OED* only gets down to serious business in its third definition, where it defines envy as "the feeling of mortification and ill-will occasioned by the contemplation of superior advantages possessed by another," in which usage the word *envy* first pops up around 1500. It adds a fourth definition, one in which the word is used without "notions of malevolence," and has to do with the (a) "desire to equal another in achievement, or excellence; emulation," and (b) speaks to "a longing for the advantages enjoyed by another person." Aristotle, in *The Rhetoric,* writes of emulation as good envy, or envy ending in admiration and thus in the attempt to imitate the qualities one began by envying. Yet it must be added that envy doesn't generally work this way. Little is good about envy, except shaking it off, which, as any of us who have felt it deeply knows, is not so easily done.

Both the *OED* and *Webster's* definitions are inattentive to the crucial distinction between envy and jealousy. Most people, failing to pick up the useful distinction, mistakenly use the two words interchangeably. I suspect people did not always do so. H. W. Fowler, in his splendid *Modern English Usage* of 1926, carries no entry on either word, suggesting that formerly there was no confusion. Bryan A. Garner, in his 1998 *Dictionary of Modern American Usage,* says that "the careful writer distinguishes between these terms," but does not himself do so sufficiently. He writes that "jealousy is properly restricted to contexts involving affairs of the heart, envy is used more broadly of resentful contemplation of a more fortunate person."

With deep pedantic delight one takes in trumping a recognized usage expert, it pleases me to say, "Not quite so." The real distinction is that one is jealous of what one has, envious of what other people have. Jealousy is not always pejorative; one can after all be jealous of one's dignity, civil rights, honor. Envy, except when used in the emulative sense mentioned by Aristotle, is always pejorative. If jealousy is, in cliché parlance, spoken of as the "green-eyed monster," envy is cross-, squinty-, and blearily red-eyed. Never, to put it very gently, a handsome or good thing, envy. Although between jealousy and envy, jealousy is often the more intensely felt of the two, it can also be the more realistic: one is, after all, sometimes correct to feel jealousy. And not all jealousy plays the familiar role of sexual jealousy. One may be jealous — again, rightly — of one's reputation, integrity, and other good things. One is almost never right to feel envy: to be envious is to be, ipso facto, wrong.

Apart from emulative envy, the only aspect of envy that does not seem to me pejorative is a form of envy I have myself felt, as I suspect have others who are reading this article: the envy that I think of as faith envy. This is the envy one feels for those who have the true and deep and intelligent religious faith that sees them through the darkest of crises, death among them. If one is oneself without faith and wishes to feel this emotion, I cannot recommend a better place to find it than in the letters of Flannery O'Connor. There one will discover a woman still in her thirties, who, after coming into her radiant talent, knows she is going to die well before her time and, fortified by her Catholicism, faces her end without voicing complaint or fear. I not long ago heard, in Vienna, what seemed to me a perfect rendering of Beethoven's Ninth Symphony, and was hugely moved by it, but how much more would I have been moved, I could not help wonder, if I were in a state of full religious belief, since the Ninth Symphony seems to me in many ways a religious work. Faith envy is envy, alas, about which one can do nothing but quietly harbor it.

Envy must also be distinguished from general yearning. One sees people at great social ease and wishes to be more like them; or feels keenly how good it would be once more to be young; or longs to be wealthier; or pines to be taller, thinner, more muscular, less awkward, more beautiful generally. All this is yearning. Envy is never general, but always very particular — at least envy of the kind one feels strongly.

The envious tend to be injustice collectors. "Envy, among other ingredients, has a love of justice in it," William Hazlitt wrote. "We are more angry at undeserved than at deserved good fortune." Something to it, but, my sense is, not all that much. Much more often than not, envy expresses feelings more personal than the love of justice. In another useful distinction, Kierkegaard in *The Sickness Unto Death* wrote that "admiration is happy self-surrender; envy is unhappy self-satisfaction." Envy asks one leading question: What about me? Why does he or she have beauty, talent, wealth, power, the world's love, and other gifts, or at any rate a larger share of them than I? Why not me? Dorothy Sayers, in a little book on the seven deadly sins, writes: "Envy is the great leveler: if it cannot level things up, it will level them down . . . At its best, envy is a climber and a snob; at its worst it is a destroyer — rather than have anyone happier than itself, it will see us all miserable together." A self-poisoning of the mind, envy is usually less about what one lacks than about what other people have. A strong element of the begrudging resides in envy, thus making the envious, as Immanuel Kant remarked in *The Metaphysics of Morals,* "intent on the destruction of the happiness of others."

One might call someone or something — another's family life, health, good fortune — "enviable" without intending rancor. In the same way, one might say, "I envy you your two-month holiday in the south of France" without, in one's mind, plotting how to do the person out of it. Or one might say, "I don't envy him the responsi-bilities of his job," by which one merely means that one is pleased not to have another's worries. There probably ought to be a word falling between envy and admiration, as there ought to be a word that falls between talent and genius. Yet there isn't. The language is inept.

Nor ought envy to be confused with open conflict. Someone has something that one feels one wants — customers, a high ranking or rating, government office, a position of power — and one con-tends for it, more or less aggressively, but out in the open. The openness changes the nature of the game. Envy is almost never out in the open; it is secretive, plotting, behind the scenes. Helmut Schoeck, who in *Envy: A Theory of Social Behavior* has written the most comprehensive book on the subject, notes that it "is a silent, secretive process and not always verifiable." Envy, to qualify as envy, has to have a strong touch — sometimes more than a touch — of malice behind it. Malice that cannot speak its name, cold-blooded but secret hostility, impotent desire, hidden rancor, and spite all cluster at the center of envy. La Rochefoucauld opened the subject of envy nicely with a silver stiletto, when he wrote: "In the misfor-tune of our best friends, we always find something that is not dis-pleasing to us." Yes, really not displeasing at all. Dear old envy.

JAMES FREDERICKS

Masao Abe: A Spiritual Friendship

FROM *Spiritus*

SOME YEARS AGO, I enjoyed a fine Japanese lunch with my friend and teacher, Masao Abe, the great exponent of Zen Buddhism and leader in the dialogue among Buddhists and Christians. Professor Abe has taught me wonderful things about Buddhism for some twenty years now. I gathered with him and his wife, Ikuko Abe, in a traditional restaurant in Kyoto. We had a private room with a low table and sat on *tatami* mats. Abe Sensei ("Sensei" is a term of endearment and respect for a teacher used in Japan) had been somewhat pensive and withdrawn for most of the meal. Mrs. Abe and I had been bantering about how late the *tsuyu* rains had been that year and the effect it was having on Kyoto's hydrangea. Suddenly Sensei began to speak with an unusual tone of voice, as if saying something of great importance to no one in particular. "It is not enough," he said. Mrs. Abe and I fell silent and attentive. He repeated himself in the same voice: "It is not enough." I knew immediately what my teacher was talking about. In his old age and after a long and distinguished career of teaching and lecturing about Zen in the West, Abe Sensei was talking about a Buddhist teaching dear to his heart, "the standpoint of emptiness." Out of politeness, I did not want to indicate that I understood his meaning so directly and sat, wondering what I should say in response. Finally, I settled on something like this: "I will continue to study; Sensei, please continue to teach." I spoke in the most formal Japanese I could muster out of respect for my teacher, but also out of friendship.

I am not sure how I should describe my relationship with Masao Abe. To call us colleagues in the dialogue among Buddhists and Christians hardly does justice to how dear he is to me. To call me his *deshi* (disciple) does not fit the expectations this word conjures in Japan. He and I disagree professionally over many important matters. Besides, Sensei is a Buddhist and I am not. Is Masao Abe my friend? He is thirty-five years my senior and a distinguished scholar. In Japan at least, calling us friends *(tomodachi)* would be presumptuous. I will stick with friendship, however, and will try to justify the term by qualifying it. My friendship with Abe Sensei is a *spiritual* friendship. I want to write about this spiritual friendship and reflect on what my teacher meant that day in Kyoto when he said, "it is not enough."

Friendship is a familiar theme in Christian spirituality. This is hardly surprising. Friendships humanize. Friendships must therefore be related in basic ways to our spiritual lives. The one who is without friends is poor indeed. More specifically, I am interested in spiritual friendships with those who follow other religious paths. I think we should look on these "inter-religious friendships" as a form of Christian spiritual practice. Friendships that reach across the boundaries of community, doctrine, scripture, asceticism, and liturgy that separate religious believers should rightly be recognized as new opportunities for exploring Christian spirituality. Certainly this is the case with my friendship with Masao Abe. Sensei's Buddhist path is central, not incidental, to our friendship. Inter-religious friendships are not common. They are not unheard of, either. Gustav Weigel's friendship with Rabbi Abraham Heschel and Thomas Merton's friendship with D. T. Suzuki (one of Abe Sensei's mentors) come readily to mind.

Friendships with those who follow other religious paths contribute to human flourishing. They are a way of building up new forms of solidarity between religious communities. The virtue of inter-religious friendship also helps us to resist vices, like our propensity to fear those who are different. In our sinfulness, fear leads us to demonize, caricature, or simply ignore the Other. A spiritual friendship with someone who follows another religious path helps us to resist not only intolerance, but also our penchant for developing elaborate theological schemes that reduce the Other to what

David Tracy calls "simply more of the same." Spiritual friendships with those who follow other religious paths help us to resist vices such as these.

Every friendship, no matter how good or how old, once involved making a hospitable place in our lives for a stranger. After all, every friend, no matter how good or how old a friend, was once a stranger. This practice has spiritual value. Welcoming a stranger entails a de-centering of the self. We are moved off our home ground. The sovereignty of the ego is undermined. In welcoming a stranger, we have to make room for another way of imagining the world and acting within it. Sartre was unable to see the advent of the stranger as anything but a threat. Emmanuel Levinas, reflecting Jewish tradition, saw the stranger not only as threat, but also as beatitude. Welcoming the stranger brings a loss of security, but also a loss of hopelessness; the ruination of autonomy, but also a liberation from self-absorption.

Every friend was once a stranger. Less obviously, friendships of lasting value and depth retain a sense of the stranger in the friend. This is very true of my friendship with Masao Abe. Years ago, I spent an evening with Professor and Mrs. Abe in their home in Kyoto. Sensei was unusually gregarious and informal that evening. He wore a summer kimono. In July, the taste of cold noodles goes nicely with the drone of cicadas in the garden and the clean smell of the *tatami*. Not knowing any good Japanese word for what I was trying to say, I told Mrs. Abe that everything was *gemutlich*. Sensei laughed as he tried to translate it into Japanese for us. In the alcove was a very simple flower arrangement and a hanging scroll with Chinese characters painted in a spontaneous hand. I asked Sensei about the calligraphy. The scroll contained only a few characters: form, emptiness, emptiness, form. Now able to read the scroll, I was left with a sudden sense of what a stranger Masao Abe remains for me.

"Form is emptiness, emptiness is form." This famous teaching comes from the Heart Sutra and tells much about why my cherished teacher and friend is still a stranger to me. According to this teaching, sensible forms, the objects we fashion out of our passions and obsessions and call "reality," are in fact "empty." They are illusions fashioned by what the Buddha called "the mind on fire." All our pretensions to selfhood — our construction of racial and national identity, our preoccupation with status, our obsession with autonomy — are but fleeting forms without substance, founded on nothing. They do not endure. They are empty. Clinging to such forms as if they were real and enduring only entangles us in a world that will never be satisfactory. This is *samsara,* what the Lotus Sutra calls the "burning house" of sorrow. The path of wisdom, the path that leads to an extinguishing of the fires that inflame the mind, entails renunciation. Clinging to empty forms will never be satisfactory. When clinging ends, empty forms no longer constitute a prison of our own construction. The forms become just transient manifestations of the emptiness that characterizes everything. Wisdom, for a Buddhist like Masao Abe, means finding freedom in the realization of the emptiness of all things through non-attachment.

Form is emptiness, but according to the Heart Sutra, the reverse is also the case. Emptiness itself is merely form and has no existence apart from the fleeting and ever-changing shapes taken by the world. This means that emptiness is not a transcendent realm beyond this world. Awakening to the emptiness of all things does not entail an "ascent" of the soul into a realm beyond the world. Form is emptiness — and emptiness is simply the myriad forms themselves. Therefore, in speaking of emptiness, Sensei likes to use phrases strange to me, such as "the original naturalness of all" *(jinen)* and the "true suchness of things" *(shin-nyo).* For my friend, things have no "beyond." Visible forms are not symbols that speak of what is "higher." In a way that would have been utterly foreign to the Psuedo-Dionysius, my friend does not live in a world in which appearances open up into a redeeming transcendence. Form is emptiness and emptiness is form — nothing more. There is nothing beyond empty forms because there is no beyond.

For many years, in our discussions, Masao Abe and I have tried to find a place for my God in those Chinese characters. Neither one of us has succeeded to the degree we had hoped. Form is emptiness. Emptiness is nothing other than form itself. In the asymmetrical grace of a flower arrangement, in the play of textures, tastes, and sounds of the tea ceremony, in the spontaneous hand of the calligrapher — there is the suggestion of a kind of intimacy of all things. In the "true suchness of things" and the "original naturalness of all," the perfectly ordinary finally becomes numinous in itself, without bearing the burden of pointing to a transcendence beyond it. Zen is witness to an immanence so radical and uncompromised that the otherness of the Christian God is overcome.

At the dedication of the Temple in Jerusalem, Solomon had to deal with the unimaginable otherness of God: "Even the heaven and the highest heaven cannot hold you, how much less this house that I have built!" (1 Kings 8:27). The "true suchness of things" negates the unimaginable otherness of Solomon's God. The "original naturalness of all" deconstructs the transcendence of the God of Zion. In my friend's Buddhist world, there is neither a Creator nor a creation that witnesses to the Creator. The heavens do not declare the glory of God. There is only the drone of cicadas, the clean smell of *tatami,* and the taste of cold noodles, in Kyoto, in July, underneath the hanging scroll. Form is emptiness — but emptiness does not lie beyond form. Nothing lies beyond the intimacy of forms. But unlike my friend and teacher, I cannot abide contentedly in this "original naturalness" that is without transcendence. The hound of heaven will not allow me to rest in this intimacy with the ordinary. In this, Sensei is not like me. He does not know what it means to be pursued by such a hound. For all our friendship over the years, there still are times when we look at one another in what only can be called an appalling bewilderment. This friend of mine remains a stranger.

So, as I began to discern the shape of those Chinese characters on the hanging scroll with Sensei's help, a poorly alloyed mixture of regret and gratitude began to arise within me. My dear friend and teacher, Masao Abe, for all his erudition about my God (he studied theology with Tillich and Niebuhr), does not know a God beyond the world of forms. He does not know the subjectivity that arises by being addressed by the Holy One of Israel, as Abraham was. Beyond the "true suchness of things," there is no transcendent One who creates and redeems, who judges but also relents. The regret arises because I recognize the goodness of the Buddhist path but cannot embrace that path as a believer and practioner. I am not a Buddhist. To say so would be not only pretense, but harmful to Buddhism. I will not hurt my Buddhist friend. The gratitude arises in the fact that my Buddhist friend has been such a patient and generous teacher. I cannot be a Buddhist. I can, however, be a

friend to Masao Abe. My spiritual friendship with this Buddhist is a
way to embrace and honor what I cannot become.

There is something paradoxical in my friendship with Masao Abe.
In no small way, our strangeness to one another is the bond that
holds our friendship together. Sensei, I think, would agree. I have
other friends who manage to inhabit the world of Zen and the
world of Christian theism with little difficulty. No doubt, this is a
grace and should be accepted as such by those to whom this grace
is given. I have never prayed for such a grace. On reflection, I suppose the reason I do not pray for such grace is the fear that this
might corrode my friendship with Sensei. Our strangeness to one
another has brought a depth of spiritual purpose to our friendship.
This depth of purpose, however, has been a pearl purchased at
great price. My friendship with Masao Abe has required me to find
my way in territory uncharted by my own religious tradition. This
calls for some explanation.

My faith, tutored by the Catholic sacramental imagination, teaches
me to watch for epiphanies. We should live life always ready to take
off our shoes. In a world where the Word is always becoming flesh,
my deepest spiritual instincts beg me to recognize in Sensei's Otherness yet another wondrous trace of the divine. Do I not see in the
face of my friend the presence of a Mystery that both summons and
beatifies? Is not this Mystery the same Otherness that led Anthony
into the desert and Juan de la Cruz to an ascent into *Nada*? As a
child, I was taught that the redwood trees prayed to their Creator
— and that I could hear them pray if only I would quit the trail and
listen hard enough. If this is true of redwood trees, how much
more must this be true of my Buddhist friend? Sensei certainly invites me to quit the trail. If only I could listen hard enough, I would
hear in Sensei's voice a hymn to the Creator.

Absorbing Masao Abe's Buddhist life into the encompassing Mystery of God, however, would be a betrayal of our friendship. The
betrayal would not lie in the fact that my teacher has repeatedly
told me that Buddhist emptiness cannot be identified with the God
of Christian faith. Sensei and I have plenty of theological disagreements. The betrayal would lie in the loss of the Otherness that
forms the basis of our friendship. The great Jewish thinker, Emmanuel Levinas, has taught me much in this regard. Levinas speaks

of the Other as a "face" *(le visage)* that is "defaced" by incorporating it comfortably into our pre-existing view of the world. By defacing the Other, we render the "face" harmless, pressed into service of the self and the world it has constructed for itself. For my friendship with Masao Abe, this would constitute a monumental loss. Appeasing my need to make theological sense of the world would come at the expense of an enriching, if troubling, friendship. This is too high a price to pay by far.

My Buddhist friend has run me off my theological roadmap. The greatness of Buddhism, which comes to me not in any book, but in the concrete form of my devoted friend, must be the work of God. And yet, this very friend assures me that this is not the case. Learning to live off the roadmap is what makes this inter-religious friendship such good, if difficult, spiritual practice. A friendship with someone who follows another religious path calls for a spirituality that resists the attempt to overcome difference and to incorporate the Other into "simply more of the same." The strangeness of my Buddhist friend is not merely provisional. His Otherness is not something to be overcome. My friend's Buddhist life cannot be situated comfortably within my Christian understanding of the world without doing violence to Buddhism and to our friendship. My spiritual practice of inter-religious friendship, therefore, is not so much a quest for understanding as a disciplined practice of listening. By "understanding," I mean here the attempt to assimilate the Other into my Christian grand narrative. "Listening," in contrast, means to let the Other appear as a "face," to resist my need to deface, and above all, to dispose myself to become one who is addressed by that face, not one who addresses.

What I speak of here is something more than Christian humility before another religious tradition. Like humility, honoring my friendship — even at the expense of theological coherence — is a form of spiritual practice. In this respect, I have been changed by a great Buddhist truth and Masao Abe has been a great teacher of this truth. But to tell of this, I must tell more about my Buddhist friend.

Sitting on the *tatami* mats in that Kyoto restaurant was not the only time that Sensei has ever said "it is not enough." In April 1942, four months after the beginning of the Pacific War, Masao Abe entered Kyoto Imperial University (now Kyoto University) to study the philosophy of religion. He was twenty-seven years old, buffeted by criticism for not enlisting in the army, and fearful of the power of nihilism at work in his militarized society. In Kyoto, he was much attracted by the lectures of Tanabe Hajime, who was already filled with foreboding over Japan's impending defeat and looking to Pure Land Buddhism for guidance. Zen is focused on unflagging effort on the meditation pillow and sudden *satori*. The Pure Land path, in contrast, is a Buddhism of repentance and faith in the compassion of Amida Buddha who rescues us from our egocentricity. Tanabe's comment, "Amida is not far from here," brought Abe to weep inconsolably in the realization that it was he who was moving away from Amida even as Amida was moving toward him. Even still, Sensei would eventually find the Pure Land path "not enough" for resisting the forces of nihilism in the world and in himself.

After the war, Abe joined a Zen meditation group that met at Reiun-ji within the great temple complex of Myoshin-ji in Kyoto. The group was directed by Hisamatsu Shin'ichi, a Zen layman and lecturer on Buddhism at the University. In December 1951, Abe had a violent encounter with Hisamatsu that people still talk about. Zen had begun to erode Abe's Pure Land faith and in the resulting personal crisis, the threat of nihilism had returned to him in force. One evening, in great agitation, Abe rose from his meditation pillow and lunged toward Hisamatsu, screaming, "Is this the true self?" He was restrained briefly and then left the room. Later, Abe recalled the anguish of that dark night. "It's all a lie!" he told Hisamatsu. Still later, Abe said in despair, "I cannot find anyplace where I can stand." Hisamatsu answered: "Stand right at that place where there is no place to stand." Zen calls this the standpoint of emptiness.

This "place where there is no place to stand" is where my friend has stood for more than half a century. Hisamatsu introduced Masao Abe to D. T. Suzuki who was already corresponding with Thomas Merton about Zen and Christian contemplation. Abe would eventually teach at great universities in the United States and Europe and become one of the leading figures in the dialogue among Buddhists and Christians. At the heart of all of this has been Abe Sensei's unwavering commitment to expounding the standpoint of emptiness.

In honoring my friendship with Masao Abe — even at the expense of theological coherence — I too have had to learn how to stand in "the place where there is no place to stand." Without ceasing to be a Christian believer, my friendship with Masao Abe has required me to move off my Christian theological roadmap. In doing so, I have not become a Buddhist. Nevertheless, I have been changed profoundly by the Buddhist truth of emptiness. My Christian friends have little understanding, and in some cases, little patience with my attempt to stand in this "place where there is no place to stand." Christianity, they remind me, is an encompassing vision that interprets the world completely. How could anything lie beyond the roadmap? Abe's Buddhism must be the work of the Holy Spirit. Even though Buddhists do not realize it, they too give praise to the Creator of heaven and earth. In this, of course, my Christian friends speak a great Christian truth. Nothing created by God has been abandoned. No corner of reality is God-forsaken. While I stand within this Christian theological roadmap, however, the face of my friend and teacher is no longer recognizable. Looking on Masao Abe as an "anonymous Christian" does violence to our friendship. The sacramental instincts of my Catholic spirituality pose a great temptation to redraw the lines of my friend's face into my own image and likeness.

I cannot abandon my Christian faith and I will not abandon my Buddhist friend. Therefore, in my own way, I have had to learn how to stand in the "place where there is no place to stand." This has not meant forsaking my trust in God and replacing it with the "original naturalness of all" and the "true suchness" of things. The practice of my faith, however, has been changed profoundly by the truth of Buddhist emptiness. This brings me to a final reflection on what my friend meant when he spoke in that restaurant in Kyoto and said, "it is not enough."

Sensei's favorite passage from the New Testament is the *carmen Christi* (Phil. 2:6–11). Singing of the savior, the hymn begins, ". . . though he was in the form of God, he did not regard equality with God something to be grasped. Rather, he emptied himself, taking the form of a slave . . ." Abe Sensei and I discussed this passage one afternoon, drinking green tea in his office. He wanted to know what "emptied himself" meant to me. I must have said something about the Incarnation of the Word in reply — I no longer remember. Sensei spoke even more softly than usual that day. "I think it means," he began, "that Christ is a kind of bodhisattva." I was deeply touched and, after a respectful moment, I said, "Sensei, please understand that this bodhisattva-Christ who takes the form of a slave is the only God that Christians know anything about." Abe Sensei closed his eyes and made the whole room very quiet.

Of Buddhism's many impressive teachings, the bodhisattva ideal must be one of the most wondrous. A bodhisattva is one who, in the quest for enlightenment, has come to the threshold of nirvana itself. Ready to enter into bliss, the bodhisattva renounces nirvana and turns back to *samsara*. This return to *samsara* takes the form of a vow to work skillfully for the benefit of every sentient being. In the bodhisattva's vow, Buddhism teaches a great and paradoxical truth. Since attachment is the birthplace of sorrow, wisdom requires that attachment be renounced. In the quest for liberation from sorrow, however, the bodhisattva is the one who has overcome every attachment save one, the attachment to nirvana itself. If the bodhisattva is to attain enlightenment, all attachment must be renounced, even the attachment to nirvana. Herein lies the paradox: only in renouncing this last attachment, our desire to abide in nirvana, can nirvana be attained. According to the bodhisattva ideal, true enlightenment involves not an escape from *samsara*, but rather a return to it in order to work skillfully and compassionately for the benefit of all sentient beings. Therefore, only by turning away from nirvana does the bodhisattva become fully enlightened. In living the vow, the bodhisattva uproots the last taint of egocentricity, the desire to find personal bliss by escaping *samsara*.

Sensei sees in Christ this paradoxical truth of the bodhisattva. Christ renounces divinity and takes on the form of a slave in order to benefit sentient beings. Because of this great renunciation, Christ is raised up and exalted. The bodhisattva is truly enlightened only by renouncing nirvana. Christ is truly divine only by abandoning divinity. By entering the world of form the transcendent monarch becomes the living God of Christian faith. According to the epigram from the Heart Sutra on Sensei's hanging scroll, emptiness is truly emptiness only when it empties itself and becomes the world of form. According to the *carmen*, Christ is truly the Christ only by renouncing his divinity and entering into the world of form.

In the bodhisattva teaching, emptiness becomes a spiritual practice, not merely a metaphysical assertion about the nature of things. In fact, when it is merely an assertion about the nature of things, emptiness is no longer empty. The bodhisattva's practice of emptiness is what Buddhists call "hard practice." Only by renouncing nirvana, understood as an escape from *samsara* and the suffering of sentient beings, is nirvana attained. Only in renouncing emptiness as a metaphysical belief is emptiness truly realized as a spiritual practice. Therefore, bodhisattva practice means standing neither in *samsara* nor nirvana, but rather in the "place where there is no place to stand." This takes the concrete form of selfless compassion.

In the restaurant in Kyoto, when my friend and teacher said "it is not enough," and I realized that he was talking about his life's work in spreading the Buddhist teaching about emptiness, that feeling of gratitude and regret came over me again. The regret flowed from the pathos of an old man as he realizes that this life will end before the quest is over. Masao Abe knows that he has been more creative in imagining Christianity anew with Buddhist insight than in his quest to renew Buddhism with Christian insight. The doctrine of emptiness, the place where Sensei has stood for so many years, cannot encompass the God of Abraham, Isaac, and Jacob. It is not enough.

I felt gratitude as well — the gratitude every Christian should feel before a bodhisattva. My teacher has had to do much renouncing over his almost ninety years of life. In his youth, the threat of nihilism drove Masao Abe to the Pure Land path of faith. But this was not enough. Only with much anguish and at great personal cost my friend renounced his attempt to live by faith. Later, in the confrontation with Hisamatsu Shin'ichi, Masao Abe began to stand in the "place where there is no place to stand" — the standpoint of emptiness embraced by the Zen path. By standing "where there is no place to stand," Sensei has lived a Zen life that has taken him to classrooms and lecterns in the West and to friends, like myself, who follow the path of Christ. But now, in his old age, my wonderful friend has realized that even the standpoint of emptiness is "not enough." In the paradoxical wisdom of the bodhisattva, this last attachment must be renounced. The quest to become truly empty demands it. I do not presume that Sensei will stop being a Zen Buddhist. On the contrary, his words came to me as a kind of promise that he will continue to be a good Buddhist for my benefit. I am so grateful for this. "It is not enough" was the vow of a bodhisattva, the voice of a true Buddhist, struggling to realize the truth of emptiness as compassion.

Sensei wants me to be a good Christian. Anything less would do violence to our inter-religious friendship. My friendship with Masao Abe, however, requires me to stand where there is no place to stand. Let me then take the path of Christ, as Sensei has taken the path of the bodhisattva. I will empty myself and take the form of one who has no place to stand — the form of a believer and a friend.

In Kyoto, sitting on the *tatami* mats, halfway through lunch, while his wife and I bantered about *tsuyu* rains and hydrangeas, my teacher took the bodhisattva path, vowing to work for the benefit of all sentient beings, including his Christian friend. Sensei is now very old — too old for dialogue meetings. His life of formal dialogue has come to an end. But his vow of compassion continues. In this, Masao Abe is a true friend, a skillful teacher, and a stranger to be welcomed. What is to be said in the face of such compassion? "I will continue to study; Sensei, please continue to teach."

PETER FRIEDERICI

Fifteen Ways of Seeing the Light

FROM the *Georgia Review*

". . . the natural limitations of light sempiternally deny the satisfaction of
desire. For this is the inherent irony of vision, that it reveals to us the space
beyond our bodies, and the shortness of our grasp. Visual perception makes
it possible for us to grasp for what is beyond, and, *at the same time,* to realize
that we cannot reach it."
— F. Gonzalez-Crussi, *The Five Senses*

Talisman

A SMALL ROUNDED STONE in my pocket: dark brown, no larger
than a half-dollar. It looks quite the same as approximately
1,600,000,000 other stones that you could pick up for free in the
southwestern quarter of Arizona. I carry it with me.

Here. Hold it in the light. See the rich brown coating of desert
varnish, almost black, that glazes its surface, baked and bronzed by
the centuries and millennia of undiluted sun. See how it glints and
gleams, lustrous as if coated with a thin sheen of oil, glossy as skin
glistening with sweat. See how the light reflects and shimmers and
seems almost to break into its prismatic components.

The stone is worn as smooth as if it had been thumbed by dozens
of worried generations. I finger it as I walk, a desert rosary. Maybe it
is cold outside and I am walking to an office, but in my mind I see
the desert sun glinting off of thousands, millions, of stones like
this. They cover the rounded, finger-shaped berms between the
narrow washes that run green with low shrubs, stunted paloverde
trees, and a few scattered and ancient ironwood trees. The iron-

woods, huge and scruffy, are beginning to bloom in delicate lavender; the bees gather 'round. In the distance, ragged mountains, hard and timeless. My mind stretches but fails to comprehend that all this expanse of stones has been worn from those mountains over the eons.

The desert varnish itself has perhaps taken thousands of years to form, built up of the slow metabolism of bacteria that live on the rock surface and that over uncounted generations cement a fine coating of manganese and other minerals above themselves — perhaps for protection from the ferocious light, a natural sunscreen. The varnish throws back the sun, and collectively the stones throw back the heat. On a late spring day, with the ironwood blooming in the washes, walking on the desert pavement feels like taking a stroll on a griddle, all heat and light.

I don't much go out of my way for rock but this one I carry as a talisman. It glints and glimmers and even in a dim room, even in winter, reminds me of the places where I used to work, reminds me of sun on my face, silence, spareness and fullness, the glare of wide spaces, distant mountains painted with light.

Sunrise

If you were to awaken at first light, you might think it a pool of acid that quietly slipped along the horizon and was rising now to leach away the no-color of night, first into paleness and then into incandescence. Blackness gives way to translucent gold, the one tone as rich and deep as the other.

As the sound of a lone cricket dies away, a rock wren starts singing *geech-geech-geech* and *teeper-teeper-teeper.*

It takes some time before the land picks up much of the color of the sky. It is a gray almost-monotone dotted with darker patches of brittlebush, the wispy silhouettes of paloverde. The landscape nearby is indistinct, but in the distance the mountains are flat and gray-blue, etched so sharply against the sky that it's as if there were nothing at all behind them. As if they demarcated the end of the earth.

A house finch sings his unpredictable burbling song. A little color comes on in the rocks: ocher, burnt umber, beige, tan, white flecks. Earth tones. The distant mountains deepen, purple-blue.

The light comes on up and announces its subtle vegetative disguises: brittlebush, paloverde, creosote, barrel cactus, bursage. The sky turns from gold to palest blue. A bat flutters along the base of the hill, ending its night. Sunlight hits the mountains directly now, green shrubs peppering salmon rock. Angular black silhouettes of saguaro and paloverde jut from the ridge to the east. The spines of the closest barrel cactus grow deep red.

The sun, now, and even in the first moments after its arrival, there is a hint of the heat to come. Time for a quick breakfast, and time for me to be off looking for birds this spring morning: my job, my passion.

Photons

It begins with random atomic collisions in the heart of the sun, where the temperature exceeds 15 million degrees and the pressure is great enough to fuse hydrogen atoms, four apiece, into helium. A thousand billion pounds of hydrogen converted to nuclear energy every second, year upon year, eon upon eon, each pound as potent as a trainload of coal. The sun is so big and so crowded that this energy, which is light being born, spends an average of a million years bouncing into other particles inside the star. At last it reaches the surface, evades the sun's considerable gravity, and like some pent-up adolescent heads pell-mell away from its birthplace. At 186,000 miles per second it only takes eight minutes to reach the surface of our small blue world. Every second, the rain of photons continues, trillions of them striking a human body of average size every second out in the desert on a cloudless day.

Light vibrates at various frequencies. Much of it pelts our skin and our clothing directly and causes vibrations that feel like heat: the infrared. A small percentage consists of the dangerous ultraviolet rays that point up the human predicament by supporting sunscreen manufacturers and tanning spas alike. The x-rays are even more powerful but do not make it through the filter of our atmosphere. And nearly half of the light that arrives on the desert floor is in the visible spectrum.

Some of it lands, say, on a paloverde tree on a ridge and bounces off and into my eye, where it lands on my retina and causes rhodopsin, a complex biochemical formed of protein and vitamin A, to break into two parts, a reaction that stimulates electrical impulses that travel at a comparatively lethargic but fully adequate seven miles an hour through the optic nerve and into the brain and in the aggregate translate into: spiky branches. Smooth and supple bark. Spiny tips. A hue of pale green. A clump of mistletoe orbiting in the tree's branches, near the top. And in a high crotch, just low enough to peer into, a dark mass that just may be the nest of a shrike, outlined against a bright blue sky made up of light a million years old.

Family History

"The value of exposure to light cannot very easily be overrated." That's what my grandfather wrote, in 1930, in the *New York Times*. A half-page in the *New York Times* to reproduce a lecture he'd given! He'd done quite well for himself, having come to this country from Germany only ten years earlier. He was poor then, and young, and had come to promote the beneficial qualities of the new x-ray machines. Their radiation, he was persuaded, could heal a wide range of ailments. It "breaks down abnormal, diseased tissue and stimulates the normal, healthy tissue," he wrote. "By increasing assimilation and dissimilation it accelerates the vital processes."

It increased his assimilation, all right. He got a good tenured university job and launched his career. He was a physicist but retained a great interest in how the human body responds to its environment. He did not like what he saw in the twentieth century. He saw cities swathed in smog and men dressed in forbiddingly thick layers of tight wool clothing (women, he said, dressed more lightly and hence more sensibly), denying their skin access to the stimulating qualities of light and air. "[O]ur civilization with its houses, closed automobiles, smokescreens over cities and eight-hour working day does not permit us to make full use" of light, he wrote.

And so he advocated more light, more air: we should all go to the beach whenever possible, and strip as nearly naked as society would allow. He saw nothing better than being nude outdoors, bathing in light.

I never knew him. He died before I was born. He may not have realized the detrimental effects of x-rays, or of ultraviolet light. But overall he was on the right track. The reaction of sunlight with certain chemicals in the skin produces vitamin D. We need it for strong bones. Too little light is indeed debilitating.

With that background, how could I have become anything less than a full-fledged photophilic?

Clarity

The crispness of the light in the desert is my hunger, especially in the morning, when the rays slant in sidewise as if from a giant floodlight and throw every plant, every rock into sharp relief. It is a severe and yet mellow light, not yet charged with the overwhelming force and sapping heat of the middle part of the day. Away over on a distant ridge every paloverde and saguaro stands out in that light as if each were the type specimen of its kind, perfect and discrete and immutable. The crenelated rocks on the ridgeline are coruscant, glittering in the light. It's as if the surfeit of photons supercharges the landscape with electromagnetic radiation of all kinds, making it reek with information. No mist, no veiling, no fuzziness. Even at hundreds of yards it seems to me that I ought to be able to count the individual cactus needles, or see a golf-ball-sized hummingbird nest in a tree's green crotch. No wonder the early Christian hermits chose the Sinai and other deserts for their meditations: on a clear morning it seems that the sun's light could pierce any veil separating us from the truth.

It's a trick, of course. Maybe the hawks can see that well; I cannot. But this clarity defines the morning light of the desert. I look around me an hour after sunrise, and it seems to me that I will never tire of looking, so sharp and detailed is my view of the world.

The view makes me think of Thoreau: "If you stand right fronting and face to face to a fact," he wrote, "you will see the sun glimmer on both its surfaces, as if it were a cimiter, and feel its sweet edge dividing you through the heart and marrow, and so you will happily conclude your mortal career. Be it life or death, we crave only reality." I imagine Henry David sauntering through this desert, plucking saguaro needles to test their tone, probing the sharpness of paloverde twigs, perhaps even seeing the light glint from all their surfaces at once and then running himself through to feel the pain and joy of ultimate reality. In the sun-washed excess of a desert morning, there is no way not to think this: surely truth, if it exists for us to uncover in this world, is no different than a flood of light, out there for us to see but far more than we can take in.

Enskyment

Light is information. The physicists read its body and learn what makes up the star whence it came. The engineers corral it into glass cables that carry our conversations, images, hopes, dreams. My job is to translate its vibrations into the specific plumages of birds and their eggs.

Light is the fastest thing we know, and indestructible until it hits something. Imagine, then, a million years, a near eternity of bumping and jostling in the fierce body of the sun. Robinson Jeffers considered the sun to be made up of a species of animal:

> . . . they would look monstrous
> If we could see them: the beautiful passionate bodies of
>   living flame, batlike flapping and screaming,
> Tortured with burning lust and acure awareness,
>   that ride the storm-tides
> Of the great fire globe. They are animals, as we are.

Imagine escaping the tumult, breaking free after so long and entering the cold desert of space. Imagine silence, imagine emptiness. Imagine such an enskyment, to use Jeffers' term. We know that it often is the growing light of spring that stimulates birds to migrate north and to lay their eggs, but imagine that the physicists and biologists perhaps do not know the full extent of the information a photon can carry.

Imagine a celestial glide that could go on for billions of years to the far reaches of the universe, but that through the happenstance of the regular orbits of rocky spheres molded by gravity is broken in only eight minutes, just a short fall, really, and then a photon with its near-infinitude of cohorts crests the sharp-cut mountains of morning, and down, and after a million years its trip comes to an end on the smooth green and lustrous bark of an aged paloverde tree. And sure enough, that is a nest, and there lie its five shiny eggs, perfect as photons, reddish-brown on white, and there is a shrike, agitated, worked up over me, calling *bzeep!-bzeep!* over where it sways on a nearby ocotillo branch.

Ultraviolet

At noon a billion photons of ultraviolet light hit an average-sized human body each second. Who says it never rains in the desert? This is a torrent, a downpour. They carry sufficient energy to knock electrons away from atoms and molecules in the upper layer of skin: it would be wise to wear sunscreen. It's been estimated that a day in full sunlight can damage between 100,000 and 1,000,000 sites in the DNA of a single exposed skin cell. So much ultraviolet radiation is also scattered by the brilliant desert sky at noon that as many photons again hit a hiker's body from it as directly from the sun: it might be wiser, then, to wear a sombrero, and long sleeves.

Ultraviolet in the right doses is beneficial, creating vitamin D, preventing rickets. "We drink light as vitamin D," says the artist James Turrell. But that's not the kind of thirst we feel in the desert. In the wrong doses ultraviolet light causes itchiness, sunburns, cataracts, skin cancer, melanoma, death. Face it: it's dangerous out there. The good things so easily go bad: the sensual feel of sun on skin, the cleansing aridity, the heat that at first feels pleasurable but can so easily get to be too much.

Confession: there have been days on which I have not worn sunscreen for no good reason at all. I hurry from the skimpy shade of one paloverde tree to another. There is no reason for this but sloth and fatalism. Even when you know the cost, the lure of what we still consider a healthy-looking tan can be insurmountable.

"I'll get skin cancer, no doubt, but it's been worth it," one middle-aged desert rat told me once as we admired another spectacular sunset. He was wrinkled before his time. His allegiance shone on his face. He loved the sun too much.

Who would not? Like so many desert rats, I spend some winter days wondering what price I will pay for my indiscretions.

Ravens

The ravens fly together, always paired up. Except for their glinting eyes, they are charcoal-black, an animated absence of light, but at noon their wings flash like liquid mercury as they fly down the dry canyon. They fly west, into the sunlight, two crosses of burning whiteness against the burnt rock walls.

Mirage

The light of the morning has intensified enormously, all its color leached away. The sun pulses, the sky glares, the pale sand bounces back the light. The desert is white, all reflection, gravel, mirage. No shade, no shelter: a sorry bleakness. Except for a high-circling turkey vulture, the birds have vanished. The patches of shade thrown by the saguaros have shrunk until they will barely shelter a jackrabbit. I still try to stand in them. Sweat drips into my eyes. Gnats pester them, seeking moisture. I squint and tie a bandanna under my eyes, bandit-style, to ward off some of the painfully brilliant reflection from below. As the Sahara's Tuareg do, I regard the bright world from a narrow slit.

The distant mountains appear smaller now, flattened by this ocean of light. They are sawtoothed ranges, steep and ragged, but in the heat their edges seem to waver. The rock-ribbed solidity of early morning is long gone. It's as if they were projected visions of mountains rather than the real thing. The ridgelines quiver; the short steep canyons creep this way and that. Even when magnified in my binoculars the mountains wriggle. What solidity is this, I wonder, and wish myself back at camp, in shade, drinking something cool.

The mountains are not really moving, of course, at least not in any way that human eyes can perceive. Nor is it any fault of light. Photons travel in straight lines except, as Einstein posited, when their path is bent by some powerful gravitational field. As far as we here on Earth are concerned, they fly straight. They follow the laws of physics. They are predictable. It is not their behavior but that of the air, gathering in cold or hot masses that reflect or refract the rays, that causes the desert's mirages. At midday hot air is rising like so many carnival balloons from the superheated ground of the creosote flat between the mountains and me. As the light enters those bubbles it is bent as if passing through water, causing the ridges to waver. Sometimes in hot weather the creosote basins appear filled with water because a layer of hot air pools low and refracts the light just as a lake would. Walk toward it, and its shore recedes, ever and always outrunning your thirst. Yes: people have died in this way.

The midday light of the desert is an awful, wonderful excess that overwhelms everything else: the rocks, the plants, the birds. It is no longer a tool whose clarity illuminates the unvarnished reality of beautiful surroundings; it has become those surroundings. The light of what had seemed truth dissolves into something much greater, and there is nothing to do but give yourself over to it: until evening, at least, there is nothing but light, heat, sky, the present moment.

Deception

"[T]he chief glory of the desert is its broad blaze of omnipresent light," wrote John Van Dyke in his 1901 classic, *The Desert*. This short, luminous book lyrically explores the low deserts of California and Arizona, forsaken places that at the time had not yet been made destinations for the aesthetically minded.

No one ever wrote more vividly or eloquently of light in the desert than Van Dyke. He was an art critic who knew how to describe what light did to the senses. The desert was, he wrote, "the most decorative landscape in the world, a landscape all color, a dream landscape. Painters for years have been trying to put it upon canvas — this landscape of color, light, and air, with form almost obliterated." Sunsets were "a reek of color." Mirages were "rose-colored dreams." Nowhere else but the desert would the traveler see "such opaline mirage, such rosy dawn, such fiery twilight."

But Van Dyke did not just paint a pretty postcard. He wrote of his travails in the desert, the awful waterless treks to distant pools of fetid water, the raging heat, the loneliness. In *The Desert*, beauty and toil and terror are inseparable. When armchair aesthetes immersed themselves in it, they too felt a little sweat, a little sand between their toes. *The Desert* became a classic that informed a modern century's appreciation of exotic scenery and an environmental movement that sought to protect such places.

Words, though, are more deceptive than light. Van Dyke, it turns out, never explored the desert the way he claimed, never had the experience of striking out across a parched plain toward a rumored waterhole in a distant porphyry mountain range and wondering whether he would make it. He made his book up. He faked it. As the scholar Peter Wild has written, he made his fine and sensitive observations from the windows of first-class Pullman cars, and invented his supposed adventures of whole cloth. Many of his natural history observations are pure fabrications; a naturalist can find dozens of grievous errors of fact. What's more, he didn't really care that much for the desert, as he wrote similar lovestruck prose about many other places.

But still. He wrote a great book, one that is enough to instill a love of the desert in many who have never been there.

Watching for Eagles

For a while, on the job, all we had to do was watch eagles, so as a wet spring was slowly baked into the crispness of summer, I scanned the sere landscape all afternoon for a glimpse of broad wings. With a job such as that one has time to think and to gather superstitions, and I came to believe that the best way to find eagles is to not look, to empty the mind of all expectation. But still I looked. I looked and my eyes struggled for a grip on a distant speck the way a drowning man at sea might search the horizon for a ship, or even the slightest smudge of smoke, until with the very effort of looking the whole afternoon grew flat, and I was unable anymore to focus properly, to perceive any real depth in the jumble of mountain and canyon rock.

"Sometimes it seems there's nothing but light out there," said Jean, who sat looking for eagles with me.

Half-dizzy, I lay down and squeezed my eyelids almost shut, thinking of the time I found a screech owl roosting in a tree during the day, gray as bark, eyes squeezed shut but head revolving to follow my sound, too sun-dazed to look around. In the pale slit of light that drizzled in through my eyelashes, the specks I saw were the shapes of birds, winging fast.

Migraine

It begins with something as slight as a glimmer from a smoothed stone reflecting the sun, or the gleam that bounces off a milk-white chunk of quartz in a wash bottom. Sometimes it's the rays of the sun itself, caught by accident in the corner of the eye. Always the result is unexpected: I am stabbed by a spear of light.

The afterimage remains on the retina, a glowing patch of green or orange or yellow that floats and bobs and is as real as it is insubstantial. It lingers and grows. It's as if a piece of the distant landscape had slipped its moorings and gone to look around, except that I can't quite get a fix on what's loose. It's always toward the edge of my vision, and floats off as I shift my eyes. It's as annoying as finding a ridge in an otherwise smooth panel of wallpaper.

The midday light is far too bright, even shrill. The heat pounds. I can't quite focus on anything. It's as if there's too much information coming in with the light reflected from each glimmering grain of sand and piece of stone. The floating chunk multiplies, two, four, eight, dozens, as if all the mirages held captive in the hard desert landscape had broken free. They zip back and forth like tiny sci-fi spacecraft or gather into bands that twist and writhe like snakes. They grow thicker.

I squeeze my eyes shut. It doesn't help. The fuzzy images remain.

Migraines are caused by the abnormal constriction and dilation of arteries that carry blood to the brain. No one really knows why this happens, though red wine, chocolate, menstrual cycles, stress, and genetics are all suspect. Most often there is no way to predict them, except for their immediate precursors — most notably the weird visual phenomena. In my case I usually blame the too-bright light of noon.

Sometimes the floaters can be anything I want them to be. Here comes an ocotillo wand, waving its red flowers, and here comes a storm of hummingbirds to hover around it. Here come some of the national flags I used to love to color when I was a child: is it Gambia? Sierra Leone? They are red and green and black, African. Here come Germany and Sweden. There's Argentina: blue, white, and sunshine yellow. It's a United Nations of headaches out here in the creosote.

If you are quick enough in catching a migraine as it starts, you can sometimes avoid the splitting headache that follows the visual effects. There are drugs for this, of course, though lying down with eyes closed in a quiet place also helps.

The sand feels warm on my head under the dappled shade of a big blue paloverde tree. A shade-rimmed wash is one of the best places to spend a sunny desert afternoon. Colored lines pulse through my vision, echoing my heartbeat. A bit of the bright afternoon filters scarlet through my closed eyelids. Thousands of ceiling fans are spinning, up as high as I can look. If I look closely they transmute themselves into lists of all the things I need to do. They have nothing to do with photons or the sun. They are lies of light, or at least of the way my body processes light, but there they are all the same. I want them to stop as much as I want to feel their cooling breeze.

There is nothing else to do with a migraine but wait it out. The sun arches over, more felt than seen. My entire body is all eye, taking in the heat. Above me a verdin perches near its spiny nest, as spherical as the earth, and sings its clear three-note song: *si-pa-pu,* over and over again, reciting the Hopi term for the place where the world began. This *is* the center of the earth, to the verdin. A black pinacate beetle scrabbles in the loose sand by my right hand. Nothing exists but this present moment. *Linger, you are so fair,* said Faust. *Go, you are so foul,* I feel like saying, trapped in the present with my brain and body doing what I don't want. It's profoundly disconcerting to lose control over what you see. Even if the pain never arrives the world beyond seems to move away a notch. It's as if the specks and squiggles were designed to remind me: here you are, encapsulated, separated from the rest of the world and very much on your own. Remember that. Have a nice day!

With time the colored lights and ceiling fans pulse and shrink and fade. Shadows lengthen and the light deepens: it's mid-afternoon. You can read this in the way the glare of the midday sky and sand fade away. It's as if the desert were a photograph slowly appearing in a tray of developer, brought back into substantiality. Colors reemerge. I sit up and rub my eyes, sopped and exhausted as some dried-out husk. My skull feels delicate, fragile as an eggshell, and I am relieved that the encircling rock-ribbed ranges don't waver anymore.

Van Gogh in Arles

What happens is that in the glare of afternoon eyes physically do tire. When rhodopsin is broken apart in the eye by the energy of light, it needs to be put back together again for later use, a reaction that works best in darkness or when the eyes are closed, and so it is a perfectly natural reaction to close the eyes for a few moments.

You don't have to be in the desert to experience that. But out there the strong southern light bounces back in such abundance from the unshielded soil, yellow and buff and white.

Some of us crave this. "For the stronger light and the blue sky teaches you to see, especially, or even only, if you see it all for a long time," wrote van Gogh from Arles. He was possessed by the bright carmines and dark cypress greens and wheatseed yellows of the south, where the purity of color was not veiled by the moisture of northern skies, where the purity of the toilers in the soil had not yet been spoiled by the strivings of the middle class. He was poor and he lived and breathed and ate color as much as any bread. Toward the end, during his attacks, he really did eat paint and drink turpentine.

In the end it was enough. It was too much. The cloak of the reaper cutting the ripened wheat was velvety black, so rich and pure. Van Gogh heaped the paint on with tectonic passion, forming small peaks and mesas and ridges. "[T]he emotions that come over me in the face of nature can be so intense that I lose consciousness," he wrote in his last year, struck dumb by light.

Then, silence. But in the galleries the impasto of his last impassioned paintings flickers even when no one is there to see it.

Sunset

The sun falls to the west and the body comes alive again. The shadow of the mountains is a solid thing with a life of its own. Moving ever more quickly, it prowls across the flats, settling itself, cool and dense. I covet it. On many days I have bemoaned how swiftly time passes, but as the shadow nears, the afternoon cannot tick along quickly enough.

The shadow arrives, and the skin breathes its relief: another twelve hours, now, before things get tough, before it's time to close up again. Coolness falls from the air. All the senses open up. There's the scent of a distant flower. Birds sing again. The light mellows and grows deeper, bringing out the texture of rocky slope and silty flat, of pleated cactus rind and gnarled creosote bark. What was flattened and exposed comes to seem lush and intimate. The eyes reacquaint themselves with the depth of the desert and of the universe. What feels like home is no longer the delicate shade of a single tree, but rather the whole place.

Evening arrives quickly in the desert, or at least seems to because of the body's relief, and before too long the last golden light pours over the mountains, palpable enough that it seems you could walk on it, or at least reach up and touch it. As the sun sets, the mountains turn to violet and seem larger than under the suffocating light of midday. Along the ridgeline to the west the saguaros and paloverdes stand against the saffron sky, etched as sharply as if with acid, absolutely black, and yet each twig and needle perfectly sharp and distinct if your eyes are clear enough.

The blue of the sky deepens further, soon becoming a deep indigo richer than any emperor's cloak. A crescent moon falls through it to the west, a bright planet above it. In the clear air the dark portion of the moon, faintly lit by earthshine, is visible next to the bright fingernail paring that's illuminated directly by the sun. The depth of that great round rock, too, is palpable, and especially after hiking through the desert much of the day, it is not difficult to imagine its rocky terrain, its rugged crater lips and dusty flats.

The sky grows lusher still, most heavily saturated in these final moments before it loses all color to the black of night: deepest blue-violet above, shading to a flame of orange above the mountain rim. In the distance an owl hoots and begins its day. There is a temptation for me, too, to roam all night, if only because of the beauty of the enormous and silent desert after the relentless assault of the day. The desert night is a soft whisper after being in a noisy crowd all day; it is a hint, a suggestion that draws us out of ourselves, questing and questioning. On a beautiful still evening in the desert, in the heat, the body resists its own weariness.

Night, Stars, the Universe

What's dark? I was in the caverns at Carlsbad once when the ranger pulled that old trick of turning the lights out on our tour so that we all could experience absolute darkness for once, as we can't in our ordinary lives because of the light bleeding out from the stars, the moon, and our own banal lighting. She flipped a hidden switch and sure enough it was as if our eyes had quit working. It was a blankness. My eyes grew hungry for any morsel of light. It *was* dark. But not empty. We were all too aware of the depth of rock above our heads, of the nervous expectation of our neighbors. After a few seconds there were a few little laughs and titters, and then after ten seconds or so the lesson dissolved in irritation at the yahoo who felt this was the right time to take a flash picture.

But out in the desert there is no such thing as darkness. In the desert there is nothing to block the sky, and so every night the light falls from the stars, the planets, the moon, and from the increasingly bright orange penumbras that blossom over Phoenix, Tucson, Yuma, and even small towns. The human eye can detect as few as eighty photons coming in per second, a vanishingly faint light that is far less that what comes in on the darkest and most overcast night — the ghost of a light. Even on a dark night lacking a moon, the sandy ground shines and the outlines of the mountains stand black against the paler sky.

Even what looks to us like emptiness, like the darkness I saw (or did not see) in the caverns, is not really. In all the known universe, the physicist Henning Genz has written, there is no space that is truly empty of matter and energy: "Let us assume we can remove all matter from some region of space. What will we be left with? A region of empty space? Not necessarily. In the universe, between galaxies, each atom is at a distance of about 1 meter from its next neighbor. Still, the space between these atoms is not empty; it is bright with light and other radiation from very different sources. It is only in the absolutely empty space of our imagination that no light, no radiation penetrates." Those Christian desert fathers sought an analogous emptiness in the imagination of their Sinai, a place so bare of life that it did not distract from the work of seeking the face of God. This, though, was no experience of darkness or of the void, but rather of its opposite, as we gather from Joseph of Panephysis: "The old man stood up and stretched his hands toward heaven. His fingers became like ten lamps of fire and he said, 'If you will, you can become all flame'" — a desert radiance of fullness rather than of emptiness.

The only real emptiness must lie out beyond the boundaries of the universe, where no matter and no energy have yet penetrated. It is that place beyond places, the time beyond time, that is the true desert. Nothing there: no time, no space, no light, not a particle of anything, not a thought. And if we were to add up all the light in the universe, the physicists say, it would constitute a pale beige, barely off-white. Imagine, then, some unimaginable observer out there in the true darkness, the greatest desert of all. And here comes the universe out of nowhere: a fuzzy ball crackling and glowing of its own luminescence, beige against black like a ball molded of the warm and dusty ground of Arizona. How could that onlooker conclude anything else but that this unthinkable manifestation itself was the face of God, rich with the potential of its own seemingly endless energy?

It is a feat of great elegance that the human eye is so well adapted to the conditions of the universe and in particular of the surface of the Earth, able to make sense of the flood of light of desert noon, the trickle of desert midnight, and everything in between. This is something to celebrate when the new moon and Venus set, leaving the sky dark with its bright pinpricks of stars. On some nights in the desert I've seen the Milky Way so dense with our neighbor stars that I thought at first it must be a cloud bank — but no, not in this heat and dryness. Those were all stars like our own, sending their light and information out to unknown lands. On some nights, even in the heat of summer when the days are a trial by fire, I've taken great comfort before sleep in the knowledge that the whirling of the Milky Way and of the constellations was really our own Earth's whirling toward the dawn, a perpetual easting toward the ever-new possibility and fullness of sunrise.

DAVID GELERNTER

Judaism Beyond Words: Conclusion

FROM *Commentary*

JUDAISM IS THE STORY God chooses to tell the Jews, and they choose to hear.

But Judaism is in grave trouble today, because it has difficulty saying what the point of the story is. What *is* Judaism's message to mankind? Jews make it their business to confront man on behalf of God, and (more foolhardy still) God on behalf of man. In practice Judaism is halakha, a "way of going," the religious law. But why should a Jew who knows nothing about Judaism set off down this path? The Jewish nation is the senior nation of the Western world, by rights the spiritual leader; but where does it lead? From the broadest to the timeliest, most concrete terms, Judaism's mission has never been plainer or more pressing or less well understood.

This is the last in a series of essays attempting to explain the essence of Judaism. It may seem bizarre to claim that this "essence of Judaism" has yet to be explained adequately, but Judaism has no portfolio of doctrine to offer, and its scholarly discussions are mostly about halakha and literary interpretation and history, not theology. This is one way in which Judaism is incompatible with Christianity, fundamentally different in character. (The magisterial eleventh edition of the *Encyclopedia Britannica* of 1910, admired for its scrupulous seriousness, has an article on "Christianity" and one on "Jews." None on "Judaism.") In Judaism you live a certain way, unconscious (or barely conscious) of doctrine or theology — because to be conscious of a thing is to be one step removed from it.

Jews are like farmers: they practice an exacting way of life where details matter and transcendent spiritual value lies too deep for outsiders to see. Like farmers, Jews are *attached* — they always know the time and season. They always know when the sun sets, when *Shabbat* starts and when it ends. "But it's hard work; why bother if you don't have to?" Yes, some do get tired and give up. Some never pick up the signal. Many laugh off the whole idea. To be a farmer or an Orthodox Jew, you have to be born to it, or be a serenely incurable romantic, or both.

Jewish doctrine arises implicitly, in the mind of each practicing Jew; in fact, in the back of his mind. Just as deep, broad truths about (say) medicine might arise in someone's mind as a result of practicing medicine — in the form of "living" rather than textbook doctrine — deep truths about Judaism arise as a result of practicing Judaism. Thus, Rabbi Yitzhak Twersky summarizes (in 1996) the view of his father-in-law, Rabbi Joseph Soloveitchik: "Direct religious experience guarantees absolute certitude. . . . The religious consciousness is not to be subservient to or derivative from any philosophic impetus."

But doctrine "in the back of the mind" is still doctrine. And today Judaism must haul its doctrines not merely into full consciousness but out of the ocean of mind altogether, onto paper. In earlier times, troubled Jews demanded, "I want to be Jewish but don't know how; tell me." The Mishnah and the great law codes, including Maimonides' Mishneh Torah, were compiled in response to such questions. Today the body of halakha is secure, but troubled Jews have a different question: no longer "I want to be Jewish but don't know how"; today, "I want to *want* to be Jewish but don't know how."

For many Jews, this is a moment of tense silence, like a child's in the presence of an aged relative to whom he desperately wants to talk but cannot. Many Jews wish to (or long to) embrace Judaism, but cannot bring themselves to do it. They would as soon enter a mosque as a synagogue. They would like to have a seder on Passover, but the ceremony — already threadbare in their parents' generation — comes to pieces in their hands. The intellectual problems seem even greater. Evil strikes them as so palpable, it crowds God out like a suffocating poison cloud. Science is so formidable it seems to crush the life out of religion, leaving Judaism no space to breathe. Thus the parched sinister ramifying silence, like cigarette smoke. . . . Is *this* the final scene?

God forbid. But if Jewish theology is a theology of experience, if Jewish doctrine exists at the back of the mind — in vivo (so to speak), not in vitro, and in the form of discoveries each practicing Jew makes for himself, not abstractions divined by divines — how do we present such doctrine? How to describe (or transcribe) a thought? Different thoughts in different minds take different forms. But we cannot repeat the lazy error of too many psychologists and philosophers and assume that thoughts are routinely made of words.

In previous essays I have laid out four "picture themes" of Judaism like a merchant flourishing rugs in a *souk*. Each is intended to represent (roughly) one of the "doctrinal thoughts" that develop in Jewish minds in response to Jewish life. Each captured thought-image (like a beating butterfly trapped in your cupped hands) represents one doctrine arising from Judaism's theology of experience. My problem has been to transfer these thoughts from mind to paper, like trapping, killing, and mounting a butterfly. (Yes, killing is part of it: the doctrine on paper can never be alive the way doctrine-in-the-mind is alive.) Of course images described in words are not thoughts; but images in general do have certain thought-like properties. You can glance at an image for an instant and still get some impression of what it holds. You can refine and develop an image over time without ruining its compactness. An image can capture movement. You can hold one in mind for years without ever reducing it to words.

Intellectual life has long been half-choked by our refusal to take pictures into our expressive universe. Since Marshall McLuhan, we have called ourselves a visual society; but think of the pejorative way in which we say "image." Thinkers have reputations; politicians have images. In his *Language of Thought* (1975), the philosopher Jerry Fodor does acknowledge what some other philosophers refuse to — that thinking *must* involve images; but even Fodor conceives such images as embedded somehow in a grammatical framework. He seems not to grasp that a thought-passage might consist *purely* of images; consider a painter mulling a picture — inventing, elaborating, simplifying, and superimposing images with no recourse to anything like a grammatical or logical structure.

What do my assertions about pictures (that we often think in pictures, that transcribed pictures are a good representation for a certain type of thought) have to do with Judaism? Nothing, some say. The literary philosopher George Steiner (1997) writes that Judaism "fears the image; it distrusts the metaphor." He is exactly wrong.

I have hinted in earlier pieces at Judaism's visual bias — have mentioned, for example, some of the images that drive the biblical narrative forward (the dove with the olive leaf in its beak, a burning bush, the split-open sea, a flaming torch of a mountain). I have mentioned the luxuriant richness of Judaism's graphic vocabulary: not just menorah, star of David, tablets of the law, and four Hebrew letters of God's proper name, but shofar, lion of Judah, lulav and etrog, and so on. (France got its fleur-de-lys from the Crusaders, who took it from the stylized lily that was a popular motif in ancient Israelite Jerusalem.) I have mentioned the finely wrought visual detail in the Bible's descriptions of tabernacle and Temple, and the originality and power of the classical European synagogue interior. Jews even dote on the precise visual characteristics of the alphabet in which Hebrew is written.

Another hint: the best adjective for Jewish literature, from the Bible onward, is "translucent." Old texts are visible through new ones; newer texts quote older texts and add to them. When you look at a classical Midrash or a book of medieval mysticism or a nineteenth-century Torah commentary, you are looking through literary stained glass, which superimposes its own colors and patterns without obscuring what lies beyond.

Such "translucence" is itself just a metaphor — but you can see it embodied in practice. The Vilna edition of the Talmud (1835) became fundamental to yeshiva study. It puts the base text (mishnah or gemara) in a block at the center of each printed page, with the two most important commentaries on either side and other notes and commentaries surrounding those — making a dense, austerely beautiful carpet page. Many separate texts occupy your visual field simultaneously — a practical approximation of textual translucence. Students and scholars recognize and recall particular pages by their appearances. Of course this style of layout has been used elsewhere, too — but nowhere else has it become so fundamental to study.

Judaism "fears the image"? Maybe Steiner fears it. The Jewish mind is quintessentially visual. It might just be *because* the Jewish mind is so inherently, exuberantly visual that graven images of the Lord are so forcefully prohibited.

Returning now to my four "picture themes," which of course I can only describe in words — I stress that they are not Judaism's *only* themes. But arguably they are the most important.

Here they are, in outline.

(1) Separation — as in the splitting open of the Red Sea. The unifying theme of halakha is the creation of separations, and thus of holiness.

(2) The veil that separates God and man — like a bridal veil, or the curtain that hangs before the holy ark in synagogue. The veil itself is important because it is God-given, but ultimate importance attaches not to the veil but to what lies beyond it.

(3) The act or motion of turning inward, going inside, entering. God has withdrawn out of history into the human mind; for Judaism the "religious stance" is not believing but *listening* — to the "still small voice" inside you.

(4) The force field between male and female, which lets human beings imitate God and finish creation. From a husband and wife joined in love you get not merely the beast with two backs, a male plus a female, but something wholly different and otherwise impossible: a man.

Each of these four picture-themes implies a doctrine.

First, the doctrine of man's transcendence. Man is not part of nature; man is defined over and against nature. He must struggle out of nature and away from nature, toward God; must struggle out of nature like a baby struggling to be born. And this struggle is the meaning of holiness.

Jews defy nature by defying its most fundamental impulse — the mad onrush of chaos, reducing all things to one level, abolishing all divisions. In my theme-image, the forced-apart waters of Creation become the upright water-walls at the split-open Red Sea, which become (eventually) the upright standards of the rolled-open Torah in synagogue, and the forced opening of birth itself. Separation is life, holiness, halakha.

Halakha seems (to the outsider) complex and arbitrary. But it has a unifying theme, which applies to kashrut and family purity, Sabbath and festivals, kiddush and havdalah, planting land, weaving cloth, making marriages. The theme is *separating*, in space and time.

Jews convert the mere physical act of separation into a moral proclamation. By relentlessly making separations they say: we do not surrender; we choose freedom. A Jew must do things *in public* that mark him out and separate him off as a Jew. That is his most basic religious obligation. To eat only kosher food is mandatory, and central to Judaism; for a man to wear a yarmulke is much less important. Yet to eat kosher food inside an Orthodox community is less praiseworthy than to walk through Paris in a yarmulke.

Second, the doctrine of God's transcendence. What the world calls "Judaism" is only a reflection in a window. You cannot see through the window, because the far side is black (or at any rate, invisible). But you must grasp that it *is* a window, there *is* a far side — and the far side is God. God is transcendent: cannot be seen, described, imagined. All you can imagine is the windowpane. All you can know is that it *is* a windowpane.

Yet the God of Judaism is no cold, remote abstraction — because of the windowpane, the "veil" itself, which might be the most remarkable religious device ever conceived. Jews believe in a transcendent God Who does not part the veil and become human but does invite (indeed, implore) man to approach.

The veil proclaims that God's ineffable, transcendent presence can be closer to you if it is separated from you. You cannot see or know God but you can see, know, and approach the veil, knowing that God is on the other side. The veil symbolizes God's inconceivableness and (simultaneously, paradoxically) draws God and man close.

In my theme-picture, the veil is the tallis worn at prayer, the mask Moses wears after encountering God; the two curtains of the Holy of Holies, the curtains before the holy ark in any synagogue; the opaque tefillin boxes or the mezuzah hiding biblical texts; the ark of the covenant, screened by cherubs' wings, hiding the tablets of Sinai. The veil is present in the wordless, tuneless sound of the shofar, the overpowering blank of the Western Wall, a Jew's refusal to pronounce God's name.

Third, the doctrine of inner listening and, by association, the religious legitimacy of doubt.

If you look for God in history, you will not find Him. The problem of evil is man's problem; the central question is not why God hasn't saved the world but why *you* haven't. Jews are expected to accept God not like children who look to their parents for miracles but like adults who pull their share, who freely accept *ol malkhut shamayim,* the yoke of heaven's kingdom. To find God, Jews try to make out the "still small voice" that the prophet Elijah heard: the echo of God's voice, an *inner* voice.

After the destruction of the Second Temple in 70 C.E., after Bar Kokhba's revolt against Rome some six decades later, the Jews were driven out of their Judean homeland and a remarkable thing happened — something unprecedented in human history. Jews never wanted to, never planned to — but (in effect) they left home and grew up.

Israel's spiritual and material support was gone. In the black sobbing ruins, Jews looked around and discovered they were on their own. Had God abandoned them? No, God had not. God had moved inside. Henceforth, He was embodied in Israel itself. He was no longer the maker of fires, storms, and earthquakes; henceforth He was a still, small voice. Israel had depended on God, and always would. But from now on God must depend on Israel, too. Having been created, reared, and protected by God, Israel would now show what it had learned and what it was worth. God became the Jews' responsibility.

For many people the problem of "theodicy" (Leibniz's term), of God's justice, is the hardest and most important problem of theology. How could a just God countenance this evil world? But for Jews there is no such theological problem, because God does *not* countenance this evil world; man does. Judaism tells us an obvious yet startling fact: *"lo ba'shamayim hi,"* the Torah is not in heaven; it is on earth, is mankind's to interpret and apply and enforce. Yet another startling fact from the Talmud: "From the day the Temple was destroyed, the Holy One Blessed be He has nothing in His universe but the four *amot* of halakha alone," where "four *amot*" is the space occupied by one human being. God has nothing in His universe but the mind of the Jew.

Nothing is harder than listening to yourself, to your own mind. Your mind says too many things you do not want to hear. Nothing is easier than to be vaguely aware of what your mind wants to say but to drown it out, sweep it away, ignore it. Conscience (the devil once said) is a Jewish invention (and he was right). But doubt is part of Judaism, too. The Bible and Talmud are records of the Jews doubting God and God doubting the Jews and the Jews doubting themselves and (in one famous passage in the talmudic tractate *Menahot*) God doubting Himself.

But doubt functions differently in Judaism than in any other of the great religions Judaism fathered. It is inside, not outside. For a Jew, the path is clear (not simple, but clear): doubt, but act.

Fourth: the doctrine of man's twoness, and (by association) of inductive morality.

God is one but man is two: not male *or* female but male *and* female. Husband and wife create a whole man out of two halves. Their sexual union is inherently blessed whether a child is engendered or not. The cult of the couple has given marriage in Judaism a supreme (and unique) importance.

In Judaism, male and female are perfectly asymmetric. The force field between maleness and femaleness creates marriage and colors the whole universe. To attempt to make the two sexes interchangeable, to short out the battery that operates civilization, to wire its two poles together, is an act of nihilist hatred directed against beauty, humanity, and God.

The purpose of life is to marry and rear a family. The modern world's idea that career and not family is the point of life is un-Jewish — and for Jews it is therefore wrong. (Not a choice one disagrees with; wrong.) Because man cannot exist except where male and female are one, the Jewish "self" is a strange, unfamiliar self, made of two separate beings. And a self that includes another person is a hint or foretaste of a self that includes God.

Jewish morality starts with the ground case and works outward. You approach the goal step by step. It is no accident that the verse in Leviticus does not merely say, "love your neighbor"; it says, "love your neighbor *as yourself*." You know how to begin; now, move forward. The ground case (loving yourself) is your basis for the inductive step (loving your neighbor).

Philologists and Bible critics once thought they were scoring points against Judaism by arguing that the biblical word "neighbor" refers not to "fellow man" but to a member of your own group or tribe. But this is a glory of Judaism, not a limitation. Judaism gives you a *method* for approaching goodness. (Many have noticed that those who are filled with love for mankind tend to be the least loving of people in practice.) From Leviticus it follows directly that, in Judaism, self-love is required; otherwise you are failing in a religious duty.

Here, then, are my four themes. They show the Jewish nation coming to terms with nature, history, man, and God. Their underlying colors are defiance and celebration — a color-harmony that is unique to Judaism. Jews celebrate nature, but defy it; will not be part of it. They celebrate history, but defy the seemingly crushing problem of theodicy, of God's justice in an evil world. They celebrate sexuality, but defy it to turn them into animals; they put the married couple at the center of the universe. They celebrate God (ineffable and transcendent), but defy God's unknowable transcendence to scare them into silence, or keep them at a distance. Their duty as Jews is to go forth like Abraham and embody God on earth.

Thus, four mounted butterflies — not as brilliant as live ones, but inducements to set off down the trail and discover the live ones for yourself.

But how do we know there *is* a God? It is strange and wonderful that such a hard question should seem in the end to have such a simple, universally agreed answer — "universally" meaning implicitly.

Although we have been living for generations in the age of atheism (or so it has seemed), this atheism turns out to have been phony — professed uncritically and without thinking, the way medieval peasants professed Christianity. The idea that our ethical principles are merely *reasonable* has been raised and batted down so many times that today it can safely be called dead as a doornail. These principles are not "only reasonable," they are not per se useful, they are certainly not obvious — and they are no mere preferences or whims. Saying "I prefer that no one be tortured to death" is not like saying "I prefer orange juice for breakfast." It reflects a moral absolute, independent of anyone's opinion or whim or preference. Virtually no serious person denies this.

But to insist that such principles are "absolute" or (in other words) "transcendent" or (in other words) "sacred" is just another way of saying "I believe in God." And not just any god; in the God of these principles, which is to say the God of Israel. Some intellectuals will go to any lengths to deny it, but there has been no way around this truth at least since the day Nietzsche (in his blazing intellectual integrity) parked the pickup truck of his moral philosophy square in the middle of the intellectual Autobahn. By acknowledging that to reject God, as he did, *forced* him to reject "Judeo-Christian morality," as he also did, he gave the game away. God and transcendent morality are inseparable.

Modernism (on the other hand) is the idea that you can close your bank account and keep writing checks. Modernism is a lie. Without God in the bank, your moral checks are drawn against nothing. A modernist who denies God while insisting on the absoluteness of Jewish ethics — which, of course, he will call something else — has proclaimed *himself* god.

Nietzsche prophesied that one day a "madman" would announce the death of God, that mankind had killed Him. (He was parodying, unawares, a central doctrine of Christianity.) Today some of our foremost thought-leaders are no longer out to kill God (they think they have put paid to that job); now they seek the death of man. It is a three-step process. Modern science thinks to have abolished "man's uniqueness." Now we are trying (in dead earnest) to abolish the distinction between male and female. Soon, genetic engineers will offer parents the chance to custom-tailor their babies. Jews have a unique duty to put everything they have into saying no to this project. Judaism *requires* that they say no.

Nietzsche used the phrase "Judeo-Christian morality," and was neither the first nor the last to do so. Many casual observers believe that the underlying ethics of Judaism and Christianity are basically the same, that the differences between the two religions center on religious law and on Jesus. Wrong. I have already pointed out their sharp disagreements on sexuality, marriage, and family. Their dispute about the character of morality is just as basic.

The argument between Judaism's morality of action and early Christianity's morality of passion, of suffering, is no mere academic disagreement. It is a schism running right down the center of Western civilization. In the action morality of Judaism, you *must judge* your fellow man — it is a moral obligation. Refusing to judge (being "nonjudgmental," in the ugly cliché) is callous, cowardly, and wrong — although, the great Pharisee Hillel warns, "Do not judge your fellow man until you have been in his place." Understood: a man might judge mistakenly; if so, he will have to face the consequences. Such are the responsibilities of adulthood.

Why does Judaism insist that to judge is mandatory? One part (only one) has to do with mental health. Nietzsche explains: "When a noble man feels resentment, it is absorbed in his instantaneous reaction and therefore does not poison him." Unexpressed resentment (in other words) can turn to poison in the metabolism of mind. The Bible anticipates this sharp observation by *outlawing* Nietzschean resentment: "Thou shalt not hate thy brother in thy heart; thou shalt rebuke yes *rebuke* thy neighbor" (Leviticus 19:17).

And you must also defend yourself: your "self" naturally including your family and your extended family, possibly your whole nation and, ever since the careers of Israel's prophets, spreading uncertainly outward toward the whole of mankind. Of course Judaism believes what Isaiah taught, that in the end of days nation will not lift up sword against nation. But in the meantime, ever-increasing moral maturity means more and not less fighting, more and not fewer wars. In Judaism, pacifism is immoral; it is the unindicted co-conspirator of wickedness.

Not so in Christianity. To the critic and philosopher Michael Tanner (1994), "Resist not evil" is one of Jesus' "most impressive precepts," and one that is (naturally) "in sharp conflict with the law" — meaning Jewish law. Why does Judaism nonetheless reaffirm the law and reject this most impressive precept? Because the Bible says: "Choose life and live, you and your children!" (Deuteronomy 30:19).

Early Christianity was associated, as Tanner notes, with a different morality — I've called it a morality of passion, born of suffering; it insists that you must not judge your fellow man and must *not* defend yourself, however you define "self." There is support for this passive morality in the New Testament. Respecting judgment: "Judge not, that ye be not judged" (Matthew 7:1). "He that is without sin among you, let him first cast a stone" (John 8:7). "Wherein thou judgest another, thou condemnest thyself" (Romans 2:1). Regarding pacifism: "Whoever shall smite thee on thy right cheek, turn to him the other also" (Matthew 5:39). "Blessed are the meek, for they shall inherit the earth" (Matthew 5:5). And of course, "Resist not evil" (Matthew 5:39).

Jewish thinking is not just different, it is opposite. Christianity: "Whoever shall smite thee on thy right cheek, turn to him the other also." Judaism: "If I am not for myself, who *will* be?" (Hillel's famous statement in Mishnah Avot). Jewish morality is warrior morality: it is no accident that Abraham, Moses, and David, the Bible's greatest heroes, should all have been described as warriors.

But this hardly puts Judaism on the side of Nietzsche's cruel "patrician ethics"; Judaism is equidistant from Christianity and Nietzsche. Hillel did not say, "If I am not for myself, who *will* be?," and stop there. He continued: "If I am only for myself, what am I?" Jews do not pray (quoting the Psalm), "May the Lord give strength to His people," and stop there. They continue: "May the Lord bless His people with peace."

All four of my themes inhabit one summary image. Rabbi Shimon bar Yohai was a hero of the Talmud and a bitter enemy of Rome. When he spoke against Roman hegemony in Israel, spies overheard and reported him, and Roman soldiers sought his life. He took refuge in a cave with his son; they were forced to remain in hiding for twelve years.

The Zohar is the basic text of Jewish mysticism. It was composed in Spain by Moses de Leon in the last three decades of the thirteenth century. But the Zohar puts many of its thoughts in the mouth of Rabbi Shimon, and is written as if *he* wrote it. By the time modern scholarship established its real origin, the idea was firmly established that the Zohar was Rabbi Shimon's work, composed in the dark of his cave.

This legendary cave with Rabbi Shimon inside composing the Zohar is Judaism's perfect emblem. It brings my themes together; it is the nutshell with infinity inside: "I could be bounded in a nutshell, and count myself a king of infinite space," says Hamlet, "were it not that I have bad dreams." But Judaism's dreams are not bad. They are dreams of salvation.

Yet something is not quite right on the world's balance sheets. Something doesn't quite compute. The cold war pitted the democratic West — part Christian, part post-Christian modernist — against the Marxist East. The one thing Christianity and Marxism had in common was that they were both Jewish inventions. In significant part, "secular modernism" was a Jewish invention, too. Today's post-cold-war conflict pits the West — part Christian, part secular postmodern — against radical Islam. Judaism is again deeply implicated, in the creation both of Islam and of postmodernism.

Not that I want to assign credit to Judaism for all these developments. That would be a slur, not a compliment. Obviously, Jews and Jewish ideas are only partly responsible, are only the launch pads for these mammoth intellectual rocket ships — and, like all launch pads, have been scorched and blasted at liftoff. Nonetheless: if we were forced to choose just one, there would be no way to deny that Judaism is the most important intellectual development in human history. And we *are* forced to, because the world's leading scholars, Gentile and Jew (especially Jew), presume to write the history of civilization without knowing anything at all about Judaism.

Which is yet not wholly surprising because, after all, the first two of my themes have to do with separation and the other two with inwardness. Cave walls symbolize the Jew's separation from society at large and (in a different sense) from transcendent God. Yet the Jews, shut up and shut out as (traditionally) they were, have always had infinity in view: a microcosmic infinity. The infinity of daring voyages venturing inward rather than outward, deeper and deeper.

The cave is symbolized itself by the oldest surviving European synagogue, the Altneuschul in Prague. It dates roughly from 1280, though parts of the building are older. The insides of medieval churches are centrifugal, drawing the eye outward toward windows and wall decorations; dead center, beneath the crossing, is often empty. Synagogues are centripetal, directing the eye inward toward the bimah at the center, where the Torah is read in the midst of the congregation. The Altneuschul seems strikingly cave-like inside, narrow and tall and full of soft dusty light coming through small windows set too high to see out of. Its grave beauty and whispery grandeur and the lights in its eyes are all striking; the inside is densely decorated with metal grillwork around the bimah, hanging lamps, carved wood, the golden-red banner presented by Charles IV in 1358, an elaborate menorah, the ark. A perfect image of Rabbi Shimon's cave: an inner infinity, separate from the world, where the mind travels inward toward God without stopping.

One of the old seats along the rim of the small room is marked as the Maharal's place — the seat of Rabbi Yehuda Bezalel Loewe, a chief rabbi of Prague, celebrated sixteenth-century scholar of astronomy and philosophy and Torah. Just as the Zohar appropriated Rabbi Shimon as its honorary author, a folktale about the mysterious Golem appropriated Rabbi Loewe. The Golem was a huge, man-shaped creature of coarse clay, a latent automaton sculpted by the rabbi to protect the Jews of Prague from persecution. It came to life when he slipped into its mouth a paper inscribed with the four Hebrew letters of God's name. Otherwise, it only *looked* like a man.

Why has the folktale always seemed so inevitable and so right to Jews? Because they know (at least subliminally) that *they* are the slip of paper bearing God's proper name; that Jews were created for no other purpose than to make the coarse clay of humanity come spiritually alive, to make it man. And the trick works — or has so far. But we had better be careful. Should the Name ever be allowed to disappear, mankind's spiritual life will be over.

NATALIE GOLDBERG

The Great Spring

FROM *Shambhala Sun*

I LIVED FOR A YEAR and a half recently in St. Paul, Minnesota, practicing Zen with one of Katagiri Roshi's dharma heirs. Roshi had been dead for a long time and still I missed him and did not know how to complete the relationship that had begun over twenty years before. I was frozen in the configuration we had together when he died — he was always the teacher and I forever would be the student. Now over a decade had passed. I wanted to move on, and in order to do that it seemed I had to move back to that northern state of long winter shadows, a place I left fifteen years earlier to plant my roots in Taos, New Mexico. It seemed I had to go back to that cold place in order to unfreeze.

A few months before the move, though, I pulled a muscle in my groin that would not let me cross my legs in the traditional zazen position. This did not please me. I'd been sitting cross-legged for twenty-five years, so my reflex even at a fancy dinner party was to have my legs intertwined on the upholstered oak chair under the pink linen tablecloth.

Structure in the zendo had been everything to me: straight back, butt on black round cushion, eyes unfocused, cast down at a forty-degree angle. Bells rung on time. Clip, clip. Everything had order. In a chaotic world it was comforting. Sitting in a chair in the zendo with feet flat on the floor seemed silly. If I was going to sit in a chair, I might as well have a cup of tea, a croissant — hell, why not be in a café or on a bench under an autumn tree.

So I did go every single day, like a good Zen student, except in the wrong direction — not to the Zen center in downtown St. Paul, but to Bread and Chocolate, a café on Grand Avenue. I walked there slowly, mindfully, and it was grand. I didn't bring a notebook. I just brought myself and I had strict regulations: I could only buy one chocolate chip cookie. And I ate that one attentively, respectfully, bite after bite at a table next to big windows. I felt the butter of it on my fingers, the chips still warm and melted. In the past, seven good bites would have finished it off. But the eating was practice now, the café a living zendo. Small bites. Several chews. Be honest — was this mindfulness or a lingering? This cookie would not last. Oh, crisp and soft, brown and buttery. How I clung. The nearer, the more appreciative was I, as it disappeared.

"Life is a cookie," Alan Arkin pronounced in *America's Sweethearts*. I fell over the popcorn in my lap with laughter. One of the deep, wise lines in American movies. No one else in the theater was as elated. No one else had eaten the same single cookie for months running. I gleefully quoted Arkin, the guru, for weeks after. I could tell by people's faces: this, the result of all her sitting?

But nothing lasts forever. My tongue finally grew tired of the taste day after day. Was this straw in my mouth, this once great cookie? In the last weeks I asked only for a large hot water with lemon and wanted to pay the price for tea, but they wouldn't let me. I had become a familiar figure. So I left tips in a paper cup, and I sat. Not for a half hour or until the cookie was done — I sat for two, often three hours. Just sat there, nothing fancy, alongside an occasional man chopping away at a laptop, a mother, her son, and his young friends, heads bent over brownies, eating their afterschool snack, an elderly couple sighing long over steaming cups, a tall, retired businessman reading the *Pioneer Press*. I sat through the whole Bush/Gore campaign and then the very long election, through a young teenage boy murdered on his bike by the Mississippi, the eventual capture of the three young men who did it for no reason but to come in from the suburbs for some kicks, and the sad agony of the boy's parents who owned a pizza parlor nearby.

St. Paul is a small city with a big heart. If I was still enough, I could feel it all — the empty lots, the great river driving itself under bridges, the Schmidt brewery emitting a smell that I thought meant the town was toasting a lot of bread, but found out later was the focal point of an irate neighborhood protest. In early fall when the weather was warm I sat on the wood-and-wrought-iron bench that was set out in front of the café under a black locust. I even sat out there in slow drizzles and fog when the streets were slick and deserted. After fifteen years in New Mexico, the gray and mist were a great balm.

Sometimes if I was across the river in Minneapolis I sat at Dunn Brothers Café on Hennepin, and then, too, at the one in Linden Hills. Hadn't this always been my writing life? To fill spiral notebooks, write whole manuscripts in local luncheonettes and restaurants? But now here was my Zen life, too, happening in a café at the same square tables, only without a notebook. Hadn't I already declared that Zen and writing were one? In and out I'd breathe. My belly would fill, my belly would contract. I lifted the hot paper cup to my lips, my eyes now not down on the page but rather unfocused on the top of the chair pushed under the table across from me.

My world of meditation was getting large for me. By leaving the old structure, I was loosening my tight grip on my old Zen teacher. I was finally letting go of him. I was bringing my zazen out into the street. But who wants to let go of something you love? I did all this, but I did not recognize what was happening to me.

There is a recorded interview of me on a panel with an old dharma friend on December 21, 2001. It was a Saturday evening, the second winter of my return to Minneapolis, and the weather had tipped to thirty below. I'd just been driven across town by a kind young Zen student. No, not driven — the car slipped across black ice. I was so stunned by the time I was in front of the audience, most of my responses to the moderator's questions were, "You can find the answer to that in one of my books." I only knew no matter how deluded you may be, the land told you you would not last forever. As a matter of fact, driving home that night might be the end of you.

By the last days of February, even the most fastidious homeowners — and believe me, St. Paul is full of them — had given up shoveling their walks. In early March I looked out my apartment window to the corner of Dale and Lincoln near posh Crocus Hill and watched the man across the street blaze out of his large, many-floored, old, pale blue clapboard house, jacket flying open, with a long ax in his hand. While bellowing out months of confinement in piercing yelps, he hacked away at the ice built up by the curb. Behind him stood a massive crabapple, its branches frozen and curled in a death cry.

I had scheduled, for mid-April, a daylong public walking and writing retreat. I doubted now that it would take place. Where would we walk? In circles around the hallway of the zendo? My plan had been to meet at the zendo, write for two rounds, then venture out on a slow mindful stroll, feeling the clear placement of heel, the roll of toes, the lifting of foot, the bend of knee, the lowering of hip, as we made our way through the dank, dark streets of industrial St. Paul, across railroad tracks and under a bridge, to be surprised by a long, spiral, stone tunnel, opening into Swede Hollow along a winding creek and yellow grass (after all, when I planned it the year before, wasn't April supposed to be spring?), then climbing up to an old-fashioned, cast-iron, high-ceilinged café with a good soup and delicious desserts where we could write again at small tables. I would not tell the students where we were going. I would just lead them out the zendo door into the warehouse district with cigarette butts in wet clusters, gathered in sidewalk cracks. We would walk past the Black Dog Café and the smokers hunched on the outside stoop and near the square for the Lowertown farmers' market where impossible summer and fresh-grown produce would arrive again.

In this city of large oaks, magnificent elms and maples, I managed to return to practice Zen at a zendo surrounded by concrete, where one spindly young line of a tree gallantly fought by a metal gate to survive. I'd renamed the practice center "The Lone Tree Zendo." And, yes, in truth, I did actually go there early mornings and Saturdays and Sundays, for weekend and weeklong retreats. I was working on koans, ancient teaching stories that tested the depth of your realization. I had to present my understanding and it never came from logic or the thinking brain. I had to step out of my normal existence and come face-to-face with images from eighth-to tenth-century China: a rhinoceros fan, a buffalo passing through a window, an oak tree in the courtyard. The northern cold penetrated me as deeply as these koans. No fly, no bare finger could survive — even sound cracked. I was gouged by impermanence.

The first miserable weekend in April came. I looked at the roster of twenty-four faithful souls who had registered for the writing retreat. Two women from Lincoln, Nebraska, were flying in. A woman from Milwaukee — a six-hour drive away — was leaving at

3:30 A.M. to make the 9:30 beginning. Such determination. Only in the Midwest, I thought. I noted with delight that Tall Suzy and her friend from Fargo were coming. She'd studied with me back in New Mexico. Mike, the Vietnam vet, from Austin, Minnesota, was driving up too. I nervously fingered the page with the list of names.

The workshop date was the Saturday before Easter. The day came and miraculously it was in the low sixties. I hustled over early to Bread and Chocolate to grab a cookie and touch the recent center of my universe, and then arrived a few minutes late for class. Everyone was silently meditating in a circle. I swirled into my place.

"We are going out for most of the day. You'll have to trust me. Remember: no good or bad. Just one step after another. We'll see different things. This is a walk of faith."

After two initial writing sessions we bounded outside, eager to be in the weak yet warming sun. But the weekend desolation of industrial St. Paul sobered us. One step after another. This was a silent walk so no one could complain — not that a Midwesterner would do such a thing. But I, an old New Yorker, had to shut up too. I couldn't encourage, explain, apologize. We just walked bare-faced on this one early April day, slow enough to feel this life. Over the still frozen ground to the tracks, crushing thin pools of ice with our boots. A left foot lifted and placed, then a right. The tunnel was ahead. Half of us were already walking through the yellow limestone spiral, built in 1856, a miracle of construction that seemed to turn your mind. Eventually we all made it through to the other side, to sudden country, the hollow, and the first sweetness of open land. Long, pale grasses, just straightening up after the melting weight of snow, and thin, unleafed trees gathered along the lively winding stream.

We had walked an hour and a half at the pace of a spider. I'd forgotten what this kind of walking does to you. You enter the raw edge of your mind, the naked line between you and your surroundings drops away. Whoever you are or think you are cracks off. We were soul-bare together in the hollow, the place poor Swedish immigrants inhabited a hundred years ago in cardboard shacks. Some people broke off and went down to the stream, put their hands in the cold water. I sat on a stone with my face in the sun. Then we continued on.

We didn't get to the café until almost two o'clock. The place was empty. We filled the tables and burst into writing. I remember looking up a moment into the stunned faces of two people behind the counter. Where did all these people suddenly come from? And none of them are talking?

I'd forgotten how strenuous it was to walk so slow for so long. I was tired.

When it was time to leave, I had planned to follow the same route back. Oh, no, the students shook their heads and took the lead almost at a trot. A short cut across a bypass over noisy 94 to the zendo. We arrived breathless in twenty minutes. Back in the circle, I inquired, "How was it?" — the first spoken words.

I looked around at them. My face fell. I'd been naïve. They ran back here for safety. That walk had rubbed them raw. One woman began: "When we reached the tunnel, I was terrified to go through. It felt like the birth canal."

Another: "I didn't know where it would lead. I looked at all of us walking like zombies and began to cry. I thought of the Jews going to the chambers."

I remembered two kids in the hollow stopping their pedaling and straddling their bikes, mouths agape, staring at us. I had taken comfort in numbers and didn't worry about how we appeared to the outside. Of course, we must have looked strange.

What happened to us? they asked.

I checked in with my own body right then. Oh, yes, I felt the way I did after a five- or seven-day retreat, kind of shattered, new and tremulous. They were feeling the same.

One woman said, "I physically felt spring entering the hollow. It was right there when I slowed up enough to feel it. I opened my hand and spring filled it. I swear I also saw winter leaving. Not a metaphor. The real thing."

They were describing experiences I'd had in the zendo after long hours of sitting. But I'd thought that only within the confines of those walls and with that cross-legged position I loved, could certain kinds of openings occur. I'd wanted so badly to cling to the old structure I learned with my beloved teacher, the time-worn, true way handed down from temples and monasteries in Japan, that he'd painstakingly brought to us in America. Yes, I loved everything he taught me, but didn't the Buddha walk around a lot? What I saw now, with these students as witnesses, was that it was me who had confined my mind, grasped a practice I learned in my thirties, feeling nothing else was authentic.

Nat, what about writing? You'd said it was a true way, but even you didn't truly believe it. You only wanted to be with your old teacher again when you came back to Minnesota a year ago. You'd returned to St. Paul, it turns out, not to let go, but to find him. Like a child, you'd never really believed he'd died. Certainly you'd discover him again up here, but your body couldn't sit in the old way. You happened upon him, but all new.

What was Zen anyway? There was you and me, living and dying, eating cake. There was the sky, there were mountains, rivers, prairies, horses, mosquitoes, justice, injustice, integrity, cucumbers. The structure was bigger than any structure I could conceive. I had fallen off the zafu, that old round cushion, into the vast unknown.

I looked again at these students in a circle. This day we were here, and we experienced we were here. I could feel Roshi's presence. I thought he had died. No one had died. And in a blink of an eye none of us were here, only spring would move to summer, if we were very lucky and no one blew up the world. But maybe there were other summers and winters out there in other universes. Nothing like a Minnesota winter, of course — that single solid thought I probably would die clinging to, like a life preserver, the one true thing I'd met after all my seeking.

After the last student left, I bent to put on my shoes. I was tired of being pigeonholed as a writer. Limited to one thing. Not Zen separate from hamburgers, not writing divided from breath. Only the foot placed down on this one earth.

If we can sit in a café breathing, we can breathe through hearing our father's last breath, the slow crack of pain as we realize he's crossing over forever. Good-bye, we say. Good-bye. Good-bye. Toenails and skin. Memory halted in our lungs: his foot, ankle, wrist. When a bomb is dropped it falls through history. No one act, no single life. No disconnected occurrence. I am sipping a root beer in another café and the world spins and you pick up a pen, speak, and save another life: this time your own.

That night at 3:00 A.M., one of those mighty Midwestern thunderstorms suddenly broke the dark early sky in an electric yellow. I gazed out the cold glass pane. Either in my head or outside of it — where do thoughts come from? — three words resounded: The Great Spring. The Great Spring. Together my students and I had witnessed the tip of the moment that green longed for itself again. I realized in all these years, Roshi had never been outside of me.

ALLEN HOEY

Essay on Snow

FROM the *Hudson Review*

For Debi

> The task is not to find the lovable object,
> but to find the object before you lovable —
> — Kierkegaard, *Works of Love*

1

In a small room in a small flat, in a small
town, beside the Quaker Meetinghouse, the first
flakes of a blizzard that will, the news predicts,
bury us in snow to the depth of feet drift
outside the window. Still, the parking lot fills,
Volvos and SUVs nosed onto the grass
yellow from the sodden winter. Congregants
bundle themselves against the wind, furtively
glance toward the lowering sky as they hurry up
the stairs to sit in silence unless — until —
the Inner Light and not some querulous fear
translates into quietly impassioned speech.
An hour. Perhaps a little more. Despite these
slowflakes gaining speed each minute, what difference
can an hour make? Yesterday, they stood in lines
sprawling down the aisles almost to the frozen
food section, carts brimming with food, with soda,
bottled water, the produce aisle picked clean, not
a single pack of skinless chicken breasts

remaining by mid-afternoon. The pantry's
filled. Candles stocked against the threat that snow
will down the power lines. Quiet now. They set
aside — or try — their fears of slickened roads that
their brand-new all-season radials will fail
to navigate. Hush. Still the fear that Inner
Light might find a stillness in which to kindle
into loving flame. God is in His heaven,
Pippa knew, all must be right, here, in His world.

2

Here, in this world, His or not, I glance from my
cave of books at flakes swirling in the updraft,
large, blinding white. The cars have left their shadow-
selves in the patches of grass that mark the lawn.
Just past noon, the sky dark with evening violet
and flakes spinning reflected light from street lamps
lit this early. Already, on the main street
beyond the auto shop, sanders clank and growl.
The few cars slalom on the street below, find
their traction, then spin tires and fishtail again
at each stop sign up the block. Snow squalls whiten
the dulled brick wall across the street, flakes freezing
on contact. Setting aside another book,
I imagine that other melancholy
Dane snowbound in København, the fury
of his mind matched by the flakes driving in off
the North Sea. His nib catches the paper's grain
and a small blot spreads. He stops. Peers at the stain.
Lets his eye travel from dark mar to darker
window, flakes battering the pane like swarming
doubt. "And what," he'd written, "about Love?" Seeing
the fisherman's hand dip into the clear cold
water and lift the hooked trout shuddering from
the stream, its speckled sides heaving and gleaming
still wet in morning sun, seeing with his eyes,
feeling with his hand the throbbing life. Too small,
perhaps he thinks. Not yet. Dipping his fingers
in chill current before he grips it soft yet firm

and gently works the hook from its mouth, panic
glazing the lidless eyes, then lowers, with love,
lowers it back and watches the single flip
of caudal send it lost in the dark current.
The smoke drifting from his cigar across years
mixes with the sweet Honduran smoke from mine,
swirling as snow swirls outside both our windows.
"There are a *you* and an *I* and yet no *mine*
and *yours!* — Remarkable! — without you and I
there is no love; yet with mine and yours — no love."

3

Purity, purity, keens the Preacher. Yet
what is "purity"? Even driven snow has
at each flake's heart a speck of soot around which
the crystal coalesces. Black at the core
of white, white because of black. Every snowflake
falls where it falls, perfectly, here, not elsewhere,
blossoming from emptiness around the shard
of matter, drifting, falling, swirled and melting —
here and now, now and then. The street lamp's beacon
lost in blinding white. Form becoming void, void
composed of form. Glyphs and figures scrawl across
the pavement, words in an uncertain syntax,
blurred, drifting, reformed. Squint as you will, eyes pinched
tightly, the sentences will not resolve, will
shift, will teem with endless meaning, then dissolve.
Now, the air full beyond fullness, not as though
flakes fell — soft music of atoms suddenly
born from nothing to light. A brightness, like love,
at the window, that softens the earth's edges.

4

Although as a rule, I dislike mentioning
poems in poems (although as a rule I dislike
rules), I remember the first poem I wrote that
someone forced me to make a poem, not well-placed
words amounting to nothing. I wrote about

snow, the terror of driving at night in snow
so thick and blinding white I couldn't see — not
road, not trees that marked, I knew though I couldn't
see them, the edge of road. With deft irony
of late youth, I recounted promises made
to the God I didn't then, as I'm still not
certain, I believed in. It made, I believe,
a good poem, though the promises so lightly
made and broken haunt me, as the poem does not
convey. So many promises, God invoked
at the darkest moment of the darkest hour.
Then what? No atheists in foxholes, the last
generation claimed. No more than that? My sleep
for forty years troubled by the fleeting thought
I had at eight, buried in covers, trying
to imagine *infinity*. The ease with
which my Lutheran teachers let the word roll
off their tongues. *Infinity. Eternity.*
But lie in bed, the steam pipes rumbling complaints
like the house's voice buried deep in its guts
sounding just outside my door, hordes of trampling
feet on the staircase, in the walls. Emptiness
as far as my small mind could take me. Within
voidness, form that gave way to a deeper void.

5

Each time it snows again, the dog spins and barks,
snapping at flakes, ploughing through drifts, as if this
were the first snow she'd ever seen. Her black fur
coated, her eyes wide as a puppy's. Faced with
such exuberance — such joy — even I, tired
by too close to fifty winters full of snow
to be shoveled, lugged, brushed, and scraped from windshields,
feel a little of the boy's delight, tumbling
before the galoshes are firmly snapped, out
the door and into snow fit only for deep
tunneling through the mountains my father's back
provided in the yard. Years before he talked
my mother into a gas-powered blower,

he shoveled the full width and length of our drive,
hauling from the farthest side to heap the next
load on the pile. Do I remember winters
wrong? It seems the days were filled with snow, one hill
hardly gone before the next shards of heaven
showered done. Crystal in the street lamp's glimmer,
glassy vistas from the backporch's vantage.
By March, I tired of it. Too much of any
good thing. Now, back inside, the dog having rolled
herself dry on the throw rug, I watch the flakes
fall, drift on updrafts, and let my mind follow.

6 (*After Huang Po*)

*How often does the world around you hinder
your perceiving perfect Mind? The least mishap
blurs your sense of deeper principles. Often,
then, you try to blot the world, to forget what
troubles you to quiet your mind or to grasp
principles that elude your thoughts, as the moon
eludes the fisherman's net. But don't confuse
the world with Mind or mishaps with principles.
If you let your mind become empty, the world
will seem the emptiness it is; if you let
principles go, the mishaps will pour away.
No — don't use your mind in this perverted way!
Don't fear that, when emptying your mind, you will
lose yourself in emptiness. Your own mind is
emptiness. Only the foolish abandon
the world and cling to thought; be wise — let go of
your thoughts and drift like a snowflake in the world.*

7

My students, I fear, would not approve of this
as an essay. Where, they might well demand, are
the sentences to declare the topics? Where's
the thesis to help readers chart the course through
the title's subject? What do we learn about
snow we didn't know before we began to read?

And, here, as I face their puzzled and perhaps
annoyed to the point of almost-angered looks,
rows of them in the far-from-orderly rows
of cramped seats in the too-hot classroom of my
imagination, I simply shrug. "Snow." Pause.
"Snow," I repeat, not entirely convinced
by my own conviction, "defines the subject.
Essay means you try — simply try." Then, without
a heartbeat's passing, the voice of Zen master
Yoda, stern as the aging German pastor
at Emanuel Lutheran church, intrudes,
insisting, "Do or do not; there is no try."

8

Snow, then, is the subject. Snow the occasion.
This snow turned sleet that rattles against the panes,
tattoos a rhythm on the roof intricate
as Elvin Jones on the ride in Trane's *A Love
Supreme.* The dog looks more than a little worried,
come from the softness of the sofa to curl
beside me on the hardwood floor, turning toward
the window when the sleet increases tempo
or volume. Settles her head back on her paws
at a reassuring word. Tell me, Søren,
can love be simple as a single spoken
word? All those volumes composed in a frenzy
less than Buddha said when, catching Kasyapa's
eye, he twirled a single lotus bloom. And smiled.

9 (*What Hölderlin in His Madness Might Have Said*)

*wandered, from godhead, down where the rivers flow,
downward, sideways, the slow spiral, straightways, too,
over the snow-capped Alps, from the fragrant wilds
of Indus, flying across the sea, waves frothed
and flecked like snow off the ragged tors, glinted
in sunlight broken through the red clouds, swirling
snow off the rockstill mountains. The jagged rock*

good for pasture, what's dry for drink, what is wet
for food. Dwell on wind-chiseled steps where a house
hangs down near the water, there spend your days, small
days in a small house, small warmth of the hearth.
What comes to the surface by day in deep sleep
you find it again, eyes covered, feet bound, bare
field, the mild view and torrents of snow. One day
simply of rest. New words. The dead words in spring
sending out fragrant shoots, the dazzle of snow.
And what's yours — what's yours — is to draw another

10

breath. Visible in the thick blue smoke of yet
another cigar. Predictably, the snow
is not what they predicted. What ever is?
"The one thing you can count on," my father said,
leaning on the shovel, "is what you never
counted on." Meaning three feet of snow. Meaning
Søren, you might concur, the nib of your pen
still hovering above the page, the hidden
overflow of love, spilling down the way these flakes
tumbled from the sky, unexpected, the cloud's
burden dropped without effort. The North Sea's gale
stilled a moment, as you peer through the murky
pane, a light across the way gleaming brightly.
Who's there? Who's ever there? The hidden spring in
a mountain pool. Soon enough, the ploughs will come
to scrape the crust away, the sun will smolder
through the clouds and melt the rest, unseen moisture
pouring upward to restore the inner dome.
What's left to say can't be said. It never can,
however hard we try. Like snow that blossoms,
falls to melt, silent in the darkness, quiet
in the daylight, emptying, filling, like love,
a look, a touch. Her eyes the way they glance that
certain way, another thing I've got no words
to explain. A touch, I offer, soft as snowflakes brushing down the softness of her soft cheek.

ANDREW HUDGINS

Beneath the Apple

FROM the *Iowa Review*

The house a-tilt with laughter, jazz,
and tipsy friends, I eased
into the yard, and took a breath
of dark, chill evening, pleased

to leave drink, smoke, and my old friends.
I lumbered to the apple
in the darkest corner, near the fence,
and underfoot, a windfall,

crushed to paste, infused the air,
its sweetness lush with rot.
(I ought to take it down, the apple.
But that's an afterthought.)

Too much to drink and my house full,
I leaned against the tree,
and stared back into yellow windows,
perplexed — why now? — to see

my friends, whose lives I know too well
and who know mine. We share
long histories but decreasing time.
We make good laughter bear

what laughter can, which is a lot.
I saw my smiling wife
finger an old friend's bright new hair
and risk an honest laugh.

A hundred feet away in darkness —
and I knew what she'd said
and what her laughing friend said back,
her hair a fevered red.

I leaned into the teeming tree,
fumbled, and emptied myself
onto its peeling bark. The dog
strolled over, took a sniff

and emptied himself too — two mammals
depositing their salts
against the boundary tree. I named
and then unnamed my faults

as I stood under unplucked fruit —
a spiteful woodland god,
I thought. Or tried to think. The god —
or was it I? — guffawed.

I sauntered up the lawn in joy,
a ghost. Nothing was mine.
The house, the friends, the night. I loved
that moment: Dead. Divine.

PICO IYER

Grandmothers

FROM the *American Scholar*

SOMETIMES, FROM MY DESK here in Japan, I see boys in the park across from me, hitting and hitting a ball with a large blue baseball bat. Their grandmothers sit in the sun, on benches, the gold and russet leaves coming down around them like confetti. A woman sits by herself on another bench, sketching the colors in front of her, and a flock of Boy Scouts is sent to gather all the trash (nonexistent, as far as I'm concerned), their yellow shirts fluttering across the clean green spaces.

I walk across the park in the autumn sunlight and feel a foreigner's sense of wonder. The convenience stores are placed along the small, shiny street as if they were just more vending machines; the two-story houses, tidily guarded by walls, are lined up along the narrow roads like salarymen in business suits waiting for the future. Every trace of the old is expunged as efficiently as the trees and the rice paddies once were, here in this place where hope means the West and tomorrow.

All this, I know, is foreign only for a foreigner: the kids around me, in their hip-hop gear and surfer shorts, regard baseball as a Japanese invention, as Japanese as the McDonald's outlet down the street ("Did you see cannibals?" Africans ask one another when they come back from Europe, Ryszard Kapuscinski writes). Yet just behind the sleek new stores, at the edge of the neighborhood, where the streets run out, there is a deeper foreignness, foreign even to the native: dark gullies, often, or slopes of untrimmed trees. The visitor steps up to the wild space, and then steps back, and retreats to the shiny machines he knows and trusts.

I go sometimes to the local train station — its platforms lined with banks of TVs that broadcast all the cable channels of the world — and take a ten-minute train ride. When I get out, at the final stop, I step into Nara's celebrated Deer Park, an open space so large and wild it takes up the entire center of the ancient capital, much as the Imperial Palace does in Tokyo and its ghostly predecessor still does in Kyoto.

By day, the park — which runs all the way from the station, the noisy arcades, and the tall department stores to the hills — is full of tour buses that have brought schoolchildren here to visit their collective past, foreigners anxious to see the last untouched part of old Japan. But as soon as dusk descends, the place empties out, and, walking toward the hills, I can feel as if I'm the only person in the world.

A couple, perhaps, is peeping through a fence at the great Buddha temple, said to be the largest wooden structure in the world. A salaryman is walking home, jacket over his shoulder, past the white-globe lanterns. A foreigner extends his arms, a temporary king, under the high ceremonial orange torii gate, built for ghosts and giants.

No one else is visible. I follow a stone path into the darkening woods, and all noise, all commotion falls away. There are only deer, on every side, coming out onto the path after nightfall, as if to reclaim their territory. They stand stock-still amid the trees, ears cocked, noses alert, to see where I am going. Occasionally, a great gust of them — thirty or forty or more — takes off in a silent canter and disappears into the farther darkness.

The deer, aggressive in their demands for food by day, are perfect Japanese hosts by night. They don't come close to me; they don't step away. I walk toward the flight of wooden steps that leads up to a temple on the hill, and they simply stand on every side of me, attentive. On the gravel path, among the trees, behind me in the dark, they wait for the trespasser to leave.

A festival held here every winter dates, they say, from the time when Nara was the Buddhist capital, thirteen centuries ago. Men in white robes run along the terrace of the great temple on the hill, which overlooks the city, and their torches shake in the night and make the wooden building seem to tremble. With great fanfare, they place the torches on the edges of the terrace, and sparks rain down on the people who have collected below, many of whom scramble in the darkness for auspicious ashes. Again and again, silently, the men carry their torches across the platform — gold streaks across the blackness — and send stars scattering down as the temple shivers in the heat.

The deer stay quiet for the duration of the festival, waiting patiently in the trees for the crowds to pass. After ten or fifteen minutes of gold-running, the people disperse, hugging themselves in the cold, rubbing mittened hands together as they walk back to the station. You know, the old ladies tell the children beside them, that the deer are sacred messengers; they bring us news of the gods, who live somewhere in the hills.

An automated voice announces the next express train, and the teenagers with yellow hair pour in from the pachinko parlors and the bars. The visitors go back to their homes, and the deer step out again in the dark.

One bright, chill autumn morning, I notice, as I walk along the path in my neighborhood, that thick sweaters are everywhere. All around me are the very old and the very young; the others are off tending the fires of official Japan. I see old ladies leaning on canes, out to get exercise as the leaves come down. By their sides are tiny grandchildren, pointing out this cosmos flower or that dog in its winter coat. The old and the young live on the edge of things in Japan, close to the dark. They can talk, or make up stories, about the creatures still known here as *kamisama*, or nature's gods.

The grandmothers weren't such good parents themselves, perhaps, when they were young, but nature is affording them a second chance. They have time now — in the short term — and freedom, while it lasts, to pass on whatever their own grandmothers passed on to them, to tell the toddlers at their sides that the fox who waits at the edge of the trees isn't a fox at all, or that the stranger who sits in a frame on the public shrine isn't a stranger, but their emperor's grandmother. The children, lost in their own games, don't bother to say that there isn't a picture of an old woman on the shrine — Grandma's eyes are fading. And of course the foxes on TV aren't real — cartoons never are. That's what makes them special.

They listen, because that's what they're supposed to do; perhaps they nod. And, being natural lawbreakers, they tell their grandmothers a thing or two, about what that animal is saying to its owner, and what the secret name of that tree is. Their fathers are seldom visible, and their mothers are chafing against the conflicts of a world of 7-Elevens and feudal rites; but the deer, the foxes stay the same.

When I was the same age as the children in my neighborhood, I was asked one summer to take a small part in a local production of *A Midsummer Night's Dream*. We lived in Oxford, often known as the center of England's largest motor works — Great Britain's Detroit — but in one corner of the industrial city, Neville Coghill, the distinguished Chaucerian and friend to C. S. Lewis and J.R.R. Tolkien, summoned the dormant spirits of the soil to life and asked them to resume their pagan duties. Spirits flitted through the trees of Worcester College, and the Queen of the Fairies took her leave of men by drifting across the college lake. Puck danced across the night, and the ghosts of ancient Greece jumped across the centuries and walked among us.

I saw the *Dream* again last night, in Nara, on a rented video from the Tsutaya Culture Convenience Club, and wondered if the scenes would seem strange to my neighbors in the park. Even the young, in their backward baseball caps or their Chanel, go to shrines where they buy temple charms from women dressed in white, like vestal virgins. They walk around the pond and look at the *O-tsuki-sama* — in the kind of honorific translation that made us laugh when we were young, the "Most Honored and God-Like Moon." They address the heavenly body, in fact, almost as Pyramus and Thisbe might.

I walk into the park — the light is failing now, the evenings are coming early — and I think the boys playing baseball would have no trouble believing that fairies could put spells on mortals to make us fall in love with the first person we see upon awakening.

Every morning, in my home, my Japanese companion rings a bell and lights a stick of incense in the shrine she's made next to her Panasonic boom box. She closes her eyes, says something very fast — or nothing at all — and I remember how, when first I met her, I took her to an amusement park, and she came out of the haunted house genuinely shaken. Ghosts are real to her. Behind the flashing lights of Japan is something dark, and very old.

I look at all this strangely, perhaps. Growing up, I had no grandparents within several thousand miles and took that to be a liberation, a chance to make my own future (even to choose my own past — I could take my gods and elders, the global order told me, from Japan as much as from my ancestral India). Those born into the modern world are free, at times, if sufficiently comfortable and sufficiently modern, to sketch their own futures, as their grandparents never could (though what they draft on their blank pieces of paper sometimes looks surprisingly close to what they might have drawn through inheritance).

Yet as I walk around this small park in the autumn light, everything blazing and about to pass away, I wonder what it means to get one's grandparents, one's ghosts, vicariously, because one lacks grandparents and old wives' tales — lacks, in effect, those pieces of collected wisdom passed down from age to age that we laugh at even as we're secretly committing them to memory. We go, some of us, to places on holiday where we can live for a few weeks by candlelight; we pick up a novel by a Chinese woman in San Francisco who reports that her mother saw the whistling of the wind as a wailing from her old nursemaid in Shanghai, decades ago. Gods and ancestors are all mixed up in the old cultures, where grandmothers may be taken, as much as deer, to be messengers from somewhere else. A belief in ghosts, the shrine by the boom box says, is just a way of having faith in what you cannot see.

One morning, under an immaculate sky, I go out again, past the long line of tearooms, past the souvenir stores where glove puppets in the shape of Buddhas and deer are sold, to a small wooden gate that leads into a shy, largely forgotten temple. A white board tells how the temple remembers the time a deer stole in, a thousand years ago, and ate a piece of calligraphy. A monk, seeing the intruder, threw a stone at it, and the deer collapsed. The monk, who was thirteen years old, was condemned to death, by Nara custom, for slaying a messenger of the gods. Now the stone turtle in the temple garden asks people to pray for the young boy who would otherwise go unmourned.

When I return to my apartment, the light still radiant, my partner tells me that she just went to see her closest friend, and the woman, hardly older than herself, held her and said that they would never meet again. She'd been told that she had cancer, in its final stages.

My friend silently lights her stick of incense, and rings a bell, over and over. Her eyes remain closed long after the bell stops ringing.

Outside, the days turn and the leaves come down. The people in my neighborhood change their futons, pull out their heaters. Autumn brings festivals in commemoration of the old and the very young. Winter will bring another set of rites, colorful occasions whose meanings have been forgotten but whose observance continues amid the video games. People do things here because they do things, the way we used to sing hymns in church: indeed, autumn makes the least of us philosophical, even if our philosophy says the same thing every year. And the saying of that same thing, over and over, becomes part of the shape, the natural pattern of our world.

I walk down the street and wonder if a large part of the human enterprise is not just the task of fitting ourselves into the larger order, adjusting to a scheme that will roll on long after we have been replaced. In England, when I was growing up, we thought of life as a play: we were given a script at birth, asked (quite politely) to play our part as convincingly as we could, and then told (no less politely) to retreat gracefully and make room for someone else. This can mean — in Japan, it usually does mean — fitting oneself into a social order, a family, a community, a company. But for those of us who choose not to be a part of that — who choose to be permanent foreigners, you might say — it means only reconciling ourselves to, and around, the larger cycle. The woman who was sitting at my dinner table a few weeks ago, apparently in the prime of health, is about to die. The last warm days are about to pass.

One virtue of grandparents, or seasons, or deer who come down from the hills is that they remind us that we don't know everything and can't make the world up entirely from scratch; much of it — most of it — is beyond our reach, even beyond our reckoning. In the larger view of things, available to grandparents and ghosts, trivial things have fallen away, and important things never change.

The old are in the best position to appreciate this, as well as to understand what the reviving freshness of the young can bring.

And the lady who is (I hear) setting up a spirit house on her lawn in West Hollywood is telling us, without saying anything, that we can all save time by remembering the lessons of those who've gone before us, and that a large part of who we are isn't very individual at all.

As autumn gives way to winter, I pick up Ryzsard Kapuscinski's most recent book on Africa, with its musing on cannibals, and read that the elephant, on what is said to be the oldest continent in the world, is treated as a sacred animal, in part because he has no enemies, and also — so the legend has it — because he never dies. He just gets exhausted and walks into a lake, never to be seen again. His death is never seen or talked about; in that sense, it never happens, or it happens only in the invisible world. I read such things — I've never been to the country he's describing — and feel I'm hearing news from a distant radio station I can hardly catch.

Then I think of the deer, not far away — the area in which I live is called the Southern Slope of Deer — their ears cocked, their eyes watching from the trees. In Oxford, at the college where I studied, a college I'd visited often as a small boy, growing up in the city, there was a deer park, and forty or so animals walked among the elm trees beside the buildings where professors held their weekly tutorials. The deer were protected by a fence, but we could touch them through the gratings and see them as we walked to class.

It was said that the number of deer must always match the number of Fellows in the college, leading to an easy joke about what might happen every time a deer died. And once a year, in the autumn, some of us were invited to a great feast of venison, after it was decreed, for whatever reason, that the number of deer had to be brought down. I didn't know the meaning of the phrase "tutelary spirit" then, and even if I had known it, I would not have paid heed to it or stopped to think what it might connote. Now, however, half a world away, I think of what happens when the darkness falls on Nara Park, and almost nothing is visible but the outline of the great temple and the stone steps leading up into the night. Outside the temple, in the emptiness, you can see the large stone guardians taken from China as emblems of protection; everywhere else, the deer, stepping through the trees.

PHILIP LEVINE

The Lesson

FROM the *Atlantic Monthly*

Early in the final industrial century
on the street where I was born lived
a doctor who smoked black shag
and walked his dog each morning
as he muttered to himself in a language
only the dog knew. The doctor had saved
my brother's life, the story went, reached
two stained fingers down his throat
to extract a chicken bone and then
bowed to kiss the ring-encrusted hand
of my beautiful mother, a young widow
on the lookout for a professional.
Years before, before the invention of smog,
before Fluid Drive, the eight-hour day,
the iron lung, I'd come into the world
in a shower of industrial filth raining
from the bruised sky above Detroit.
Time did not stop. Mother married
a bland wizard in clutch plates
and drive shafts. My uncles went off
to their world wars, and I began a career
in root vegetables. Each morning,
just as the dark expired, the corner church
tolled its bells. Beyond the church
an oily river ran both day and night
and there along its banks I first conversed

with the doctor and Waldo, his dog.
"Young man," he said in words
resembling English, "you would dress
heavy for autumn, scarf, hat, gloves.
Not to smoke," he added, "as I do."

Eleven, small for my age but ambitious,
I took whatever good advice I got,
though I knew then what I know
now: the past, not the future, was mine.
If I told you he and I became pals
even though I barely understood him
would you doubt me? Wakened before dawn
by the Catholic bells, I would dress
in the dark — remembering scarf, hat, gloves —
to make my way into the deserted streets
to where Waldo and his master ambled
the riverbank. Sixty-four years ago,
and each morning is frozen in memory,
each a lesson in what was to come.
What was to come? you ask. This world
as we have it, utterly unknowable,
utterly unacceptable, utterly unlovable,
the world we waken to each day
with or without bells. The lesson was
in his hands, one holding a cigarette,
the other buried in blond dog fur, and in
his words thick with laughter, hushed,
incomprehensible, words that were sound
only without sense, just as these must be.
Staring into the moist eyes of my maestro,
I heard the lost voices of creation running
over stones as the last darkness sifted upward,
voices saddened by the milky residue
of machine shops and spangled with first light,
discordant, harsh, but voices nonetheless.

B. K. LOREN

Word Hoard

FROM *Parabola*

ONCE, I BECAME APHASIC. "Synapses," my neurologist explained to me, "are an all or none proposition." Mine were none.

Fish: *Bagel.*

Lion: *Table.*

Pelican: *Funicular.*

This is the way I named things. *The funicular skimmed the surface of the ocean searching for bagels.* Ocean was big enough, usually, to fit on my tongue and palate, to dance on my tongue and groove. The rest of the words I've filled in after the fact, like we usually do with memory (aphasic or not). We like to be understood. What I really might have said may have involved "funicular" and "bagel," but the words between would have been gibberish. My brain was an unplanned language poem and I a woman who tires easily of language poetry for its insistence upon intrinsic ambiguity. When you don't have it, language becomes unflinchingly precise.

Signifier: Signified: Bullshit.

Words carry on their backs their entire histories. This is what I learned the day they packed up and left me languageless. No forwarding address, no wish-you-were-here postcard.

Postcard: *Night Cream.*

Yard: *Breast.*

Water: *Orgasm.*

Holy shit. I was dead in the water without language.

As it is with any lover, I didn't see my words packing their bags to go. If I had, I'd have tried to stop them. I'd have begged, "Let's work this out, you and me. Let's find a middle ground."

I didn't see the verbs colluding with the nouns, the adverbs separating off, the adjectives running like lemmings to the cliff of my lips. I went to bed one night with a congregation gathering in my throat to sing me awake the next morn, and I woke with a stale mix of nonsense in my mouth, Fruit Loops instead of the promise of eggs hatching thoughts in my brain for breakfast.

My doctors were flummoxed.

A year into it, and I was depressed. I do not mean sad. I mean looking for the word *gun* daily, something to put in my mouth. I'd studied classics instead of writing in college. I couldn't stand to see words played with as they were in some writing workshops.

I needed to know the genetic origin of words. Their family tree. I mean, without that, all words are adopted. They grow up angry foster children wanting to burn things down. I wanted to know their mother and grandmother. I wanted to know their Adam, their Eve, their Eden, their original sin. Knowledge.

When you use the word *flummox,* for instance, your tongue rolls across the same territory of every person who has ever spoken that word. It carries every sentiment every flummoxed person has ever implied, plus your own.

Muriel Ruckeyser has said, "The world is made of stories, not atoms." They say that every third breath you breathe contains at least one of the same molecules Caesar exhaled as he was dying. Think of the words, then, the same words you breathe that have been inhaled and exhaled throughout history. If you're looking for a link, there it is. They are only shapes and noises formed into meaning. But how many shapes and sounds have crossed the tongues of those who have come before? And this exact shape and sound has crossed centuries to come to you, fully formed, Athene from Zeus's head (or so you believe as it transforms itself even as it leaves your lips). Words say simultaneously too much and too little. This is why they are perfect for communication, most people's lives operating in the balance between too much and too little. Nothing more precise.

In those years without language, I was limbless. I had no way to reach out. I had no way to touch others or myself. Water: *Orgasm.* My body had no reason to come or go anywhere.

Words are my nourishment. They are the molecules that seethe in my veins. They are the light that filters through the rods and cones of my eyes to create color and dimension. They are my resting heart rate, my tulips, my knives, my forks, my spoons.

My art, to me, means food. Means sustenance. If I had another choice, I tell you, I would make money. It's a catch-22. You must eat to live, must live to work. I eat my art for breakfast because I know what it is to go wordless, to be naked on the tongue and groping for a story that makes sense.

Towel: *Meridian.*

Apple: *Bird.*

Chalice: *Fly.*

Write: *Live.*

Silence: *Die.*

It's a cliché. But here's what I know. I have come into existence alongside words. Others have come into existence alongside business or sculpture or music or humor or science. Words carry with them a unique challenge. We use them daily, whether we love them or not. And so, loving them is a fix. Unless you're stuck in a Hollywood musical, people do not usually sing to you as a form of communication. Unless you are Neanderthal, they do not usually draw. But people will talk to you with words even when you're a writer. They'll toss your medium around willy-nilly. They'll use it to bad ends. They'll use it to create wars, to manipulate leaders, to rape people, to sell.

You will be tempted to think your medium mundane, sometimes evil. You will be forced to discipline yourself against this. It will make you poor.

Once, I was aphasic. The condition lasted, to some extent or another, nearly ten years. When I came back to words I came back like a lover who'd had a mistaken affair. Once the damage is done, it's done. But there's a carefulness that follows. You don't take things for granted. You speak from the soles of your feet, a current of meaning running through your body, each word carrying with it its history and the intimate mouths of your ancestors speaking it. Their lips touch yours as the word leaves you.

This is what connects you to who you are. What you love. What you caress. Whatever it is that leaves you and in its absence makes you lonelier than God.

When it returns, it becomes holy. When it returns, you see the sacred in the profane. You do not fall prostrate before it. You hold it close. You let it go. You live with it. You live.

THOMAS LYNCH

Good Grief

FROM *Christian Century*

IT'S SUNNY AND 70° at Chapel Hill. I'm speaking to Project Compassion, an advocacy group for end-of-life issues, on an unlikely trinity of oxymorons — the *good* death, *good* grief, and the *good* funeral. "What," most people reasonably ask, "can ever be good about death or grief or funerals?" The 150 people in this room understand. They are mostly women — clergy, hospice and social workers, doctors, nurses, and funeral directors — and they work, so to speak, in the deep end of the pool, with the dying, the dead, and the bereaved.

We begin by agreeing that the good death is the one that happens when we are among our own, surrounded not by beeping meters and blinking monitors but by the faces of family and people who care. It is the death of a whole person, not an ailing part. It is neither a failure nor an anomaly; it is less science and more serenity. The good death, like the good life, does not happen in isolation. It is not only or entirely a medical event, nor only or entirely a social or spiritual or retail one. The good death engages our entire humanity — both what is permanent and what is passing. So I am thanking these women for the power of their presence — as nurses and doctors and hospice volunteers, as pastors and rabbis, priests and imams, as mothers and daughters, sisters and wives — for their willingness to stand in the room where someone is dying, without an easy answer, without a cure or false hopes, with only their own humanity, to bear witness and to be present. The power of being there is that it emboldens others — family and friends — also to be present to the glorious and sorrowful mysteries.

And grief, *good* grief, we further concur, is something about which we have little choice. It is the tax we pay on the loves of our lives, our habits and attachments. And like every other tax, there is this dull math to it — if you love, you grieve. So the question is not so much whether or not, but rather how well, how completely, how meaningfully we mourn. And though we do not grieve as those who have no faith grieve, as people of faith we grieve nonetheless. We talk about the deeper meanings we sometimes find in the contemplation of these things and how we sometimes feel God's presence there, and sometimes God's absence.

And everything is going very well. We are all nodding in warm consensus. It's like preaching to the choir — until I come to the part where I talk about a *good* funeral.

A good funeral, I tell them, serves the living by caring for the dead. It tends to both — the living and dead — because a death in the family happens to both. A good funeral transports the newly deceased and the newly bereaved to the borders of a changed reality. The dead are disposed of in a way that says they mattered to us, and the living are brought to the edge of a life they will lead without the one who has died. We deal with death by dealing with the dead, not just the idea but also the sad and actual fact of the matter — the dead body.

Here is where some of the audience stops nodding. Brows furrow, eyes narrow into squints, as if something doesn't exactly compute. The idea of death is one thing. A dead body is quite another. An Episcopal priest in the third row raises her hand to ask, "Why do we need the body there? Isn't it, after all, just a shell?" She is speaking, she tells me, from a Christian perspective.

This "just a shell" theory is a favorite among clergy of my generation. Their pastoral educations on death and bereavement began and, for many of them, ended with *The American Way of Death* — Jessica Mitford's 1963 best-selling lampoon of funerals and funeral directors. It was an easy and often hilarious read. Mitford made much of the math of caskets — how much they cost, how profitable they were, how devious or obsequious the sales pitch was. She disliked the boxes for their expense. And she disliked the bodies in the boxes for the untidy and unpredictable feelings that surrounded them. She recommended getting rid of both caskets and corpses, and letting convenience and cost efficiency replace what she regarded as pricey and barbaric display.

The bodies of Mitford's first husband, who died in the war, her first daughter, who died in infancy, and her first son, who was killed by a bus in Berkeley, California, all "disappeared" — dispatched without witness or rubric and never mentioned in *The American Way of Death* nor in two volumes of autobiography. Their names were erased from the books of her life for fear of the feelings that might linger there. Fearful that the sight of a dead body might trigger overwhelming emotions, she downsized it to "just a shell" to be burned or buried without attendant bother or much expense.

This was a welcome notion among many of the clergy coming of age in the latter decades of the last century. It aligned nicely with their sense that, just as merchants were removing Christ from Christmas, morticians were removing faith from funerals. What need have Christians of all this bother — caskets, flowers, wakes, and processions. Aren't the sureties of heaven enough? The "just a shell" theory furthermore articulated the differences between the earthly and heavenly, the corruptible and incorruptible, the base and blessed, sacred and profane, sinful natures and holy spirits.

Human beings are bodies and souls. And souls, made in the image and likeness of God, are eternal and essential, whereas bodies are mortal and impermanent. "There is," the scripture holds, "a natural body and a spiritual body." In life, we are regarded as one — a whole being, body and soul, flesh and blood and spirit. And we are charged with the care and maintenance of both. We feed the flesh and the essence. We pamper the wounds and strive to improve the condition of both body and soul. We read and we run wind sprints, we fast and pray, confide in our pastors and medicos, and seek communion, spiritual and physical, with other members of our species. "Know ye not," Paul asks the Corinthians, "that ye are the temple of God, and that the Spirit of God dwelleth in you?"

But in death, the good priest in the third row seemed to be saying, the temple becomes suddenly devalued, suddenly irrelevant, suddenly negligible and disposable — "just a shell" from which we ought to seek a hurried and most often unseen riddance.

Like many of her fellow clergy, she finds the spiritual bodies more agreeable than the natural ones. The spirits are well intentioned and faultless; the bodies are hungry, lustful, greedy, and weak. The soul is the sanctuary of faith, the body full of doubts and despairs. The soul sees the straight and narrow path, whereas the body wants the easier, softer way. The corruptible bleeds and belches and dies, and the incorruptible is perfect and perpetual. Souls are just easier all around. Which is why for years she's been officiating at memorial services instead of funerals. They are easier, more convenient, and more cost-efficient. They are notable for their user-friendliness. They can be scheduled around the churches' priorities — the day care and Stephen Ministries, the Bible studies and rummage sales — and around a pastor's all-too-busy schedule. A quick and private disposal of the dead removes the sense of emergency and immediacy from a death in the family.

There is no bother with coffins at all. The dead are secreted off to the crematory or grave while the living go about their business. Where a dead body requires more or less immediate attention, riddance of "just the shell" can hold grief off for a few days, or a week, or a season. No cutting short the pastor's too brief vacation, no rushing home from a ministerial conference to deal with a death in the parish family. The eventual "celebration" will be a lovely and, needless to say, "life-affirming" event to which everyone is invited — except, of course, the one who has died. The talk is determinedly uplifting, the finger food and memorabilia are all in good taste, the music more purposefully cheering than poignant, the bereaved most likely on their best behavior, less likely to "break down," "fall apart," or "go to pieces" — they will be brave and faithful. And "closure," if not achieved, is nonetheless proclaimed, often just before the Merlot runs out.

The memorial service makes much of dealing with memories of the dead by steadfastly refusing to deal with the dead themselves. It is the emotional and commemorative equivalent of a baptism without the baby or a wedding without the blushing bride or a graduation without the graduates. A funeral without the dead body has the religious significance of the Book of Job without the sores and boils, Exodus without the stench of frogs, Calvary without a cross, or the cross without the broken, breathless, precious body hanging there, all suffering and salvation. It is Easter without the resurrected body.

So I asked her reverence: what if her congregants, instead of showing up to worship, left "just their shells" in bed on Sunday mornings? Or what if, instead of dressing up the children's "shells" and driving them across town to church, they assured their pastor that they were "with her in spirit"? Might she think there was something missing from the morning services? At this she looked at me, perplexed. Or what if Jesus had not raised his "just a shell" from the dead? What if he'd resurrected the "idea" of himself, say, or his personality? Would we all be Christians these centuries since?

The clergywoman was not amused.

When Joseph of Arimathea, in league with Nicodemus, pleaded with Pilate for "just" the body of Christ, he was acting out a signature duty of our species. And when the Marys came bearing spices and ointments to anoint the corpse, they too were acting out long-standing obsequies "in keeping with the customs of the Jews." It is the custom of humankind to deal with death by dealing with the dead.

The defining truth of our Christianity — an empty tomb — proceeds from the defining truth of our humanity: we fill tombs. The mystery of the resurrection to eternal life is bound inextricably to the experience of suffering and death. Indeed, the effort to make sense of life — the religious impulse — owes much to our primeval questions about the nature of death.

Is that all there is? Can it happen to me? Why is it cold? What comes next?

The funeral — that ritual wheel that works the space between the living and the dead — must deal with our humanity and our Christianity, our spiritual and natural realities, our flesh, our fears, our faith and hopes, our bodies and our souls.

Lately it seems the wheel is broken, or has gone off the track, or must be reinvented every day. Nowadays news of a death is often attended by a gathering ambiguity about what we ought to do about it. We have more choices and fewer certainties, more options and fewer customs. The culture — that combination of religious, ethnic, social, and market dynamics — seems to have failed us. We are drawn, it seems, toward two extremes — to do anything and everything or to do nothing, nothing at all.

To be sure, funerals and funeral directors can disappoint us, confusing, as they often do, the fashions with the fundamentals, the accessories with the essentials, the accoutrements with the enduring truths. The clergy and faithful have good reason to be wary. The merger and acquisition frenzy of the past two decades has had the same effect on funeral homes that it had on pharmacies and hardware, restaurants and medical care. Personal, compassionate, professional service is often lost to the "have a nice day" speak of corporate cover. The sales-pitch, bottom-line, every-sadness-a-sales-op mentality that Mitford wrote about forty years ago has not disappeared, especially among the three large mortuary conglomerates — Service Corporation International, Alderwoods, and Stewart Enterprises — that own nearly 20 percent of the funeral homes and cemeteries around the country.

The largest manufacturer of caskets in the country markets "visitation vignettes" — a kind of theater of the absurd where the dead are laid out in "lifestyle" caskets among emblems not of their faith or family but of their hobbies. There is the "Sports Dad" vignette, heavy on beer and sports paraphernalia, and one for gardeners, and the much publicized "Big Mama's Kitchen" with its faux stove, kitchen table, and apple pie for the mourners to share with those who call. And while most families want to personalize a funeral, the market almost always errs on the side of excess, too often tendering the ridiculous instead of the sublime. We would not mistake a good diamond for a good marriage, or stained glass for true faith, but we are always mistaking a good box for a good funeral. It is the triumph of accessory over essentials.

These funerary fashion blunders make most people more than a little wary. Too often, however, to avoid the fashions, the fundamental obligations are neglected — to bear witness to the life that was lived and the death that has occurred. Too often the body is dispatched by cell phone and gold card to the grave unaccompanied by clergy, family, or the company of those who care. It is a function performed by functionaries — quick, clean, cheap, convenient, and ultimately meaningless.

A good funeral is not about how much we spend or how much we save. Rather it is about what we do — to act out our faith, our hopes, our loves and losses. Pastoral care is not about making death easier, or grief less keenly felt, or funerals cheaper or more convenient. It is about bringing the power of faith to bear on the human experience of dying, death, and bereavement. And our faith is not for getting around grief or past it, but for getting through it. It is not for denying death, but for confronting it. It is not for dodging our dead, but for bearing us up as we bear them to the grave or tomb or fire at the edge of which we give them back to God.

Among the several blessings of my work as a funeral director is that I have seen the power of such faith in the face of death. I remember the churchman at the deathbed of a neighbor — it was four in the morning in the middle of winter — who gathered the family around to pray, then helped me guide the stretcher through the snow out to where our hearse was parked. Three days later, after the services at church, he rode with me in the hearse to the grave, committed the body with a handful of earth, and then stood with the family and friends as the grave was filled, reading from the psalms — the calm in his voice and the assurance of the words making the sad and honorable duties bearable.

I remember the priest I called to bury one of our town's indigents — a man without family or friends or finances. He, the gravediggers, and I carried the casket to the grave. The priest incensed the body, blessed it with holy water, and read from the liturgy for twenty minutes, then sang *In Paradisum* — that gorgeous Latin for "May the angels lead you into Paradise" — as we lowered the poor man's body into the ground. When I asked him why he'd gone to such trouble, he said these are the most important funerals — even if only God is watching — because it affirms the agreement between "all God's children" that we will witness and remember and take care of each other.

And I remember the Presbyterian pastor, a woman of strength and compassion who assisted a young mother, whose baby had died, in placing the infant's body into a tiny casket. She held the young woman as she placed a cross in the baby's hands and a teddy bear at the baby's side and then, because the mother couldn't, the pastor carefully closed the casket lid. They stood and prayed together — "God grant us the serenity to accept the things we cannot change" — then drove with me to the crematory.

Or the Baptist preacher called to preach the funeral of one of our famously imperfect citizens who drank and smoked and ran a little wild, contrary to how his born-again parents had raised him. Instead of damnation and altar calls, the pastor turned the service into a lesson in God's love and mercy and forgiveness. After speaking about the man's Christian youth, he allowed as how he had "gone astray" after he'd left home and joined the army. "It seems he couldn't keep his body and his soul aligned," the young pastor said, and seemed a little lost for words until he left the pulpit, walked over and opened the casket, took out a harmonica, and began to play "Just As I Am" while everyone in the congregation nodded and wept and smiled, some of them mouthing the words of promise and comfort to themselves.

In each case these holy people treated the bodies of the dead neither as a bother or embarrassment, nor an idol or icon, nor just a shell. They treated the dead like one of our own, precious to the people who loved them, temples of the Holy Spirit, neighbors, family, fellow pilgrims. They stand — these local heroes, these saints and sinners, these men and women of God — in that difficult space between the living and the dead, between faith and fear, between humanity and Christianity and say out loud, "Behold, I show you a mystery."

BILL MCKIBBEN

Designer Genes

FROM *Orion*

I GREW UP IN A HOUSEHOLD where we were very suspicious of dented cans. Dented cans were, according to my mother, a well-established gateway to botulism, and botulism was a bad thing, worse than swimming immediately after lunch. It was one of those bad things measured in extinctions, as in "three tablespoons of botulism toxin could theoretically kill every human on Earth." Or something like that.

So I refused to believe the early reports, a few years back, that socialites had begun injecting dilute strains of the toxin into their brows in an effort to temporarily remove the vertical furrow that appears between one's eyes as one ages. It sounded like a Monty Python routine, some clinic where they daubed your soles with plague germs to combat athlete's foot. But I was wrong to doubt. As the world now knows, Botox has become, in a few short years, a staple weapon in the cosmetic arsenal — so prevalent that, in the words of one writer, "it is now rare in certain social enclaves to see a woman over the age of thirty-five with the ability to look angry." With their facial muscles essentially paralyzed, actresses are having trouble acting; since the treatment requires periodic booster shots, doctors "warn that you could marry a woman (or a man) with a flawlessly even face and wind up with someone who four months later looks like a Shar-Pei." But never mind — now you can get Botoxed in strip mall storefronts and at cocktail parties.

People, in other words, will do fairly far out things for less than pressing causes. And more so all the time: public approval of "aesthetic surgery" has grown 50 percent in the United States in the last decade. But why stop there? Once you accept the idea that our bodies are essentially plastic and that it's okay to manipulate that plastic, there's no reason to think that consumers would balk because "genes" were involved instead of, say, "toxins." Especially since genetic engineering would not promote your own vanity, but instead be sold as a boon to your child.

The vision of genetic engineers is to do to humans what we have already done to salmon and wheat, pine trees and tomatoes. That is, to make them *better* in some way; to delete, modify, or add genes in developing embryos so that the cells of the resulting person will produce proteins that make them taller and more muscular, or smarter and less aggressive, maybe handsome and possibly straight. Even happy. As early as 1993, a March of Dimes poll found that 43 percent of Americans would engage in genetic engineering "simply to enhance their children's looks or intelligence."

Ethical guidelines promulgated by the scientific oversight boards so far prohibit actual attempts at human genetic engineering, but researchers have walked right to the line, maybe even stuck their toes a trifle over. In the spring of 2001, for instance, a fertility clinic in New Jersey impregnated fifteen women with embryos fashioned from their own eggs, their partner's sperm, and a small portion of an egg donated by a second woman. The procedure was designed to work around defects in the would-be mother's egg — but in at least two of the cases, tests showed the resulting babies carried genetic material from all three "parents."

And so the genetic modification of humans is not only possible, it's coming fast; a mix of technical progress and shifting mood means it could easily happen in the next few years. Consider what happened with plants. A decade ago, university research farms were growing small plots of genetically modified grain and vegetables. Sometimes activists who didn't like what they were doing would come and rip the plants up, one by one. Then, all of a sudden in the mid-1990s, before anyone had paid any real attention, farmers had planted half the corn and soybean fields in America with transgenic seed.

Every time you turn your back this technology creeps a little closer. Gallops, actually, growing and spreading as fast as the internet. One moment you've sort of heard of it; the next moment it's everywhere. But we haven't done it yet. For the moment we remain, if barely, a fully human species. And so we have time yet to consider, to decide, to act. This is arguably the biggest decision humans will ever make.

Right up until this decade, the genes that humans carried in their bodies were exclusively the result of chance — of how the genes of the sperm and the egg, the father and the mother, combined. The only way you could intervene in the process was by choosing who you would mate with — and that was as much wishful thinking as anything else, as generation upon generation of surprised parents have discovered.

But that is changing. We now know two different methods to change human genes. The first, and less controversial, is called somatic gene therapy. Somatic gene therapy begins with an existing individual — someone with, say, cystic fibrosis. Researchers try to deliver new, modified genes to some of her cells, usually by putting the genes aboard viruses they inject into the patient, hoping that the viruses will infect the cells and thereby transmit the genes. Somatic gene therapy is, in other words, much like medicine. You take an existing patient with an existing condition, and you in essence try and convince her cells to manufacture the medicine she needs.

Germline genetic engineering, on the other hand, is something very novel indeed. "Germ" here refers not to microbes, but to the egg and sperm cells, the germ cells of the human being. Scientists intent on genetic engineering would probably start with a fertilized embryo a week or so old. They would tease apart the cells of that embryo, and then, selecting one, they would add to, delete, or modify some of its genes. They could also insert artificial chromosomes containing predesigned genes. They would then take the cell, place it inside an egg whose nucleus had been removed, and implant the resulting new embryo inside a woman. The embryo would, if all went according to plan, grow into a genetically engineered child. His genes would be pushing out proteins to meet the particular choices made by his parents and by the companies and clinicians they were buying the genes from. Instead of coming solely from the combination of his parents, and thus the combination of their parents, and so on back through time, those genes could come from any other person, or any other plant or animal, or out of the thin blue sky. And once implanted, they will pass to his children and on into time.

But all this work will require one large change in our current way of doing business. Instead of making babies by making love, we will have to move conception to the laboratory. You need to have the embryo out there where you can work on it — to make the necessary copies, try to add or delete genes, and then implant the one that seems likely to turn out best. Gregory Stock, a researcher at the University of California and an apostle of the new genetic technologies, says that "the union of egg and sperm from two individuals . . . would be too unpredictable with intercourse." And once you've got the embryo out on the lab bench, gravity disappears altogether. "Ultimately," says Michael West, CEO of Advanced Cell Technology, the firm furthest out on the cutting edge of these technologies, "the dream of biologists is to have the sequence of DNA, the programming code of life, and to be able to edit it the way you can a document on a word processor."

Does it sound far-fetched? We began doing it with animals (mice) in 1978, and we've managed the trick with most of the obvious mammals, except one. Some of the first germline interventions might be semimedical. You might, say some advocates, start by improving "visual and auditory acuity," first to eliminate nearsightedness or prevent deafness, then to "improve artistic potential." But why stop there? "If something has evolved elsewhere, then it is possible for us to determine its genetic basis and transfer it into the human genome," says Princeton geneticist Lee Silver — just as we have stuck flounder genes into strawberries to keep them from freezing, and jellyfish genes into rabbits and monkeys to make them glow in the dark.

But would we actually do this? Is there any real need to raise these questions as more than curiosities, or will the schemes simply fade away on their own, ignored by the parents who are their necessary consumers?

Anyone who has entered a baby supply store in the last few years knows that even the soberest parents can be counted on to spend virtually unlimited sums in pursuit of successful offspring. What if the "Baby Einstein" video series, which immerses "learning-enabled" babies in English, Spanish, Japanese, Hebrew, German, Russian, and French, could be bolstered with a little gene tweaking to improve memory? What if the Wombsongs prenatal music system, piping in Brahms to your waiting fetus, could be supplemented with an auditory upgrade? One sociologist told the *New York Times* we'd crossed the line from parenting to "product development," and even if that remark is truer in Manhattan than elsewhere, it's not hard to imagine what such attitudes will mean across the affluent world.

Here's one small example. In the 1980s, two drug companies were awarded patents to market human growth hormone to the few thousand American children suffering from dwarfism. The PDA thought the market would be very small, so HGH was given "orphan drug status," a series of special market advantages designed to reward the manufacturers for taking on such an unattractive business. But within a few years, HGH had become one of the largest selling drugs in the country, with half a billion dollars in sales. This was not because there'd been a sharp increase in the number of dwarves, but because there'd been a sharp increase in the number of parents who wanted to make their slightly short children taller. Before long the drug companies were arguing that the children in the bottom 5 percent of their normal height range were in fact in need of three to five shots a week of HGH. Take eleven-year-old Marco Oriti. At four foot one, he was about four inches shorter than average, and projected to eventually top out at five foot four. This was enough to convince his parents to start on a six-day-a-week HGH regimen, which will cost them $150,000 over the next four years. "You want to give your child the edge no matter what," said his mother.

A few of the would-be parents out on the current cutting edge of the reproduction revolution — those who need to obtain sperm or eggs for in vitro fertilization — exhibit similar zeal. Ads started appearing in Ivy League college newspapers a few years ago: couples were willing to pay $50,000 for an egg, provided the donor was at least five feet, ten inches tall, white, and had scored 1400 on her SATs. There is, in other words, a market just waiting for the first clinic with a catalogue of germline modifications, a market that two California artists proved when they opened a small boutique, Gene Genies Worldwide, in a trendy part of Pasadena. Tran Kim-Trang and Karl Mihail wanted to get people thinking more deeply about these emerging technologies, so they outfitted their store with petri dishes and models of the double helix and printed up brochures highlighting traits with genetic links: creativity, extroversion, thrill-seeking criminality. When they opened the doors, they found people ready to shell out for designer families (one man insisted he wanted the survival ability of a cockroach). The "store" was meant to be ironic, but the irony was lost on a culture so deeply consumeristic that this land of manipulation seems like the obvious next step. "Generally, people refused to believe this store was an art project," says Tran. And why not? The next store in the mall could easily have been a Botox salon.

But say you're not ready. Say you're perfectly happy with the prospect of a child who shares the unmodified genes of you and your partner. Say you think that manipulating the DNA of your child might be dangerous, or presumptuous, or icky? How long will you be able to hold that line if the procedure begins to spread among your neighbors? Maybe not so long as you think. If germline manipulation actually does begin, it seems likely to set off a kind of biological arms race. "Suppose parents could add thirty points to their child's IQ?" asks MIT economist Lester Thurow. "Wouldn't you want to do it? And if you don't, your child will be the stupidest in the neighborhood." That's precisely what it might feel like to be the parent faring the choice. Individual competition more or less defines the society we've built, and in that context love can almost be defined as giving your kids what they need to make their way in the world. Deciding not to soup them up . . . well, it could come to seem like child abuse.

Of course, the problem about arms races is that you never really get anywhere. If everyone's adding thirty IQ points, then having an IQ of one hundred fifty won't get you any closer to Stanford than you were at the outset. The very first athlete engineered to use twice as much oxygen as the next guy will be unbeatable in the Tour de France — but in no time he'll merely be the new standard. You'll have to do what he did to be in the race, but your upgrades won't put you ahead, merely back on a level playing field. You might be able to argue that society as a whole was helped, because there was more total brainpower at work, but your kid won't be any closer to the top of the pack. All you'll be able to do is guarantee she won't be left hopelessly far behind.

In fact, the arms race problem has an extra ironic twist when it comes to genetic manipulation. The United States and the Soviet Union could, and did, keep adding new weapons to their arsenals over the decades. But with germline manipulation, you get only one shot; the extra chromosome you stick in your kid when he's born is the one he carries throughout his life. So let's say baby Sophie has a state-of-the-art gene job: her parents paid for the proteins discovered by, say, 2005 that on average yield ten extra IQ points. By the time Sophie is five, though, scientists will doubtless have discovered ten more genes linked to intelligence. Now anyone with a platinum card can get twenty IQ points, not to mention a memory boost and a permanent wrinkle-free brow. So by the time Sophie is twenty-five and in the job market, she's already more or less obsolete — the kids coming out of college plainly just have better hardware.

"For all his billions, Bill Gates could not have purchased a single genetic enhancement for his son Rory John," writes Gregory Stock at the University of California. "And you can bet that any enhancements a billion dollars can buy Rory's child in 2030 will seem crude alongside those available for modest sums in 2060." It's not, he adds, "so different from upgraded software. You'll want the new release."

The vision of one's child as a nearly useless copy of Windows 95 should make parents fight like hell to make sure we never get started down this path. But the vision gets lost easily in the gushing excitement about "improving" the opportunities for our kids.

Beginning the hour my daughter came home from the hospital, I spent part of every day with her in the woods out back, showing her trees and ferns and chipmunks and frogs. One of her very first words was "birch," and you couldn't have asked for a prouder papa. She got her middle name from the mountain we see out the window; for her fifth birthday she got her own child-sized canoe; her school wardrobe may not be relentlessly up-to-date, but she's never lacked for hiking boots. As I write these words, she's spending her first summer at sleepaway camp, one we chose because the kids sleep in tents and spend days in the mountains. All of which is to say that I have done everything in my power to try to mold her into a lover of the natural world. That is where my deepest satisfactions lie, and I want the same for her. It seems benign enough, but it has its drawbacks; it means less time and money and energy for trips to the city and music lessons and so forth. As time goes on and she develops stronger opinions of her own, I yield more and more, but I keep trying to stack the deck, to nudge her in the direction that's meant something to me. On a Saturday morning, when the question comes up of what to do, the very first words out of my mouth always involve yet another hike. I can't help myself.

In other words, we already "engineer" our offspring in some sense of the word: we do our best, and often our worst, to steer them in particular directions. And our worst can be pretty bad. We all know people whose lives were blighted trying to meet the expectations of their parents. We've all seen the crazed devotion to getting kids into the right schools, the right professions, the right income brackets. Parents try to pass down their prejudices, their politics, their attitude toward the world ("we've got to toughen that kid up — he's going to get walked all over"). There are fathers who start teaching the curveball at the age of four, and sons made to feel worthless if they don't make the Little League traveling team. People move house so that their kids can grow up with the right band of schoolmates. They threaten to disown them for marrying African Americans, or for not marrying African Americans. No dictator anywhere has ever tried to rule his subjects with as much attention to detail as the average modern parent.

Why not take this just one small step further? Why not engineer children to up the odds that all that nudging will stick? In the words of Lee Silver, a Princeton geneticist, "Why not seize this power? Why not control what has been left to chance in the past? Indeed, we control all other aspects of our children's lives and identities through powerful social and environmental influences. . . . On what basis can we reject positive genetic influences on a person's essence when we accept the rights of parents to benefit their children in every other way?" If you can buy your kid three years at Deerfield, four at Harvard, and three more at Harvard Law, why shouldn't you be able to turbocharge his IQ a bit?

But most likely the answer has already occurred to you as well. Because you know plenty of people who managed to rebel successfully against whatever agenda their parents laid out for them, or who took that agenda and bent it to fit their own particular personality. In our society that's often what growing up is all about — the

sometimes excruciatingly difficult, frequently liberating break with
the expectations of your parents. The decision to join the Peace
Corps (or, the decision to leave the commune where you grew up
and go to business school). The discovery that you were happiest
davening in an Orthodox shul three hours a day, much to the con-
sternation of your good suburban parents who almost always made
it to Yom Kippur services; the decision that, much as you respected
the Southern Baptist piety of your parents, the Bible won't be your
watchword.

Without the grounding offered by tradition, the search for the
"authentic you" can be hard; our generations contain the first people who routinely shop religions, for instance. But the sometimes
poignant difficulty of finding yourself merely underscores how essential it is. Silver says the costs of germline engineering and a college education might be roughly comparable; in both cases, he
goes on, the point is to "increase the chances the child will become
wiser in some way, and better able to achieve success and happiness." But that's half the story, at best. College is where you go to be
exposed to a thousand new influences, ideas that should be able to
take you in almost any direction. It's where you go to get out from
under your parents' thumb, to find out that you actually don't
have to go to law school if you don't want to. As often as not, the
harder parents try to wrench their kids in one direction, the harder
those kids eventually fight to determine their own destiny. I am as
prepared as I can be for the possibility — the probability — that
Sophie will decide she wants to live her life in the concrete heart of
Manhattan. It's her life (and perhaps her kids will have a secret desire to come wander in the woods with me).

We try to shape the lives of our kids — to "improve" their lives,
as we would measure improvement — but our gravity is usually
weak enough that kids can break out of it if and when they need to.
(When it isn't, when parents manage to bend their children to the
point of breaking, we think of them as monstrous.) "Many of the
most creative and valuable human lives are the result of particularly difficult struggles" against expectation and influence, writes
the legal scholar Martha Nussbaum.

That's not how a genetic engineer thinks of his product. He
works to ensure absolute success. Last spring an Israeli researcher
announced that he had managed to produce a featherless chicken.
This constituted an improvement, to his mind, because "it will be

cheaper to produce since its lack of feathers means there is no need to pluck it before it hits the shelves." Also, poultry farmers would no longer have to ventilate their vast barns to keep their birds from overheating. "Feathers are a waste," the scientist explained. "The chickens are using feed to produce something that has to be dumped, and the farmers have to waste electricity to overcome that fact." Now, that engineer was not trying to influence his chickens to shed their feathers because they'd be happier and the farmer would be happier and everyone would be happier. He was inserting a gene that created a protein that made good and certain they would not be producing feathers. Just substitute, say, an even temperament for feathers, and you'll know what the human engineers envision.

"With reprogenetics," writes Lee Silver, "parents can gain *complete control* [emphasis mine] over their destiny, with the ability to guide and enhance the characteristics of their children, and their children's children as well." Such parents would not be calling their children on the phone at annoyingly frequent intervals to suggest that it's time to get a real job; instead, just like the chicken guy, they would be inserting genes that produced proteins that would make their child behave in certain ways throughout his life. You cannot rebel against the production of that protein. Perhaps you can still do everything in your power to defeat the wishes of your parents, but that protein will nonetheless be pumped out relentlessly into your system, defining who you are. You won't grow feathers, no matter how much you want them. And maybe they can engineer your mood enough that your lack of plumage won't even cross your mind.

Such children will, in effect, be assigned a goal by their programmers: "intelligence," "even temper," "athleticism." (As with chickens, the market will doubtless lean in the direction of efficiency. It may be hard to find genes for, say, dreaminess.) Now two possibilities arise. Perhaps the programming doesn't work very well, and your lad spells poorly, or turns moody, or can't hit the inside fastball. In the present world, you just tell yourself that that's who he is. But in the coming world, he'll be, in essence, a defective product. Do you still accept *him* unconditionally? Why? If your new Jetta got thirty miles to the gallon instead of the forty it was designed to get, you'd take it back. You'd call it a lemon. If necessary, you'd sue.

Or what if the engineering worked pretty well, but you decided, too late, that you'd picked the wrong package, hadn't gotten the best features? Would you feel buyer's remorse if the kid next door had a better ear, a stronger arm?

Say the gene work went a little awry and left you with a kid who had some serious problems; what kind of guilt would that leave you with? Remember, this is not a child created by the random interaction of your genes with those of your partner, this is a child created with specific intent. Does *Consumer Reports* start rating the various biotech offerings?

What if you had a second child five years after the first, and by that time the upgrades were undeniably improved: how would you feel about the first kid? How would he feel about his new brother, the latest model?

The other outcome — that the genetic engineering works just as you had hoped — seems at least as bad. Now your child is a product. You can take precisely as much pride in her achievements as you take in the achievements of your dishwashing detergent. It was designed to produce streak-free glassware, and she was designed to be sweet-tempered, social, and smart. And what can she take pride in? Her good grades? She may have worked hard, but she'll always know that she was spec'ed for good grades. Her kindness to others? Well, yes, it's good to be kind — but perhaps it's not much of an accomplishment once the various genes with some link to sociability have been catalogued and manipulated. I have no doubt that these qualms would be one of the powerful psychological afflictions of the future — at least until someone figures out a fix that keeps the next generations from having such bad thoughts.

Britain's chief rabbi, Jonathan Sacks, was asked a few years ago about the announcement that Italian doctors were trying to clone humans. "If there is a mystery at the heart of human condition, it is otherness: the otherness of man and woman, parent and child. It is the space we make for otherness that makes love something other than narcissism." I remember so well the feeling of walking into the maternity ward with Sue, and walking out with Sue and Sophie: where there had been two there were now, somehow, three, each of us our own person, but now commanded to make a family, a place where we all could thrive. She was so mysterious, that Sophie, and in many ways she still is. There are times when, like every parent, I see myself reflected in her, and times when I wonder if she's even related. She's ours to nurture and protect, but she is who *she is*. That's the mystery and the glory of any child.

Mystery, however, is not one of the words that thrills engineers. They try to deliver solid bridges, unyielding dams, reliable cars. We wouldn't want it any other way. The only question is if their product line should be expanded to include children.

Right now both the genes, and the limits that they set on us, connect us with every human that came before. Human beings can look at rock art carved into African cliffs and French caves thirty thousand years ago and feel an electric, immediate kinship. We've gone from digging sticks to combines, and from drum circles to symphony orchestras (and back again to drum circles), but we still hear in the same range and see in the same spectrum, still produce adrenaline and dopamine in the same ways, still think in many of the same patterns. We are, by and large, the same people, more closely genetically related to one another than we may be to our engineered grandchildren.

These new technologies show us that human meaning dangles by a far thinner thread than we had thought. If germline genetic engineering ever starts, it will accelerate endlessly and unstoppably into the future, as individuals make the calculation that they have no choice but to equip their kids for the world that's being made. The first child whose genes come in part from some corporate lab, the first child who has been "enhanced" from what came before — that's the first child who will glance back over his shoulder and see a gap between himself and human history.

These would be mere consumer decisions — but that also means that they would benefit the rich far more than the poor. They would take the gap in power, wealth, and education that currently divides both our society and the world at large, and write that division into our very biology. A sixth of the American population lacks health insurance of any kind — they can't afford to go to the doctor for a *check-up*. And much of the rest of the world is far worse off. If we can't afford the fifty cents per person it would take to buy bed nets to protect most of Africa from malaria, it is unlikely we will extend to anyone but the top tax bracket these latest forms of genetic technology. The injustice is so obvious that even the strongest proponents of genetic engineering make little attempt to deny it.

"Anyone who accepts the right of affluent parents to provide their children with an expensive private school education cannot use 'unfairness' as a reason for rejecting the use of reprogenetic technologies," says Lee Silver.

These new technologies, however, are not yet inevitable. Unlike global warming, this genie is not yet out of the bottle. But if germ-line genetic engineering is going to be stopped, it will have to happen now, before it's quite begun. It will have to be a political choice, that is — one we make not as parents but as citizens, not as individuals but as a whole, thinking not only about our own offspring but about everyone.

So far the discussion has been confined to a few scientists, a few philosophers, a few ideologues. It needs to spread widely, and quickly, and loudly. The stakes are absurdly high, nothing less than the meaning of being human. And given the seductions that we've seen — the intuitively and culturally delicious prospect of a *better* child — the arguments against must be not only powerful but also deep. They'll need to resonate on the same intuitive and cultural level. We'll need to feel in our gut the reasons why, this time, we should tell Prometheus thanks, but no thanks.

W. S. MERWIN

To the Fire

FROM *Poetry*

How long I have been
looking into you
staring through you into
the other side
there is no way of telling

it appears to have continued
from an age of its own
this scrutiny of the bright
veil rising and the lit
corridors of the embers
in which I see the days

beyond touch beyond reach
beyond all understanding
beyond their faces
beneath your dangerous wings
you at whose touch
everything changes
you who never change

there in you one at a time
are the unknown days
turning the corners
the unseen past
the unrecognized present

familiar but already
beyond identity

expressions without selves
appearing finally within you
of whom the light is made

PATRICIA MONAGHAN

Physics and Grief

FROM *Fourth Genre*

> In nature nothing remains constant. Everything is in a perpetual state of transformation, motion, and change. However, we discover that nothing simply surges up out of nothing without having antecedents that existed before. Likewise, nothing ever disappears without a trace, in the sense that it gives rise to absolutely nothing existing in later times.
> — David Bohm

ACTUALLY," DAN SAID, "I've been reading a lot of physics." He looked down at his empty paper plate and shrugged one shoulder, then the other. "I don't suppose that makes any sense."

Dan had not spoken to me in almost a year. We'd seen each other occasionally; we had too many common friends for that not to happen. But when it did, Dan made certain to stay on the other side of the room, to find himself in need of a drink when I came near, to turn suddenly away when I tried to catch his eye.

That was the year when I was a new widow, and Dan was about to become one, his partner, Steve, descending into a hell of lesions and pneumonia and fungal invasions of the brain. Even in the blur of my loss, I felt no anger toward Dan — though anger is so predictable a part of grief — for avoiding me. I knew the cause: I already was what he most feared to become.

Six months after I was widowed, Dan joined me in that state. Steve gave up his obdurate struggle to remain alive, asking to be kept home when the next crisis hit. It was only a week. Friends told me that Steve's death was gentle and that Dan bore up as well as could be expected. Dan dropped from sight for a time, disappearing into memories and pain.

Now it was summer, and we were sitting under blue canvas at an outdoor festival. Dan had approached me with an apology for his actions. I had embraced him with understanding. We were sitting companionably together, catching up on each other's lives, when I asked him what most helped him deal with his grief.

Physics.

Dan met my eyes, and his brows came together, then raised. "Relativity. Quantum mechanics. Bell's Theorem. You know?" I think he expected me to be surprised. But I was not. It had been the same for me.

To explain how physics came to be important on my journey of grief, I have first to describe the problem with my keys. There were five of them, bound together with a wide steel ring: a big silver skeleton key, for the embossed brass Victorian lock on the front door; a round-headed key that opens the more modern deadbolt; a little golden key to the garage; an institutional "do not duplicate" key to my office; and a black-headed key to the Ford station wagon.

I remember the day — the hour — that the keys disappeared. It was late spring, less than three months after Bob died. Walking out the door to go shopping, I had reached into my jacket pocket, where I always kept my keys.

They weren't there.

At the instant, it seemed inconsequential. I'd mislaid keys before; hasn't everyone? I was inside the house, so I had used the keys to enter. They were, therefore, somewhere in the house with me. I merely had to look carefully and I would find them.

I was unperturbed. I did what I did whenever I had mislaid something. I looked in all the logical places: in my coat's other pocket; on the shelf near the front door; next to the telephone; in the kitchen near the sink. Nothing.

I was still not overly concerned. I must have been distracted when I entered, I reasoned with myself; I must have put the keys in some unlikely spot. So I began methodically searching the house. Entry hall. Living room. Pulling out furniture, looking under pillows. Nothing. Dining room. Kitchen. Opening cabinets, reaching to the back of shelves. Nothing.

Okay, then, I must have carried them upstairs. Guest room. Bathroom. Moving around each room slowly, looking especially in places where keys were unlikely to be. Behind pictures. In rarely opened drawers. Study. Nothing. Linen closet. Nothing.

In my bedroom, I suddenly grew frustrated. I needed my keys! The only key to my car was on that ring; I could not go to work without it. What would I do without my keys?

I started to cry.

I had been crying for months, ever since Bob had finally died, fighting cancer to the last. The six months before his death were exhausting. For three months I was his sole caregiver; then, during his final hospitalization, I visited him two, three, even four times each day. Economics forced me to continue working, so I had neither physical strength nor emotional resources left when he died.

In the days before Bob's death, I had been with him constantly, telling him stories of the future we should have had, praising his work and his son to him, reminiscing for him about happy times when he could no longer speak. I did not sleep for perhaps forty-eight hours as I held vigil by his bedside, leaving only for necessary moments, for he had been shatteringly fearful of being alone at the moment of death. And so I was with him when that moment came, holding his hand as his breathing slowed, singing old songs to him, stroking his face through its paralysis.

It was the hardest thing I have ever done, witnessing as he "departed from this strange world a little ahead of me," as Einstein said when his oldest friend, Michele Besso, died. When I left that hospital room, bearing with me the amaryllis that had bloomed only the day before, I felt that I was leaving all happiness behind, that my world had changed unutterably, and only for the worse.

I lived the months afterward in a trance of grief. There was a memorial service that I planned, I remember that. I remember a brick meeting hall with red tulips, a jazz pianist, readings from Bob's novels, visitors from many states. For the rest, I barely recall anything. I apparently kept working, and doing laundry, and feeding the dogs, and planting the garden. My body kept moving through the Midwestern spring. But my soul was in the desert, in winter.

That day in May, the loss of my keys reduced me to tears, though of course I was weeping for my greater loss, which every other loss would now reflect. Possibly I wept for hours; I did such things at that time. Finally the storm passed. I got up and set determinedly about to find the keys. To survive, I had to work. I needed to drive to my office. I could not manage without my keys. I would find them. I had to.

And so I repeated my search. I must have missed the keys the first time, I told myself. I started again at the front door and scoured the downstairs. Living room: no. Kitchen: no.

And so it went. After an hour or so, I found myself again in the bedroom, still keyless.

I began to weep again. This time, my desolation seemed endless. I could not stop crying. I lay on the bed, sobbing and flailing my arms. I soaked several handkerchiefs. I buried my head in pillows and drenched them with tears.

Then I became enraged. I got up from the bed and began to scream at Bob, furious at him for dying and leaving me so helplessly besieged by grief. I screamed that he was cruel and heartless, that I'd been there in his hour of need, and where was he when I needed him? I raged and wept, wept and raged.

I had not, before Bob's death, spent much time thinking about the question of whether or not there is an afterlife. I had been brought up with a conventional picture of heaven and hell. And I had studied enough other religions to realize that many wiser than I believed in some kind of survival after death. I had read believable-enough accounts of those who claimed to have been contacted by the dead. But the possibility of an afterlife was not something I dwelt upon. I did not wish to make moral decisions by weighing the possibilities of future reward or punishment for myself. Nor did the survival of my own small person seem especially important in comparison with the universe's vast majesty. So, for myself, what happened or did not happen after death was not a very important question.

Bob, by contrast, had been quite clear about his beliefs. A natural mystic, he had practiced Zen for twenty years. But he was also an unrelentingly hard-headed empiricist who believed the universe to be a mechanistic place in which consciousness was only a byproduct of the body's functions. Thus, when the body died, consciousness ceased as well. Bob believed, as Fred Alan Wolf put it in describing the Newtonian worldview, that mind — or soul, or spirit, whatever you call it — was just "a convenient byproduct of the physiology of . . . the mechanisms of the brain, down to the remarkable electrical and mechanical movements of the nerve firings and blood flows."

He never changed his belief once he entered the hospital that final time, even though I, desperate for some reassurance that our love could continue after he faded from this life, talked to him about reincarnation and other possible survivals. But Bob would be no foxhole convert; he marched gamely toward that abyss which he saw as the likely end of his being. Death was painful to him; he had much to live for; but he would not grasp at hope of continued life just to ease his pain. Unless he had time to ponder, unless he could become completely convinced, he would believe as he always had. Happy lies held no appeal for him.

One thing I loved about Bob was this: he had more integrity than any person I'd ever met. That integrity remained to the end. He met his death with his long-held beliefs intact. He was frightened, but he was very, very brave.

Because I had no personal convictions on the subject, I held true to Bob's beliefs after he was gone. It was a way of remaining close to him. I, too, would refuse to grasp at imaginary straws just to ease my pain. If Bob believed that all traces of his consciousness would evaporate at his death, that only his physical works would remain, then I would loyally uphold that belief.

And so I lived in the desert. Life has never seemed so dry and meaningless to me as it did then. I would watch lovers kiss in a coffee shop and a whirlpool of pain would open beneath me, as I thought of one of them holding the other as they parted forever. I would stare at parents playing with their children near the lake and imagine sudden illnesses and accidents, wondering how life could create such joy only to obliterate it. I wept constantly: when I heard beautiful music, when I saw painful news, when I saw new flowers, when I went to bed, when I woke up.

But I adamantly refused to settle for those happy visions that religion held out, of dreamy heavens full of harps, of other lives to come, of eventual reunion in some cosmic void. I even rejected nonreligious spiritualism. When friends said they had dreamed of Bob, or felt him near, I received the information in silent disbelief. It was their need of solace, I told myself, that caused these apparitions. They had just imagined it. I, loyal to Bob's beliefs, would not settle for such self-deluding comfort. I would tough it out, looking reality right in its cruel face.

But the day I lost my keys, I could not be brave like Bob, not any longer. Seeing those loving eyes go dim had been the single most painful moment of my life. The idea that the universe could so wantonly create beauty, could bestow upon our lives the kind of love that seems like ultimate meaning, only to destroy it in a breath, had finally become too much for me.

I wanted so desperately to believe that Bob, and Bob's love for me, still existed somewhere in the universe, that in my furious pain I flung down a challenge. Standing in the middle of the bedroom, I demanded that he come back. Find my keys, I insisted. Find my damned keys! If there's anyone there, if there's any love left in this universe for me, find my keys!

After the fury had passed, I felt mortified. I had been screaming at a dead man. Standing in my room alone, screaming at a dead man.

Worse, it was all so trivial. If I were going to throw down the gauntlet to the universe about whether there is life after death, couldn't I have chosen something more important as proof? World peace? Personal economic security? A beatific vision?

But I'd spoken. I'd insisted that Bob prove his continuing existence by finding my keys.

Even writing about that day, I feel embarrassment cover me. It was such an excess of emotion about such a small matter, about such a minor inconvenience. Why had I broken down over such a silly thing? Why had I challenged the universe over something as unimportant as a key ring?

But break down I had, and challenge the universe I had. And I could not bear the answer to be silence, negation, the absence of Bob forever, anywhere. Now I truly had to find the keys. So I resolutely began, yet again, to search. I started once more in the front hallway. But this time, I took a new tack. I might as well do spring-cleaning, I decided. I'd clean the entire house, front door to attic, and in doing so I would certainly find the keys.

There was more than a bit of desperation about all this. If I did not find the keys, all was indeed lost. If I did not find the keys, there was no vestige of Bob in the world. If I did not find the keys, I was alone in the cruelest universe imaginable.

Three days later, I was back in the bedroom. Except for that one room, the house was now clean, ammonia-and-paste-wax clean. I had taken down curtains and washed them, cleaned out closets, pulled up rugs. I had upended sofas and searched their bowels. I had repotted plants. I had pulled books from shelves and dusted both.

The house sparkled, indeed.

But I had not found the keys.

The bedroom was the final outpost of possibility. From the first corner around to the last, then spiraling in to the center, I cleaned and searched. I opened drawers and rearranged them, shaking out their contents on the floor. I moved pictures and dusted their frames. I worked slowly, with mounting despair, for the keys had still not appeared. I moved the bed and polished the floor under it. I shook out the bedclothes and aired out the mattress.

Finally, I was finished.

There were no keys.

I collapsed. This time my grief truly knew no bounds. I had asked for an answer from the universe, and I had — I believed — received one. Bob had been right. Consciousness was a byproduct of our body's functioning, and now that the ashes of Bob's body sat on the bookshelf in a white box, there was nothing, anywhere, left of the curiosity and passion and brilliance and love that had been him.

The depression that began that day incapacitated me. I was unable to work for nearly a week. Finally, however, I called the car dealership and got new car keys. I found the spare house keys. I began to reconstruct the openings to my life. I knew now that I was indeed alone, that I could not call upon Bob for help, that he was no longer present anywhere, in any form. It was a bleak and cruel universe, but at least I knew the truth of it.

What I experienced during that next year was more than simple grief and certainly more than emotional depression, although I suffered from both as well. It was stark existential despair. Life had no meaning, much less any savor. I tried to find what comfort I could in friendship, in earthly beauty, in art, in learning. But at my center was an abyss of meaninglessness. I could as easily have gambled all my resources away as built a garden; as easily have crashed my car as driven it safely across the Midwest; as easily have drunk slow poison as cocoa for breakfast. That I did one thing rather than another seemed only an arbitrary choice.

At last, however, I began to awaken from my coma of sorrow. I began to argue with Bob in my mind. As I gardened, I noticed again the resilient connection of matter and energy, how nature never destroys but only transforms. As I walked in the woods with my dog, I saw spring flowers emerging from the withered leaves of autumn.

What hubris, I began to think, to imagine that human consciousness is the only thing this universe cares to obliterate. Surely we are
not that important.

But these were fleeting thoughts, unconvincing, evanescent,
ideas which did not in any case reach to the root of my grief. It was
easy to accept that Bob's body would eventually nourish other beings, through the cycle of decomposition and recomposition. But it
was Bob's self that I'd loved — not only his body, though certainly
that. And although I knew and accepted, with piercing pain, what
had happened to his body, that told me nothing about where the
unique energy went that had invigorated it.

Every once in a while, I would think of the lost keys and sigh. I
had, after all, asked for a sign, and I had been given one.

That was when I began reading books on physics. I had been
reading a lot of spiritual literature, looking for answers to the appalling questions life presented. But I only grew more isolated,
angry at the serenity that seemed forever beyond my grasp, despairing at my continuing inability to find any sense in death's senseless-
ness. It was not that the answers which spiritual literature offered
seemed implausible or incorrect; it was simply that I could not believe them, could not make the leap into not-doubting. The more
rigidly codified the religious insight, the more it seemed to exclude
— even to mock — my anguished confusion.

I can't remember exactly which book, which author, brought me
to physics. Most likely one that pushed the boundaries of science to
include spirituality. Fritz Capra, perhaps, or Gary Zukov. One of
those wild minds who saw bridges where others saw barricades. But
it wasn't the spirituality that gripped my attention. It was the science.

Where religion had failed me, being so certain of itself, physics
offered paradoxes and complexities so bizarre that my hatred and
fear of the universe began to be replaced with what can only be
called awe. I'd known Newtonian physics before, from my days as
a science reporter, but I had never ventured into quantum mechanics. There I found the most astonishing ideas, ones which
smashed the clockwork universe just as Bob's death had torn apart
mine. Ideas that read like Bob's beloved Zen koans, statements that
strained the limits of my linear thinking. "Our universe seems to be
composed of facts and their opposites at the same time," I read in

Louis de Broglie's work, and "everything happens as though it did not exist at all."

Such statements seemed eminently sensible, reasonable, even straightforward. Yes, I responded passionately. Yes, the universe was that strange, that indescribable. Death is not an equal and opposite reaction to life; consciousness is not some strange form of inertia. I needed a new physics to describe the wild movements of my grieving soul. And a new physics I found.

Like my friend Dan, I found quantum theory immeasurably consoling. With an uncertainty-loves-company kind of logic, I lost myself in Heisenberg and the reassurances of the Uncertainty Principle. If we cannot conceivably know everything about the physical universe, then the abyss of doubt whereon I stood was as good a standpoint as any from which to view life. If we cannot know something as simple as two aspects of a subatomic particle's motion simultaneously, how can we know for certain that there is no life after death — or that there is? If our measurements may alter the reality that we measure, could not consciousness be a form of measurement, subtly altering the universe?

My deepest consolation, however, was not in speculating about whether a consciousness suffused, as mine was, with grief altered the world in a different way than one flooded with happiness. Rather, I drew solace from the dumbfounding absoluteness of Heisenberg's theory. We could not know everything, not ever, because in the moment of such knowing we may change what we know. I could not know — I could never know — if or where Bob existed, for each time I sought for him — each time I measured this universe in terms of Bob's existence or nonexistence — I was perhaps changing the conditions of the very universe through which I sought. It was as though Heisenberg, by enshrining uncertainty at the center of perception and knowledge, made anything and everything both possible and impossible at once.

Suddenly the world seemed to make sense again, although in a deeply paradoxical way. Where religion's certainties had left me bitterly bereft of comfort, quantum uncertainty allowed for unimaginable possibilities. Whatever measurement I took of the universe, I understood now, could be only partial. There would always be something that eluded my grasp. This was an enormous comfort.

It was not only uncertainty that captured me. Because this new physics was all about time and space, Einstein spoke to me like a voice from a burning bush. I, who lived in a time and space from which my love had disappeared, found respite in considering the ways that time and space were linked. "Any two points in space and time are both separate and not separate," David Bohm said. What a salvation that seemed! As incomprehensible as this new space-time was, it was more lively with possibilities than linear and planar realities. My separateness from Bob was real, but in some way, we were also still together.

In some way — this was most important to me. For this was not a metaphoric togetherness, a trick of language. This was science, after all. And not just science but the queen of sciences, physics. Physics, which did not ask me to believe, did not ask me to have faith. Physics, which observed and experimented. Physics, which offered a description of the world, admittedly bizarre but as accurate as blundering language could make it.

I did not have to believe. I only had to wonder.

The fact that, as Max Born pointed out, the quantum world is utterly unvisualizable presented no problem to me. Visions of the subatomic world were metaphors, whose richness and limitations I amply understood. But unlike religion, which seemed hypnotized by its own articulations of the ineffable, physics acknowledged that any picture we hold of the subatomic world is by definition inaccurate, limited, inexact. No one has ever seen a quark, much less a Higgs boson. But they act; we see their traces. Such quantum strangeness spoke to my condition. I had witnessed something deeply incomprehensible when Bob died. Studying what Bohm called the "unanalyzable ways of the universe" mirrored that experience.

My grief did not disappear, for grief is a chronic disease which exists in the body. My body would still regularly writhe with sudden memories: when I automatically reached for Bob's favorite juice at the Jewel, when I passed the lake where we had taken our last walk, when someone uttered a phrase he had relished. The tape loop of his last hours ran constantly in my mind, so that I would see the doctor, my friends Natalie and Barbara arriving, Bob's son Michael leaving, the amaryllis, Bob's paralyzed face, the doctor, Natalie, the amaryllis, the doctor. . . .

Because of the power of these death-watch memories, relativity especially absorbed me. The paradoxes of time preoccupied me for days on end. Einstein had seen the connection between the study of time and awareness of death's approach, arguing that death really means nothing because "the distinction between past, present and future is only a stubbornly persistent illusion." I envisioned those points in the universe where radio waves of Bob's voice, from a long-ago interview, were still new and bright. I invented scenarios in which I stretched time out like taffy, making Bob's last days as eternal as they had subjectively seemed. I relished that consoling insight that Einstein's equations were time-reversible, that perhaps time does not move in one direction but can flow backward as well as forward. I imagined moving backward through time, intersecting with a healthy Bob and recreating our life, always hopping back on the time machine before the diagnosis, living those happy times over and over and over. I knew these were fantasies, but I also knew that I no longer knew what time really was. There, once again, were limitless possibilities.

If my grief did not disappear, that crazed existential doubt did. Life no longer was so utterly senseless. It made sense again, but in a more marvelous way than I'd ever imagined. I found myself staring at graphs of the Schroedinger wave collapse, imagining a cat alive, dead, alive, dead, all at the same time — imagining Bob's continued existence as such a wave. I pondered the complementarity between particles and waves, especially the way an observer seems implicated in the emergence into reality of each. Particles dancing and leaping in a virtual world, flickering in and out of measurable existence. Or perhaps they were not even particles at all, but what Henry Sapp called "sets of relationships that reach outward to other things." To David Bohm, too, particles exist not so much as nuggets of virtual and actual matter, but as "ongoing movements that are mutually dependent because ultimately they merge and interpenetrate."

Matter disappeared, at this scale, into flashing energy, particles into momentarily observable comets of being. Bob had been composed of these miraculous particles, these miraculous relationships reaching outward toward me, these mutually dependent and interpenetrating movements. And perhaps he still was, in some way, in some unmeasurable place. Our lives together had been lived in a space and a time, within a universe through which the mighty and unfathomable river of space-time flows. Were we still connected, as Bell's Theorem hints, in some intricate and inexpressible way? Was I somehow still affected by the changes that he experienced — in whatever state those blinking-into-existence particles that had been Bob were now? And did my changes affect him still as well?

Far from compelling me toward certainty about where and how Bob still existed, quantum theory removed from me any urge toward stapling down reality within one interpretation. In the quantum world, Nick Herbert has pointed out, there are at least eight possible pictures of reality, any of which is more consoling than the Newtonian vision of the universe. Maybe there is an "ordinary reality," as de Broglie and Einstein believed; in that case the hard stuff that made up Bob is somewhere still in existence, and even now I am breathing atoms that had been part of him during his life. But the Copenhagen hypothesis of Bohr and Heisenberg questions whether there is any such "reality" at all. In their view, Bob and I had lived something like a dream together, and that dream had as much reality without him as it had with him. An alternative reading of the Copenhagen hypothesis is that we create our own realities, that reality exists only as we observe it doing so; in that case, I could create the reality of his continued existence by believing strongly enough.

These were only some of the possibilities. There was David Bohm's theory of the implicate order, which argues that there is an undivided wholeness that could wrap both Bob and me, in our varying current states, in what he called "indivisible quantum processes that link different systems in an unanalyzable way." There was the fantastic many-world hypothesis, which permitted me to envision that Bob and I still lived happily in another space-time, after he had survived cancer; in that reality, we are writing an essay together, perhaps this very one.

Or possibly, the quantum world is based upon no logic that we would recognize. In that case, life's either/or does not exist, and Bob's apparent lack of existence is no more true than his apparent existence had been. Or perhaps I created him, or he me; perhaps neither of us existed before we met, we came into being complete with memories when we created each other, and thus he continues in me, his creation. Perhaps, as Fred Alan Wolf has argued, the mind does not "exist in the physical universe at all. It may be beyond the boundaries of space, time and matter. It may use the physical body in the same sense that an automobile driver uses a car."

Or maybe all of this is simultaneously true. Maybe this world is so full of mystery that we cannot ever grasp its actual probabilities and probable actualities.

I pondered these extraordinary possibilities as I moved through my ordinary life. Slowly, the pain of my loss began not to diminish, but to find its place in my life. If I did not feel joy, at least my pain had become a familiar companion. I continued reading physics, but with less crazed compulsion. I even began to accept the cruel existence of thermodynamics, with its arrow of time that threatened my happy time-travel imaginings, once I realized how connected to the richness of chaos it was.

Every once and again, I thought of the lost keys. In fall, as I was raking the front yard, I imagined that perhaps I had gone to the car for something, that spring day, and had dropped my key ring into the crowded bed of hosta by the door. But no. In winter, when I decided to move the piano, I thought that perhaps I had missed the hidden keys during my frenzied cleaning by not moving that massive upright. But no. That next spring, after preparing for a dinner party, I sat in Bob's recliner and noticed a side pocket I had missed. There? But no: the keys were not there either. The seasons passed, and the keys remained lost.

Each time this happened, I thought to myself that finding the keys no longer mattered. That I had moved beyond the challenge I had flung out to Bob, to the universe, on that wild sad day. That unless the keys found their way back to me in some utterly strange way, I could not regard it as an answer to my desperate plea. I said to myself that finding the keys would be — just finding the keys. That if I found them in some ordinary way, it would prove nothing, one way or the other: I had lost the keys, I found them, there was no connection.

And then I found the keys.

Friends were coming to dinner, and I was sitting in my study feeling sad, as I often did, and thinking of Bob, which I always did. I wistfully imagined him being with us, thought how much he would have enjoyed it. I felt my loss again, but poignantly this time, as a sad melody rather than as painful cacophony.

Then, for no special reason, I looked at the door of my study. It was open after having been closed all day. I kept it closed to keep my dog out and to keep visitors from wandering into my private space. That door had been opened and closed scores of times in the preceding year. When I entered, nothing unusual had caught my eye.

My study door is decorated. There is a Celtic knocker in the shape of a squirrel, a St. Bridget cross made of Irish rushes, and a poster. The poster, mounted on heavy blue cardboard, is a memento from the publication of my first book. Issued by my publisher for promotional parties, it shows the book's cover, my name, and the huge black words "it's here!"

The door is one of those old wooden doors with six deep panels. The poster is tacked tightly to the middle of the door, covering the two center panels and resting on the lower. The edges of the poster are flush against the door, especially at top and bottom, with the exception of two areas on each side, halfway down the cardboard, where small gaps exist.

From one of these gaps, I noticed a key coyly poking out. I walked to the door and pulled sharply. Immediately, out tumbled the entire missing set.

I held the keys loosely in my hand and stared at them. I looked up at the poster, with its emphatic proclamation. And then I smiled and said aloud, "You always did have a great sense of humor, Bob Shea."

It would make a good story to say that everything suddenly fell into place, that all my questions dissolved, that I was somehow transported to a place of certainty and confidence in life's meaning. That I no longer felt that the universe was a place of uncertainty and chaos. That I recognized and accepted the proof of Bob's continuing existence.

But that would not be true. What I felt was bafflement and curiosity, together with a startled amusement. This could not be the answer to my crazed prayer. No. There had to be some other, more commonsense answer. The keys were behind the poster: effect. Someone must have put them there: cause. I had been alone when the keys disappeared. Ergo, I had put the keys behind the poster. I did not remember doing so; it must have happened accidentally. Somehow, it was clear, I must have dropped the keys behind that poster, that day a year previously when I'd lost them.

I set out to prove my thesis. I tried to drop the keys behind the poster. I stood at the door, held the keys up in my right hand, and dropped them on the door. They caught at first on the cardboard's edge, then bounced off the door mounding and slid down to the floor.

I tried throwing the keys at the poster from a few feet away. The same thing happened: they slid down and did not hold. I tried walking past the door with the keys dangling from my hand, to see if they would catch in the poster and hold. They did not catch and hold.

There was only one way to get the keys into the position I had found them. I had to pull the poster forward, push the keys along a little groove in the door, and shove the poster back in place. Anything else would result in the keys either not lodging behind the poster at all, or dropping out as soon as the door was moved.

I spent a half-hour trying to make the keys stay behind that poster. Natalie, when I told her the mystery of the found keys, did the same. We stood in the green-carpeted upstairs hallway, two grown women flinging keys at a door, over and over. Thinking of more and more peculiar ways that the keys might have wound up resting on that hidden shelf. Unwilling at first to accept that only careful, conscious effort could bring the keys to rest as they had been, but unable to find any other way to make the keys stay in that place.

A year previously, the answer that I had wanted was a simple one: that Bob still existed and, hearing my call for help, would return my keys to me. But once this particular and peculiar miracle had occurred, I resisted accepting it as an answer to that crazy challenge. I attempted to catalog all possibilities. I had gone into a fugue state, placed the keys behind the poster, and forgotten all about them. A visitor had found the keys and whimsically placed them behind the poster. A worker — the plumber, say — had found the keys and hid them rather than giving them to me.

These scenarios are possible, though fairly unlikely. Were this a court of law, I would argue that there was no motive for anyone else to hide the keys, and no evidence that I have either before or since gone into a state of mindless fugue. That my beloved Bob had somehow answered my request seems as likely as any of these interpretations. Also: Bob had a unique sense of humor, and he tended to procrastinate. So it would be in character for him to have taken a year to get around to giving me the keys back, and then it would be in a suitably clever fashion.

I have, many times since the keys reappeared, asked myself how I would have responded had I found the keys, in exactly the same place, during my original frenzy of grief. I would, I think, have accepted it as a dramatic proof of Bob's continued existence. Look, I would have said to myself, he returned to me in my hour of need. He loved me still; I could still call upon him and rely upon him; there was life after death. In retrospect, I am glad that I did not find the keys then. Although my pain might have been greatly lessened at the start, I would have been left with only an odd anecdote which, over time, would have grown less and less vital, would have held less and less consolation.

Instead, the loss of the keys had propelled me into discovering a way to live with the unresolvability of our most basic questions. During my period of grief, I became familiar — even comfortable — with relativity and uncertainty. Indeed, those theories polished the world so that it shone with a strange and compelling luster. The world could never again be ordinary once I had plummeted through the rabbit hole of quantum mechanics. If there was uncertainty at the basis of the universe, there was also a ravishing mystery.

After the keys reappeared, as I considered the various possibilities for how they got where they did, I did not feel compelled to prove any one or another. I did not call every visitor and worker who had entered the house in the previous year; I did not have myself examined for unsuspected fugue states. Neither did I convince myself that I had proof of life after death. I was, and I am, willing to live with all the possibilities. I will never know exactly how those keys got on my door, but it does not matter. The loss of the keys did not pose a question to me; it set me on a journey. Finding the keys was not an answer to my question; it was just another station on the way.

I once asked a techno-junkie friend where my e-mail is stored. I think I pictured a huge computer somewhere, where I had the electronic equivalent of a little mailbox. I think I pictured that mailbox sometimes full with mail, sometimes empty. But where on earth was the mailbox?

My friend guffawed. "There's no big computer," she said, "it's all in the fiber-optic network."

This answer was utterly mysterious to me. In the fiber-optic network? Where is that? How can messages be in a network, rather than in a place? My mind boggled.

But quantum theory teaches us that this is not, ultimately, a universe of hard mechanistic reality where mail has to rest in mailboxes. It is a universe of connections and relations, of particle waves in space-time where order explicates itself in form and enfolds itself in pattern. The universe is not a great machine, Jeans said, but a great thought. A great thought that expresses itself in matter and energy, ceaselessly changing places.

Whatever part of that great thought once appeared as Bob Shea still exists, I now believe, somewhere in the network of this universe. He has only "departed from this strange world a little ahead of me." Perhaps, as Einstein said, "That means nothing. People like us, who believe in physics, know that the distinction between past, present and future is only a stubbornly persistent illusion." If I cannot access the codes to find Bob in the universal network, it does not mean that he has ceased to be. But "being" in that other world must surely be something beyond our imagining in this one, something as different as messages surging through networks are from little metal envelope-filled boxes.

I am comforted by having my keys again. We live in story, and the story of the keys now has a pleasing symmetry. But I do not know what that story means. Or, rather: I know that it can mean many things, some contradictory, but perhaps all true at the same time nonetheless. And I am most deeply comforted by knowing that I cannot ever truly know, that the universe is so far beyond our understanding that miracles, even peculiar and rather silly ones like this one, are very likely to keep occurring.

SEYYED HOSSEIN NASR

In the Beginning Was Consciousness

FROM the *Harvard Divinity Bulletin*

MY TITLE MAY SOUND somewhat strange, but I chose it on purpose. I believe that we are, at the present moment, at the cusp of the curve of life — what the French call *course de vie* — of the paradigm that has dominated Western civilization since the Renaissance. And this transformation has at its heart the problem of consciousness. This change began about fifty years ago, right here on the Harvard campus, with Thomas Kuhn, a major American philosopher of science and an old friend, and a few others, including myself, who were grappling with this question of paradigm shifts. He and I did not exactly agree on what the shift was or what we meant by paradigm, but we both felt that a major change was afoot. Of course, these things do not happen quickly, as he himself pointed out in his important writings. It takes some time. But I do believe that the most important questions that face present-day civilizations involve not only solutions within the present parameters within which people think, but also those parameters themselves — that is, the paradigm within which human beings carry out their intellectual and also practical activities.

So, I speak about "in the beginning was consciousness." In fact, the original title I had thought up for my lecture was "In the Beginning *Is* Consciousness" — because "in the beginning" does not simply refer to a past time; it involves a principal reality here and now. Let me begin by quoting from several of the sacred scriptures of the world. In the Rig Veda, the oldest of all Hindu sacred scriptures, we read, "When alone is the dawn beaming over all this, it is the one that severally becomes all this." The one is Sat, Chit, and Ananda — that is, the three states of being, blessedness, bliss, and, of course, consciousness, Chit.

We find the same idea in the Tao Te Ching, the primary text of Taoism, which also influenced Neo-Confucianism. The nameless Tao is the beginning of heaven and earth, and the same Tao is the mother of the ten thousand things. So at the origin of the universe you have the Tao, which in fact is also consciousness.

And, of course, we all know the opening of the Book of John: "In the beginning was the Word. And the Word was with God, and the Word was God." In chapter six of the Book of John, Christ says, "The words I have spoken to you are spirit and they are life." So this Word is not simply word in the ordinary sense, but it is the spirit and life; it is consciousness.

Finally, in the Qur'an, in chapter 36, the surah Yāsīn, it is said, "But His command when He intendeth a thing is only that He sayeth unto it, be and it is." So the origin is very explicitly stated in the Qur'an to be the command of God, who is the knower (al-'Alīm) and is supreme consciousness.

When we turn to traditional philosophies all over the world, we see this almost remarkable unanimity in this matter. We think of the point beyond all forms and numbers associated with the Lambda of Pythagoras, or of Plato's *to Agathon* (his name for that aspect of the Divine otherwise called the Unmanifest or First Logos), or Aristotle's Divine Intellect. We can think of the *esse* of St. Thomas Aquinas, which is also consciousness, which is the origin of all things and knows all beings, and corresponds to wujūd in Islamic philosophy, which St. Thomas Aquinas knew well. And outside of the circle of Western Asia, Europe, and the Abrahamic world, we can turn to Ātman in Hindu metaphysics, which is pure consciousness, the Self, which is the origin of all things, and also the role of Tao, and the Neo-Confucian philosophies of the twelfth and thirteenth centuries. One can go on and on in providing examples.

So where is the exception to the view of consciousness being the origin of things? The exception happens to be found in the world in which we are living. Before modern times, there were philosophies for which consciousness was not primary and "in the beginning." We see it in the Greco-Roman antiquity; we also see it in certain schools of Hinduism, but these views were minor and marginal. They did not dominate the worldview of the civilizations in question. Furthermore, in all traditional civilizations, there was a mentality in which "in the beginning" did not imply only a beginning in time somewhere back there but also a metahistorical truth. That is very important. It is very significant that while in English we say, "In the beginning was the Word," in the Latin Vulgate it says, *In principia erat verbum.* So in principle was the Word, and not only temporally. These other civilizations were fully aware of this truth. The reality of the primacy of consciousness begins in modern times at the end of the Renaissance, especially with the Scientific Revolution.

Before I go further, however, it is important, if we are going to be philosophically serious, to define what we mean by "consciousness." There are those who believe that philosophy should only deal with what is operationally definable, that the word *veritas* should be removed from the concern of the philosophy department because it cannot be defined from the point of operational methods that are used in analytical philosophy.

But there are universal concepts of philosophy to which I am appealing — the traditional and the time-honored schools of philosophy — which also are very rigorous, but not necessarily rationalistically. This is because it's impossible to define consciousness operationally. Every time you try to define consciousness operationally, you have to make use of consciousness in order to do so. It is like the famous saying of Pascal, who said that one cannot define "to be," because every time one uses a sentence to define it, one says, "that is, it is, etc.," and one is therefore already using the verb "to be" in order to define being. One then has a circular argument, and this is not logically acceptable.

It is a paradox that something as obvious as consciousness cannot be externally and operationally defined. That is true. But we all know what consciousness is innately, because to know itself involves consciousness. Through a way of deluding ourselves of being the only reality, we might deny the world out there, or, through some kind of sophism, try to deny the reality of the consciousness that is making the statement about the world out there. In both cases, it is through the use of consciousness that we make a truth claim, a claim to know. Consciousness is, therefore, the most primary reality through which we know and judge every other reality.

Consciousness, for traditional civilizations, for religions and traditional philosophies, is not only a state. It is a substance and not a process. It is something that is, like Being itself, which at its highest level of reality is at once luminous and numinous. Consciousness at its elevated levels is at once knowing and knowing that it knows, knowledgeable of its own knowledge. It is at once the source of all sentience, of all experience, and beyond all experience of the knowledge that something is being experienced. That is why even the more skeptical philosophers have had a great deal of trouble negating it, even those who have been skeptics from a religious point of view.

We have the supreme example of skepticism in the famous Cartesian method. Descartes was, I think, wrong in many ways, but he was right in one thing. And that is: you can doubt everything, but you cannot doubt the fact that you are doubting. And from this affirmation, of course, comes the famous *cogito ergo sum* of Descartes, "I think, therefore I am." What follows from the "therefore" is unfortunate, because the "therefore" has other more essential consequences. Descartes should have said, "I think, therefore God is," or "Consciousness is," but he did not do so. Nevertheless, the fact remains that even if you negate everything, if you doubt everything, you cannot doubt the instrument by which you are doubting.

This idea did not begin with Descartes. The great Persian philosopher Ibn Sīnā, or Avicenna, over a thousand years ago talked about the hanging man. A man hangs in the middle of space so his feet do not touch anything; his hands do not touch anything. He does not know where he is. He can doubt the existence of the earth. He can doubt the existence of the air. There is nothing that he cannot doubt. The only thing he cannot doubt is himself, who is doubting other things. So, in fact, Descartes' argument is not the beginning of this concept in the history of philosophy. Even the skeptical philosophers in days of old did not deny the primacy of consciousness. The question was, "What mode of consciousness?" "What kind of consciousness?"

I want to get back now to the significance of consciousness metaphysically, and the consequences of the denial of its primacy, for our life, religiously and otherwise. As I have said elsewhere, I believe that it was really with the Scientific Revolution that "in the beginning was consciousness" was seriously challenged. At first it was not challenged outwardly by those who were the great masters who created modern science. Certainly, not by Johannes Kepler and Sir Isaac Newton, both of whom had even a mystical view of religion and the belief not only in God but also in a kind of mystical vision of God, each in his own way. And even Galileo the maverick could not imagine denying that God created the world. But that is not really the point.

Once having established this new worldview in which God becomes at best only the creator of the world, two issues arise. First, the levels of consciousness are all, in a sense, reduced to a single level. That is, the multileveled structure of the world of consciousness, which you had traditionally, from the Divine Consciousness, to the consciousness of the angels, of the great intellects, of the great saints, and sages all the way to the consciousness of ordinary human beings, not to speak of animals, was all reduced to a single level of reality. And people spoke of consciousness in the world as being confined to ordinary human consciousness.

The second consequence, which is even more devastating from the point of our discussion here, is that it is true that it was accepted by most of the architects of the Scientific Revolution that God created the world, and that God had consciousness, because he knew — he is the "knower," and that he has all the other attributes related to the attribute of consciousness. But after creating the world he had nothing further to do with it. In other words, "in the beginning" was understood only temporally. This is the deistic position, which came to the fore for a long time, and remained so, replacing the theistic position of William Paley and other natural theists. Natural theology came to be considered to be, in fact, an oxymoron, not having any real significance and meaning, even religiously. What lasted much longer was the deism within whose framework many people still think to a large extent.

During the last forty years we have heard constantly about the Big Bang theory. Lectures have been held on how it is related to the perspective of the book of Genesis, or the Qur'an, and the Abrahamic vision of a creator God. But the consciousness of God within his creation is irrelevant, because once the Big Bang has taken place, and the universe is here, one is no longer seen as being interested in any consciousness in the universe, and in fact the predominant scientism denies such a reality. One speaks only of energies and material particles. So consciousness is taken out of God's creation. That is what resulted from the seventeenth-century Scientific Revolution, and henceforth consciousness became an epiphenomenon in the universe limited to the human state. It was through this mechanical view of the universe, complemented by the Darwinian theory of evolution in the nineteenth century, that the category of consciousness essentially became irrelevant in the cosmos according to the new scientific paradigm. It became irrelevant, even if many still believe, that God created the heavens and the earth. It became irrelevant as far as science and our situation in the world — that scientism is so dominant today even among many people who call themselves religious — are concerned.

And it is this denial of the primacy of consciousness that led finally to the idea of always trying to explain by reduction. This reductionist outlook is one of the most important characteristics of modern thought: explanation through analysis and reduction but rarely through synthesis and integration. That is, the whole is never seen to be greater than its parts, and therefore in explaining the cosmos we are always after ultimate particles. Long ago, a well-known physicist thought that within five years we would discover all of the ultimate particles of matter. Fifty years later, we are still looking for the ultimate particles of "matter." Because of metaphysical reasons, it is not just a question of discovering a few billiard balls that happen to be very small and we just have not found the smaller ones whose discovery is around the corner. Just put material particles together and create the universe. And yet we hold on to this idea, and continue to deny higher rules of existence and the truth that "in the beginning was consciousness."

One example is found at the doctor's office. We are reduced to what the MRI shows, and our chart, but the rest of us does not count. We are reduced to our biological aspect, and the biological aspect to chemistry, the chemistry to physics, and so forth. This is reductionism at work in our personal lives. It is only recently, in fact, that Harvard University has started a spirituality and healing program at the Medical School, because at least some medical doctors have come to realize all too well that our consciousness does affect our body in remarkable ways, even if we cannot explain it according to the prevalent paradigm.

In the realm of quantum mechanics, paradoxically, we have to accept the reality of consciousness, because we cannot ever know anything without observing it. That is why some physicists now talk about psychons, but most physicists have not accepted such an idea. The idea that we have psychic "particles," consciousness "entities" or "fields," along with neurons and all the other particles that are around is itself a way of trying to come to terms with consciousness. We have ended up with the paradox that we cannot really understand the universe quantum-mechanically without a consciousness to observe the quantum.

The reality of consciousness has grabbed us once again and will not let us go. And the remarkable thing is that when we come to the end of this period of the gradual dissolution of the Renaissance seventeenth-century paradigm, the reality of consciousness enters the scene again.

Hinduism, to cite a non-Western example, is the antipode of this seventeenth-century view, for in the Hindu view everything is a level of consciousness. For example, a stone's being is a form of stony consciousness, as it were. In Hinduism, this is perfectly understandable, but in our terms, such an assertion is not understandable. The same holds true up the line, all the way to the level of human beings. In contrast to Hindu doctrines and ideas coming from other religions and philosophies of the East, in the prevalent scientistic worldview the ontological reality of consciousness is negated from everything in the world, except for some human beings, including ordinary believers in God. But in this paradigm, whether one believes in God or not is irrelevant to the situation of human beings in the world, as far as the significance of consciousness is concerned.

This banishing of consciousness from the cosmos, denying that "in the beginning was consciousness" (and also, in principal, *is* consciousness at the present moment), has had very deep consequences for the human state, for what we are suffering through and experiencing today. Let us not forget that the scientific theory posits that consciousness is an epiphenomenon in the cosmos, possessed by an insignificant species living on a very irrelevant planet, in a minor solar system and galaxy, a species some of whose members happen to be able to claim that human consciousness is irrelevant. But no one talks about how we happen to be able to make this claim. Our consciousness is not considered to be a major reality in the cosmos, although it claims to know the cosmos. We consider it to be no more than an epiphenomenon. We paint the picture of a cosmos that is not only without consciousness but is also dead. And, nevertheless, we claim that our consciousness is able to study it objectively. What a peculiar consciousness is this indeed.

What are the consequences of this denial of the principality of consciousness? First and foremost there has been the withering of religious life by the reducing of levels of consciousness to the lowest and the most ordinary, to the level of ordinary causes. I believe one of the reasons for the withering and marginalization of mysticism within Western Christianity after the Middle Ages — not only in Protestant Christianity, but even to some extent in Roman Catholic Christianity — was this loss of vision of the levels of consciousness. In medieval times, or even in the Renaissance, a Hildegard of Bingen or St. Teresa of Avila had visions of Christ and the angels, and these visions had meaning within that universe. Whereas, when Swedenborg was having his visions in Stockholm, that did not mean anything, given the dominant scientific paradigm of that time. The meaning of Swedenborg's visions in the Christianity of the seventeenth century is already very different than that of St. Teresa of Avila and the Catholicism of the sixteenth century, and the reason is the banishment of consciousness from the cosmos, and even reality as such, during the period separating these two figures.

The consequence of cutting off man's consciousness from the higher levels of consciousness, which, however, did not go away by our denying them, was the weakening of access to the transcendent. Taking away the ladder or stairs to the third floor in this building means that you will not try to go up to the third floor any longer, and gradually the existence of the third floor becomes denied. Therefore, the quest for transcendence — for the empowering and illumination of our consciousness, which was the goal of all traditional civilizations — became irrelevant, explained by many to be an illusion. The desire for the transcendent and the gaining of perfection — which defines what, if one views it from the point of view of our ultimate concerns, it means to be human — became horizontalized. It was reduced to gaining more and more information but not necessarily luminous knowledge, which meant a negative transformation of human consciousness.

Another consequence of this loss was that the truths and realities of religion themselves became lost or put in serious doubt. They became either meaningless or reduced to metaphors or simply historical accidents. It is not accidental that most of the influential philosophies of religion that developed from the nineteenth century onward were based on historical reductionism, of reducing historical realities to what can be understood materially, and denying everything that cannot be demonstrated by positive historical methods or proven in a laboratory at Oxford or Harvard. Since we cannot walk on water, then Christ could not have walked on water either. And, therefore, if the people say he did walk on water, either they were blind or they had not been as well educated as us, or it had some other meaning, and has to be interpreted metaphorically on the basis of our truncated view of reality.

The whole question of the language of religion — the way it spoke to humanity, from the greatest miracles to everyday religious life — became unreal. The turning away in droves of people from religion in the eighteenth and nineteenth centuries in the West was not at all accidental, because religion addresses humanity in the context of a universe that is full of consciousness. Not only is the divine reality consciousness, but also there are the hierarchies of angels, of various conscious beings that are now reduced to UFOs. This emphasis of religion upon a cosmos replete with conscious beings holds also true in the non-Abrahamic world, in the Buddhist tradition with the hierarchy of the various Buddhas and boddhisatvas, and all kinds of other beings in intermediate worlds, and also in the world of Hinduism with its gods and goddesses. There is no religion whose traditional universe is not filled with consciousness. Even the most rationalistic Muslims who try to interpret Islam in a very dry manner cannot deny the reality of the archangel Gabriel, without whom there would not have been a Qur'anic revelation. They cannot deny the verses of the Qur'an which speak of the angels and the jinn.

*

This became a very important issue, and the reductionism in the understanding of the language of religion and its worldview caused a panic among many people, a fervor to try to reinterpret religion. This occurred for people all the way from atheists to theists, from Karl Marx to Schleiermacher, in the nineteenth century, and in the twentieth century all different kinds of new interpretations appeared that people had not needed or confronted previously because the religious view of the cosmos had been their general worldview. They lived in a universe in which God could speak to the trees as well as to us. Angelic beings could manifest themselves and they could even transmit knowledge. Knowledge and consciousness were not limited to the human order.

This emptying the universe of consciousness even affected the relationship between human beings and God. This change did not destroy the reality of God in the minds of many people, but it did affect that relationship — even the question of prayer and how God answers prayers. Of course, in a mechanistic universe, in which consciousness is placed at the beginning in time, this is a very difficult thing to explain rationally. What are the agencies through which the divine can come into our lives and in the life of the cosmos? Most theologians in the West tried to explain this matter emotionally, without really confronting intellectually, in the most rigorous sense, the challenge of the mechanistic universe. They tried to circumvent the issue. And, of course, Christian theology suffered a great deal in the battles that were fought because one had to accept a more and more scientistic point of view.

Another important consequence of this transformation is the loss of the meaning of being human. What does it mean to be human? This is not just an academic matter. A Christian or Muslim would say the human being has an immortal soul, but what does soul mean in the accepted view of the cosmos? We have consciousness of being human, of having a human soul, and for believers God is the Spirit with a capital S. And what about our attitude toward and relation to the rest of God's creation? What does that entail? What does that mean? And also, what is the relationship between our being human as an immortal soul and our body? Since the establishment of the mechanistic worldview there has been an indifference to the body as a source of wisdom. Then there seemed to be a sudden rediscovery of the body in the 1960s, expressed through sexuality and new kinds of music, trying to reassert the reality of the body. This was a reaction to the reductionist view prevalent in Western society.

All this goes back precisely to what happened as a result of the loss of the sense of the presence of consciousness throughout reality. Moreover, not only was the sense of the sacredness of human life put into question — because the word *sacred* does not mean anything in the context of modern science; it is just sentimentality. And with the loss of the sense of the sacred came the loss by human beings of their home in the cosmos — that is, we became homeless in a cosmos that was seen as being no more than energy and matter. Historically, humanity knew its position in the universe and felt at home in it. In the West there was this Ptolemaic system, with the earth in the middle and all of the heavens above, and this did not cause hubris because man was also seen to dwell on the lowest level of the cosmic hierarchy. The Mesoamericans in the Amazon feel they know where they are ontologically, but we do not know where we are — we do not have a home in the cosmos, and we have lost our sense of orientation. The result has been a very profound sense of alienation, including psychological alienation, which is one of the maladies of the modern world from which traditional society suffered much less. Alienation is a disease like AIDS, a really modern ailment. This is not to say that no one was ever alienated before, but this strong sense of alienation today comes, to a large extent, from the fact that if we accept this reductionist worldview that came into being in the seventeenth century, and take seriously this cutting off of consciousness from the world in which we live, then we become very lonely here. The cosmos is no longer a hospitable place for us, and we are alienated from the world in which we live.

And, of course, if you calculate the probabilities for our being here, from a scientific point of view, and it comes out to be extremely small, then that makes it even stranger that we are here at all. But even if we keep that idea in a corner of our minds, we feel even more that we do not belong here. That is why in our normal lives we do not take these probabilities seriously. Any person who walks in the street and smells a flower, and sees how beautiful it is, that person is not taking this point of view seriously, even if he is a professor teaching it in his class — because our human psyche, to remain sane, has to feel somewhat at home in the world in which we live even if we have become more alienated from it than ever before.

This desacralization of the cosmos and the ensuing alienation has also made a sham of the metaphysical and philosophical basis of ethics. This is a major claim that I am making, and is really a subject for another day, but let me just say a word about it. In all periods of human history, ethics was related to a vision of reality. It had a cosmic aspect. We think of the battle between the good spirits, the *ahuras,* and the bad, the *divs,* in Zoroastrianism, of the treatise of St. Augustine on the good. We think of Neo-Confucianism. Whatever traditional world you enter, there is a permanent set of ethical norms that are never only human ethics linked to the human world. Rather, they have a cosmic aspect. For the Abrahamic world at least — you had the ternary of God, human beings, and the cosmos. And in the world of ethics there were relations and correspondences between them. Through this depleting of the cosmos of consciousness, we have made any ethical act toward the world of nature contrived and without a metaphysical and cosmological basis. Regarding Christian ethics, for example, we adhere to being respectful to our neighbor: "Thou shalt not kill." But within the scientistic paradigm what is the reason for not cutting down a tree or not killing a particular animal except sentimentality or expediency?

In the sacred scriptures, there were explanations given for an ethics encompassing the world of nature as well as that of human beings. Animals and plants were seen as God's creation, with spiritual value, as were rivers and mountains. Those notions are now scientifically meaningless, and any environmental ethics based on that view of the world is based on mere sentimentality. It is not based on reality, if you accept the scientific view of the world as reality. It's like talking about the sacredness of human life. In one breath we mention the sacredness of human life and with the next breath note that its basis is nothing but DNA. What is sacred about DNA if it is just some molecules banging against each other in certain configurations? If we reject the sacred, reject that it is the wisdom of God that is imprinted upon the DNA, that all creation bears the imprint of God — a meaningless statement in modern biology — where then does the sacredness of human life come from?

*

Even the withering away of Christian ethics, which we now see before us after several hundred years of its survival even since the Scientific Revolution, has to do a lot with the more recent consequences of the extension of the desacralized view of nature into the domain of human life itself. This is especially notable when it comes to environmental ethics, which we need to create in a serious way if we are to be able to live in the future. For now, animal activists and others like them are outside of the mainstream. They are considered "crazy" people who tie themselves to trees and refuse to come down. These acts are not part of the mainstream of society, which is not able to develop an environmental ethics that is also in accord with the worldview that dominates our lives. A similar disjunction occurs in our hospitals because of the purely mechanical treatment of the human body, and tensions are created by the fact that some people still believe they have a soul and that the human body is not just a mechanical gadget. All of these tensions present great challenges that the still dominant worldview poses for us, and are signs that this paradigm is now falling apart.

Finally, if you take seriously the rejection of the idea of consciousness being the beginning not only of time but also, in principle, of the universe, it really shatters all the deepest hopes of human beings. First of all, hopes of immortality become mere dreams. And that is why we have, for the first time in human history, the development of a society in which many people do not dare to harbor these hopes. Great fear brings these hopes back, but, over all, these hopes that relate to the deepest needs of our souls are no longer meaningful or realizable within the framework of a worldview based on the primacy of the material rather than consciousness.

If we have come into being only from the matrix of time and space, we cannot transcend time and space. There is nothing that can ever exist at the omega point that was not there at the alpha point. I have written very strongly against Teilhard de Chardin and other theologians who believe that at the beginning was matter and at the end there will be spirit, because as Christ said, "I am the Alpha and the Omega." He did not say just, "I am the Omega." If we do not have our root in consciousness, which is beyond time, which is nontemporal, we shall never attain to the nontemporal.

*

These are the deepest aspirations of human beings, aspirations for immortality — that is, for an experience beyond time and space, for we are the only beings who are aware that we shall die. Even if we are good scientists, we know we are going to die. The diversions that we create for ourselves cannot prevent us from thinking of the fact that sooner or later we shall die. No diversion can prevent us from that truth. Hence the significance of the hope for immortality, which is inseparable from the deepest nature of our souls — which are in reality created for immortality.

The reality of human life, whose terminus is the call of death, and what that implies spiritually, has, of course, been very strongly challenged by the worldview that reduces consciousness to an accidental epiphenomenon. I believe the time has come for us to take this challenge seriously, to rethink what consciousness is in relation to our life, in relation to the manner in which we live, to the world in which we live, to our way of knowing, our sentience, our experience. And also it is time to realize fully the consequences of the negation of the primacy of consciousness in all its import.

It is logically absurd to deny the primacy of consciousness, because as soon as we do so, we do it through consciousness. But a lot of people have claimed to have done so — in fact, many professors on this campus. Behavioral psychologists and the like, of course, do not believe there is such a thing as consciousness. Although it is logically absurd, they have nevertheless claimed such a view. We need to realize the consequences of this state of affairs for human beings living in such trying and difficult times.

I believe that ultimately, of course, consciousness will have the final say, but it is for us while we have consciousness — this great, great gift — to use it properly to understand what it means to live consciously, to live fully with awareness, to know where we are coming from, where we are going, and why we are here.

KATHLEEN NORRIS

The Grace of Aridity and Other Comedies

FROM *Portland Magazine*

IT'S ALL ABOUT WATER, and grace.

Our planet is mostly water, as are we: one fact of nature that astonished and delighted me when I first encountered it as a child, and which I still treasure as evidence of the essential unity of all things, is that human blood, chemically speaking, is nearly indistinguishable from sea water. While we live and breathe, we are literally at one with the ocean, and when we die, our bodies become earth. This is not New Age fancy, but science.

We human beings, however, are remarkably adept at ignoring elemental truths; we'd rather place our faith in technology, and keep playing with our toys. Every now and then I read of a survey conducted by sociologists in which Americans are asked what they couldn't live without. The answers are always things like microwaves, computers, e-mail, cell phones, and Palm Pilots. I am composing this on a laptop, and as I am old enough to remember when the IBM Selectric typewriter was high-tech, I greatly enjoy the convenience a word processor provides. But I also recognize the computer as a mere tool, a convenience rather than a necessity. The stark truth is that our lives are entirely conditional on our access to air and water. In extreme circumstances, we can subsist for weeks without food, but take away our air and water, and we quickly die.

There is perhaps another human need that we can't live without; at least the world's religions would have us believe that this is so. Without love, we are told, love of God, love of neighbor, and love of self, we are nothing, we are good as dead. Scientists who play with the atomic glue that holds our world together have revealed that at the very heart of things is the quark. They are strange little critters, for there is no such thing as one quark, but only three mutually interdependent ones. The original three musketeers, one for all, and all for one.

Now think of love as a quark: if we believe that God first loves us, then we are called to love God in return, and to love our neighbor, and to love ourselves. But these three loves, like our blood and ocean water, are inextricably connected. We can't have one without all three, and we can't let any one of the three get out of balance. Loving God, for example, does not mean that we ignore the needs of others. And loving the neighbor means just that, not just loving those we choose to love, but loving people we would not have chosen, who happen to come into our lives, in our dorms, or apartment buildings, or jobs. Like it or not, how we love these often difficult people reveals how we love God, and ourselves.

Often the love of self is the most difficult for us. That may seem a peculiar thing to say, in the context of our narcissistic culture. But, as with any of the three loves, the key is balance. Think of the person who is never wrong, who harbors an exaggerated and unwarranted self-esteem, and lives smugly. Or, contrariwise, the person who is never right, and laboring under an exaggerated and unwarranted self-loathing, lives self-destructively. For both people, their real enemy is a self-absorption that withers love on the vine. Love itself is inexhaustible — God has made sure of that — but we find that it's not easy to love. That's where grace, and the comedy, enter in.

Grace Disguised

It's easy to like the idea of grace. What's not to like? One of its dictionary definitions reads: "divine love and protection bestowed freely on people." But if grace is so wonderful, why do we have such difficulty recognizing and accepting it? Maybe it's because grace is not gentle, or made-to-order. It often comes disguised as loss, or failure, or unwelcome change. And in the depths of our confusion and anger, we ask: "Where is God? How can this be divine love and protection?" But if an accident, illness, or sudden reversal of fortune forces us to confront and even change our priorities in life for the better, isn't that grace?

The comedy of grace is that it must so often come to us as loss and failure because if it came as success and gain we wouldn't be grateful. We would, as we are wont to do, take personal credit for what is an unwarranted gift of God. But for grace to be grace, it must take us places we didn't imagine we could go, and give us things we didn't know we needed. As we stumble crazily, blindly, through this strange, new landscape — of drought, of illness, of grief, and terrifying change — we slowly come to recognize that God is there with us. In fact, God is enjoying our attention as never before. And maybe that's the point. We have finally dropped the mirror of narcissism, and are looking for God. It is a divine comedy.

"The grace of aridity" is a phrase I've borrowed from Graham Greene's tragic-comic novel *A Burnt-Out Case,* about a renowned architect whose worldly success — both in his vocation and in his personal life, as a womanizer — has left him cold. He can feel nothing, anymore, except boredom and disgust with himself and with others. The simple pleasure of human laughter has become incomprehensible to him. He finds it as irritating and offensive as a bad odor.

The story begins as the man is traveling to a remote African leper colony run by a religious order. He seeks "an empty place, a place where no new building or woman would remind me that there was a time when I was alive, with a vocation and a capacity to love — if it was love." The colony's physician suspects that the man is "a burnt-out case," comparing him to a leper in whom the disease has run its course. He may be cured, and no longer contagious, but his mutilations — in this case, inner mutilations, wounds of the soul — will prevent him from ever feeling at home again in human society. Like the other "burnt-out cases," he will be content to do odd jobs at the clinic if it means he doesn't have to return to the outside world.

The man claims to have lost any capacity for religious faith, which, ironically, only makes some of the priests and brothers at the mission admire his humility. To them he seems a great and successful man who has stooped to help them build a hospital in a lowly, insignificant place. But the more the man denies any spiritual motives for himself, the more the others see God at work in him. In one bitingly comic scene — comic because two people are talking at complete cross purposes, yet both speak truly — a priest says to him, "Don't you see that perhaps you've been given the grace of aridity? Perhaps even now you are walking in the footsteps of St. John of the Cross." The man confesses that the ability to pray deserted him long ago, but the priest (who is half burnt-out himself, and lonely) replies that he senses in him a deep "interior prayer, the prayer of silence." As this kitty-wampus conversation ends, each man retreats back into his loneliness: when the priest asks, "You really do understand, don't you?" the man can only respond with "an expression of tired despair."

Aridity as Grace

It's all about grace, and water, and those of us who reside on the American plains know a good deal about how the two go together. Ours is a "next-year country" in which we learn to be grateful even for the bitter pills we're given. Precious moisture may come in the form of destructive hail. A hundred inches of snow that buries pasture grass and makes hay for the cattle inaccessible, may contain a pitiful amount of moisture. But even dry snow is wet, and that's better than the alternative. Thus we hang on — until next year, when things will be better.

Living in a place that is marginal by the world's standards, and also in terms of climate, can be a constant lesson in grace. Plains people know the grace of living in, and loving, a place the rest of the world considers God-forsaken. They enjoy the little things, a pasque flower asserting itself on a south-facing slope in early spring. They marvel at the magnificence of the sky at dawn and sunset, and sometimes even at noon. They value the silence that can frighten visitors who are accustomed to the noise of cities.

Both in our lives and in our environment, the key to maturity is recognizing and accepting what is there. In other words, letting a place be itself. That sounds easy enough, but evidently it is not. Think of the newcomers to the American Southwest who moved there because the air was relatively free of pollen that made it difficult for them to breathe in the East or Midwest. But now we're finding that these refugees brought so many plants from "back home" and coaxed them to grow in the desert, that they brought the pollen and the health problems along with them. Think of all the pasture land in the American West, especially land close to cities, that has become suddenly trendy, where fields of sage and scrub and grass are now dotted with absurd mansions. Absurd because they have cathedral ceilings and huge windows in a place where winter temperatures reach 35° below zero, and because around each dwelling is a tiny "lawn," its greenness maintained by an assiduous watering that might make sense in Connecticut or Ohio, but in Wyoming should be a crime.

Putting this in theological terms, I'd say that such housing developments as we see in the West constitute a denial of grace. As we've been conditioned to see grassland as barren, we attempt to change it into something else. A suburban lawn. We are rejecting the grace we've been given in favor of one we've invented for ourselves. The tragedy is that the shortgrass pasture of the American West is a remarkable grace indeed: grasses that look dead to us somehow retain their nutrients over the winter, so that they can nourish the cattle or buffalo who graze there.

In our own lives, too, we all too often deny the grace we've been given in barren places. When really bad things happen, we tend to blame God or assume that God has abandoned us. "Where was God when this happened?" This is a normal and probably necessary response. But sooner or later, we must learn to deal the cards we've been given, and look for the grace that is hidden in our loss.

There were grace notes in the unspeakably evil acts of September 11, 2001. No one phoned out of those buildings in hatred or revenge. Instead, the calls and e-mails were an affirmation of life and love. "I love you; take care of yourself." "I love you and the kids, God bless you and good-bye." Or simply, "You've been a good friend." If the hijackers of September 11 inadvertently invited us to the grace of aridity, isn't that comedy? (I am employing the word in its rich and ancient sense, as inextricably linked to tragedy.)

For if the terrorists' intent was to destroy us, they failed miserably. And we succeeded in finding a measure of grace. A more unified country, at least for a time. No riots, no panicked runs on banks. We were a more thoughtful people, if only briefly. We enjoyed the grace of a week without the usual advertisement bombardment, a week without celebrity trivia. Now that we've gone back to worrying about what Ben Affleck eats for breakfast and what Jennifer Lopez is wearing or not wearing, we might recall the seriousness to which we were called on September 11, and find something meaningful there.

Death and Life

The comedy of death is that it generally leads us to a better, fuller perspective on life. The prospect of death — whether it is the death of three thousand or of a family member or ourselves — encourages us to set aside the unessentials that can fill our days and to drop the fantasy that status and celebrity have meaning. Death allows us to live in the real world and provokes us to ask the right questions: What is the purpose of life? What is necessary for a good life?

If, as we are led to believe in our culture, the purpose of life is to consume and thereby support the economy, shouldn't we pursue wealth as the ultimate value? Shouldn't we, in the words of one computer billionaire, seek to die with more toys than the next guy? Even death might laugh at that one. But if we take seriously the way we were created, with our human blood so like the ocean, shouldn't we also take more seriously our connection with other people and the planet itself? If the market is our god, such connections don't matter, and it's no tragedy that the vast majority of people on this earth have no access to clean water for drinking and cooking. Water, like anything else, goes to the highest bidder, and those who can't afford it, do without.

But is the "right to life" contingent on our ability to pay for decent air or water or basic medical care? How much water necessary for human life — water, air, our very gene pool — is truly sacred and therefore must remain outside the realm of corporate control and the profit motive? What in our economy must be held in public trust, for the common good? We are being called on to make decisions about these things as a society, and if we're not careful, we will end up with a bitter comedy that will not be to our liking.

Here's a case in point. Several years ago I read a newspaper article about how the Great Lakes are suffering from both pollution and overuse. In a search for more efficient water management, cities were looking into the privatization of their water utilities. One company aggressively pursued, and came very close to winning, a contract to manage the water supply for a large Midwestern city. The company's name was Enron.

It's all about greed, and water.

MAURA O'HALLORAN

Annie Mirror Heart

FROM *Shambhala Sun*

IT WAS DUSK when she arrived. She walked from the station through the village to the outskirts where the temple lay. She didn't know anyone where she was headed, and not a word of the language. With each step closer, the urge to turn and run became greater.

The temple steps were steep and she had to stoop to pass through the entrance. This humbling posture robbed her of her remaining confidence. The temple was silent, self-contained, awesome. She stood just inside the gate and clutched her small bundle of possessions, her one familiar token in an unknown world. She began to shiver in the evening chill. A dim light flickered on, and she marched quickly toward it. She stumbled and her bundle rolled from her arms. She tried not to cry.

She reached the light and entered a dim room where a little monk was flinging papers about, shuffling and muttering in excited Japanese.

"I'm Annie Shaw," she said. "I'm expected."

The monk's black, pajama-like robes flapped around him as he searched under the desk and on top of shelves. "Ah!" he shouted, and banged a paper on the desk before her. On it, penned in a childish scrawl, was, "Please come this way." He peered at it, straining to pronounce it: "Pleezu kumu deesu waiyu."

Then he was off, waving the paper before her nose like a carrot before a donkey, and making gestures that to a Westerner looked like "go away," but obviously meant "follow me." Stumbling through the narrow, dark maze, she felt like Alice chasing the Mad

Hatter. The little monk, whose name was Hogen, was still shuffling and mumbling, "Pleezu kumu deesu waiyu." After pulling and straining at a door swollen in its tracks, he slid it open to reveal her room.

Hogen looked proud. He had cleaned the room himself, Annie learned later, in anticipation of the lady foreigner. He had scoured the temple to find a spare desk with legs aligned and had chosen the prettiest cushion cover he could find. It was floral, with huge magenta roses.

With a majestic sweep of his arm, he ushered her into her new abode. "Oh my God," she thought. "It hasn't got a window and I won't be able to stretch my legs out across it." She wanted to collapse into an armchair or onto a bed, but there was only a hideous magenta cushion and a spartan plywood desk. The dinner bell sounded, and before the full horror of the room engulfed her, Hogen whisked her back into the black of the temple labyrinth.

He led her to a large, bare room, furnished only with eight identical benches. Two monks were watching her shyly. "How are yoo?" "You berry welcome," they said, and tittered. With the sound of clappers, they grabbed their oryoki sets. Hogen gave her a similar parcel and indicated that she should imitate him.

The monks sat and unwrapped their sets in inhuman quiet. Two bowls, a tiny side plate, a pair of chopsticks, and a cloth square were all wrapped in another square like an Oriental version of the mess kit she used in the Girl Scouts. Hogen demonstrated how to place the bowls so that contact with the bare wood of the bench made no noise. The formalities involved in just passing one's bowls for rice and soup seemed insurmountable — the order fixed, the bowls specified: three fingers, the right hand, wipe before passing, on to the palm, gassho, soup on the right, rice on the left, chopsticks point towards you, make an offering, seven grains of rice. Wait for the clackers. And they were off.

She was incredulous. They were guzzling their food with the frenzy of savages, yet making not a sound except for a stray chopstick accidentally grazing a tooth. She had expected them to eat as if seeking to become one with each grain, to chew the universe and swallow the cosmos.

She chewed her rice thoroughly, even meditatively, she told herself. Looking to Hogen for reassurance, she picked up her side plate with a little mound of brown slime on it. Greasy, oozy, it tasted lethal. She had been faring reasonably well with her chopsticks up to that point, but the viscous mess slid round her plate, resisting every attempt to be scooped or speared.

Now from the corner of her eye she could see them passing hot water, pouring, filling their bowls. Hogen was urging her to finish, yet still the slime escaped her, dripping and plopping through the sticks. Try the rice. That was gluier, and by holding the bowl near her chin, she could shovel it in efficiently. Now they were wrapping the bowls. At least her rice was nearly gone. She tried to stand when they sprang to their feet, holding their neatly wrapped bowls, but Hogen pushed her back down. She felt like a dunce in the corner. They were wiping the benches.

"Good evening," said a voice in a recognizable tongue. "Why don't you just pick it up and knock it back?" And now she really could have cried. "I'm Shonen, Go Roshi's son. You must be Annie."

Patiently, he showed her how to eat every grain of rice, how to wash the oryoki set by pouring the water from bowl to bowl, how she should drink the water in order to waste nothing. Finally came the elaborate bowing and the folding involved in rewrapping the wretched things.

Shonen invited her to his room for green tea and dried rice cakes, and she was grateful for the gesture. His room was tiny, scarcely bigger than her own hole, but bursting with books, manuscripts, and reams of practice calligraphy strewn in an arc around the desk. From the corners of the bookcases, iron nails protruded at unexpected angles, displaying wrinkled robes drooping in baggy folds.

He struck a match, then lit a stick of incense and a cigarette. Casually he stuck the incense in a brass bowl in front of a plastic Buddha, and drew on his cigarette. From outside came a voice. He bolted upright and quenched the cigarette. But it was only Hogen, who gently slid the door open, peeped inside, and grinned. Shonen threw the cigarette at him. With a loud laugh Hogen thanked him and lit it himself.

They began to chatter animatedly in Japanese. She heard her name mentioned often but was content just to lean against the bookshelf and observe. They looked comical. Two round, bald heads nodding, living a fourteenth-century existence enveloped in clouds of smoke from king-sized tobacco sticks. The monks reminded her of schoolboys puffing in the bathroom. They became giggly as they discussed her. This blue-eyed woman was to become a monk in a mountain temple of remote northern Japan. Unbelievable!

It was only seven o'clock, but to Annie it felt like midnight. She groped her way back to her cell, where she dragged out the damp-smelling futons and piled on a heavy wad of assorted bedding. Already fully dressed, she added a woolly hat and scarf and hauled the bulky spreads over her body. She wondered if she could even turn over under the weight. She stared at the void where the ceiling must be, and in her stomach she felt a hole as black as the void above her.

Did she have any idea what she was undertaking here? Yet gazing into that void, she felt that somehow her whole life had been leading up to this moment. It was no accident that she had stumbled upon a reference to this remote monastery. It was something that sooner or later she had to do. She must try. She must really throw herself into this. Still, she thought, what wouldn't she give right at this moment to be seated in front of an open fire with a whiskey in her hand?

Morning came quickly, insistent and cold. Bells were ringing. Sleepy, she tried to dismiss them, but Hogen was at the door, reading from a scrap of paper that said, "I show you get dressed." He was making squealing noises and was obviously in a hurry. When she still couldn't understand, he started dragging her clothes off. Her first reflex was to belt him, but she reasoned that he'd hardly threaten her virtue at five o'clock in the morning in a bustling monastery. She was further reassured by the sounds of washing and toothbrushing just outside.

Hogen pulled a parcel in from the corridor and shook out a kimono, gesturing that she should put it on. He showed her how the right side slipped under the left, then how to loop it up with various strings, seal it with a majiku bando, and make sure not to let the lapels bag. This, he emphasized, was most important, but it seemed to her just another ridiculous triviality. Still, she chuckled at the idea of a man dressing her so platonically, even maternally.

As he patted the lapels flat on her chest, it was apparently without consciousness that this was a woman's chest. Could there really be some corner on the earth where she might be free of her sex?

The first few days seemed eternal, and she doubted each day whether she could survive until the next. The year she had promised herself seemed unthinkable. While everything was new, there was still a depressing absence of stimulation. Nothing really happened. She was cold and bored and ravenously hungry. There were no heaters and it was December. She could never finish her meals on time, so she took only minute portions.

Today she was up at five to splash her face in the icy water of an outdoor basin, then wash by the light of the moon. Next came the frenetic morning exercises, everyone roaring the count together. By half past six she found herself outdoors, sweeping the grounds. She stared at the raw red of her toes, like so many frozen sausages around the thongs of her sandals. Perched on those wooden platforms and in dawn's grey light, she could have been a geisha stepping down from her carriage after a night's work, not a *gaijin* with a bamboo twig stabbing listlessly at fallen leaves. She wanted out.

"That's all wrong." She was startled to hear a curt Japanese accent. "Sweep like this." The monk demonstrated jerky little side whips with all the motion in the twig, the handle almost rigid.

"There is a Zen way to sweep?" she muttered to herself. "I wonder if there is a Zen way to knock your arrogant block off."

A Zen way to sweep — this was truly humiliating. Upstairs she had tried to dust the meditation hall, and the first swipe of the duster had ripped a hole in the shoji screen. Then she had swept against the grain of the tatami, instead of up and down. She seemed to do everything wrong.

On her fifth day they told her she would have her ceremony soon. Up to that time she had only seen Go Roshi at meals. He looked at his food; he ate his food. He bowed to them; they bowed to him. He went to his room, where she could hear a television blaring.

What kind of man was he? She knew something of his story. He and his twin brother had been the oldest in a large farming family. His brother was destined to take over the farm, and Roshi to become a priest. When he was about eleven years old, his twin was accidentally shot. It was no one's fault, but Roshi was then expected to inherit the farm and fulfill his filial duties. He protested that he still wanted to be a priest. They refused to let him go. He chopped off his finger to show his earnestness. They still refused. So he ran away from home, a terrible disgrace. He took to the roads, not yet a teenager, wandering and chanting all the while, *Namu myo ho renge kyo.* He roamed around the country questioning various Zen masters on the meaning of life and death. Finally he went to Daiko Roshi, who said, "When apples are ripe and falling from their branches, what will you do?" "Gather them," he said. Daiko gave him a basket and showed him to the orchard. He remained for thirty-five years.

The clock struck eight as he walked in. The monks sat in two rows. The lights were off and the shoji was open, allowing harsh winter sunshine to stream across the passage and onto the benches. It lit Go Roshi's face. He was speaking animatedly, and as he laughed, his heavily repaired teeth glinted golden. She thought of him at twelve years old, alone, on pilgrimage. It made this venture into Zen seem all the less probable for an ordinary person like herself. The little finger of his left hand was a stub.

He mentioned her name several times during his talk. No one translated. He stopped speaking, stared at her, laughed, and addressed her in English. She was flabbergasted. She thought he knew no English. "Your ceremony will be in a few days. Are you ready?"

"What ceremony?" she said.

"You become priest ceremony," he said.

She knew this would come sooner or later, but she had thought it would be later. "Well, I mean, don't I have to know something? Believe things?"

"No, the less you know and believe the better."

"But does it mean I can never leave?"

"No, leave when you please."

"But, I mean, what do I promise?"

"I only ask that you request permission for outings."

This was mystifying. A priest with no beliefs or commitments? What was a priest, anyway?

"Well," she said, "I suppose I'm ready then."

Go Roshi clapped his hands in childish glee and dragged a huge cardboard box from behind the shoji. He unwrapped it slowly, with the precision of someone dismantling a bomb. He wound up the string and tucked it in his sleeve. Then he presented her with her robes and told her to go out and try them on.

To her it felt like Christmas and playing dress-up, all rolled into one. Barefoot, swathed in the long, silk kimono, she floated back and forth the length of the corridor. Hogen transformed himself into a photographer, focusing and clicking his imaginary camera to record the latest in temple fashions. The silent, empty corridors echoed with their laughter.

Then Go Roshi went away for a few days, and she felt miserable again. The lack of communication felt like a darkness around her, as if her entire world had sunk in on her. The monks tried to talk to her, consulting their dictionaries. They said they felt comfortable with her, then conferred for the right words to tell her they were glad she had come to Shodoji. She felt a real affection for them, yet they seemed so totally foreign and unreachable. They treated her kindly, but could they possibly conceive of who she was and the world from which she came?

On the day scheduled for the ceremony, Shonen came to her room and told her to wear the white kimono. "But your hair . . ." he said. "No one has shaved your head yet."

Her thick, dark hair had always been a source of pride for her.

"Shave your head, O.K.?" Shonen said. "Hurry up, O.K.?"

"Yes, fine," she said. "It's a nuisance anyway."

"Ah so," Shonen said. "You not usual woman."

That made her laugh and she found that she felt quite cheerful about it.

Shonen began with the clippers. Her long locks looked so forlorn, strewn on the wood. Now her head felt light. She touched it, naked and bristling. Shonen gathered the locks up, still in a hurry. She could only stare at herself in the mirror. So much for bravado. Shonen paused for a long stare. "It suits you," he said. "But you are not usual woman."

He doesn't know that she doesn't even feel like a woman anymore.

"Please, fast, fast," he said. "You now become a priest. In ceremony, repeat after me Japanese words."

"But Shonen-san," she said, "what do they mean? I must know what I'm saying. This is so important."

"No, Miss Annie, words are not important. You cannot really

make promise, for you are not free. Do ceremony now and you begin life, where promise will naturally become itself. Come. Come. Never mind. Words are only words."

"Well, why the hell do the ceremony?" she thought. She could feel herself beginning to get angry. The Buddha is not a god, but the place teems with statues and altars to him. Why all the formalities and petty regulations, if one is supposed to become free? So much foolish ritual and bowing. She was getting cross. She rubbed her bald head. A small voice inside advised that she'd get nowhere by endless questioning and rejecting. The way to understand this thing is not by analysis but by immersion. But she knew that immersion sometimes results in drowning.

The meditation hall smelled of straw mats and incense. She breathed it deeply and felt calmed. She decided to avert her eyes from the gaudy altar and the huge vases of fake flowers. She could see no beauty in the statues. They were looming, grotesque, with their rows of candles and offerings. It felt like a pagan mockery of the Catholic churches of her childhood. She felt she had stumbled once again into the religious world she had left behind.

Shonen was signaling her to prostrate herself before the images. Somehow she managed. The ceremony seemed a blur. She remembered repeating in a whisper Shonen's cues. Roshi was waving something that looked like a horse's tail in her face and chanting. Everyone joined in, voices loud, the drum pounding, primitive. Their huge voices were booming with wild energy and it unnerved her. Roshi gave her a paper with elaborate *kanji* and intricate folding. The horsetail was waving again.

The shouting finally ended. She felt faint. Now she was a Buddhist priest, although no one would tell her what that meant. They went downstairs for tea. Her new priestly name meant "Mirror Heart." Everyone said this was a good name, but they continued to call her Annie.

A monk named Mochian was smiling. "One moment pleez." He rooted through the sleeves of his robes and thrust a bar of chocolate into her hands. "*Omedeto gozaimasu.*" He bowed his head to the floor. Shonen translated this as "Congratulations," then continued, "You will make excellent priest. I very happy you do us the favor become this temple priest. We grateful. Thank you. You give pure energy."

This was embarrassing. She felt like a hypocrite.

The ceremony over, it was time for work again. She went up to the third floor and climbed over the huge Buddha, dusting and polishing him. She wore five layers of undershirts and sweaters but still felt chilled to her bones. The Buddha was not smiling, only enormous and awesome. She shuddered at the prospect of wringing the rag in icy water to wash the altars and floors.

Cleaning before breakfast was even worse. For this she began at one end of the corridor with a wet rag, hands on the cloth, hips high in the air, and ran down the passage with her weight on the wet cloth. It was effective, but she was running in the smear of the water, which instantly began to ice. Her feet froze and stuck as she ran. Each step felt like the sensation of ripping a Band-Aid from a raw cut. She asked herself if she could possibly put up with any more of this. Still, the thought kept throbbing in her mind: "I'm now a Buddhist priest."

In her meditations during zazen, she counted her breaths from one to ten. When she lost count because her mind became distracted, she returned to one. She had yet to get as far as ten. Her record was six breaths. "It's my own mind," she thought, "yet I can't even quiet it to count as far as ten." She recalled the complex calculus problems her mind had fathomed at university, the theories it had probed. The mind held facts from when she was young, from hundreds of years ago, from events she'd never experienced and places she hadn't been. It could hold them more vividly than the present, apply them, relate them, sift them, and arrive at new conclusions. This wonderful mind. But she couldn't count ten breaths. For one mere minute she could not still her mind. It flew off on a thousand fantasies. Why did the mind abandon its task to replay tired conversations, or wonder if the black stuff at breakfast was seaweed, or if her mother's favorite tulips were white or yellow? Her mind seemed to be mocking her.

She sat straight and stared at the sliding screen before her. One breath, two. Was that a cat she heard? She remembered that she liked cats.

"This most intimate possession," she thought, "belonging only to me, is not mine at all. Which is the mind — this incessant prattler, or the one struggling to shut it up, to drown it with numbers? But that's not right either. Shonen said it can't be forced. But if it won't stop spontaneously and it can't be forced, it seems to be a deadlock. Yet I think that's too rational an approach. Well, damn it, I am a rational being."

The next morning Annie went to her first *dokusan*. She stood at the door to Go Roshi's room, Shonen behind her to translate. Roshi wasn't looking at her, but into space, or perhaps, she should say, through space. His gaze did not seem to have an object but rather to slice. It was at once penetrating and vacant. His robes were patched purple silk, and across his knees he held a stick. She'd heard of masters beating their students and even a story of one getting his leg broken in dokusan. Here before her was the same dear man who had laughed with her and made her feel at home, but now he was frightening. He might do anything.

But her first dokusan was an anticlimax. Roshi made the same innocent small talk anyone might make. When she went again the next day, she expected to be calm. Yet standing at the door, she felt sick. Behind Roshi loomed the immense statue of his teacher. The lighting was from the base of the statue, giving it sinister shadows. Behind her stood his son, ready to translate for them.

This time he did not smile. A small hoarse voice, hers, spoke her koan. Why did she feel dwarfed by these presences? He's only human and a very kindly one. Her temples were throbbing. Having said her koan, she waited. He paused an uncomfortably long time and cleared his throat. "You must work now on *muji* koan. Become one with muji. Never let go of muji. Throw away your head. Stop reading. Don't concern yourself with the meaning of muji. Become muji. Let it fill you like a great piston pounding up and down in your belly until you feel that you'll explode." She wanted to ask what muji was, but had no voice.

"But if I don't know what it is, how can I lose myself in it?" she asked.

"Never leave it," Go Roshi said. "Practice this koan when you clean, when you eat, when you go to the toilet. You never know when or where *satori* may strike you." He rang the little brass bell to dismiss her.

Outside the door she pounced on Shonen. "What is muji?"

"Nothing," he said.

"What?"

"I'll explain later. Now it's time for sutra service."

With gongs and drums pounding, the monks' voices chanted the sutras. Her mind pounded. Did he mean that she should become muji? Become *nothing*? Her body was quite solid and material. It was a contradiction in terms.

After breakfast Shonen called her into his room. Now it seemed to her to have a cozy homeliness about it. The altar needed dusting and fresh flowers. A Bank of Tokyo calendar was peeling off the wall. His long robes still hung at odd angles about the room. He was smiling and peeling an apple. "It's puzzling, isn't it?" he said. "Here, take this Nagano-ken apple. Most delicious. I must tell you first that your koan originated with a famous monk named Joshu. One day a young monk asked Joshu, 'Does a dog have buddha-nature?' Joshu answered, '*Mu.*' Mu is a negative answer. It means 'no, nothing, nothingness.' But in Buddhism everything has bud-dhanature, so how can Joshu say 'mu'? You live in world of things — the phenomenal world, where everything appears separate. I am here, you are there, apple is there. There is no connection. At the same time, there is essential world. There is no thing. No sepa-rate thing."

"I don't understand," she said.

"Everything is atoms, yes? Atoms are particles. Now scientists dis-cover these act both like wave and particle."

This rang a vague bell for Annie.

"Think particle has decided place, size, time. How can it be both? How infinite and finite? This is impossible. Impossible to our minds because our minds can only think in our concepts. Our concepts come through our language from our experience. Our senses say apple and Shonen and Annie are separate. This is practi-cal. This is functional. This works, so we say it is truth. Science of Newton worked, so everyone said it was true. But it is not whole truth. In everyday world we not experience whole reality. So no un-derstanding and we become very attached to finite things. For twenty-five hundred years Buddhism has taught this world what modern science now realizes. How? No special tools, computer, sci-ence buildings. Through zazen many people experience for them-selves this reality.

"You can understand, Miss Annie. You need no scientific train-ing, only patience to sit and sit. Many people have *kensho* early, sometimes after only a few weeks, but then must train a long time so understanding goes into cells."

She asked Shonen to explain what kensho was. "Kensho is first time you see essential world. First time you see yourself. For some people this is very deep and at once understanding everything. Most people this is shallow, the beginning. You work on muji koan until kensho, then train with other koans."

"Shonen, when did you have kensho?"

"Not yet, Miss Annie. I try very hard but still muji is my koan. Many young priests come and have kensho quickly, but I am patient. Last month my father give sesshin and a man, fifty-one years doing muji koan, have kensho. My father crying. This man, so pure heart, so beautiful kensho."

She felt discouraged. She munched her apple. "But you understand so well, Shonen."

"That my problem. I'm like scientists. My father say 'You understand with head. Now with your belly.'"

The monthly *Zenkai* began. For this event, people from the area assembled for one day and two nights of extra meditation, dokusan, and talks by Roshi. Hogen instructed her in the appropriate clothing to wear. He liked to fuss over her, a real mother hen. Now he made sure her collars all overlapped properly, straightened and tugged everything into place, then stepped back a moment to admire.

She went to dokusan again. Go Roshi said she was to come alone. They struggled in his primitive English. He asked, "What do you make of muji?"

"Your son explained to me many things about muji and Buddhism and enlightenment, but frankly I can't make anything of it. I repeat 'nothingness' whenever I can remember to, but don't see what it's all about."

She wondered, but didn't add, how such monotonous reiteration could lead to any enlightenment at all.

"My son doesn't know a thing about Buddhism," Roshi said.

She was astonished.

"Your approach is incorrect," he said. "You must use the Japanese syllable '*mu.*' Never mind the meaning, only concentrate, pour your entire being into it. When you scrub the floors" — he startled her by jumping up and pretending to wash the floor — "that is muji. When you wash your face" — miming again he splashed water, then jumped back in mock horror — "it's freezing, brr, brr. That's muji. 'Oh, today I'm exhausted'" — he flipped on his cushion and snored outrageously — "that's muji. Do you understand?"

"I don't know," she said.

"Good," he said. "That's best. Don't-know mind is best. Hold on to don't-know mind and fight with all your might." He shook the little handbell. She was dismissed.

"Hold on to don't-know mind," he had said. Yet apparently that's not the same "don't know" as Shonen's. Roshi said his son didn't know a thing about Buddhism. That was puzzling, too. Shonen was obviously very learned in Buddhist matters. The whole business baffled her. Why can't it all be straightforward and logical?

She went back into the meditation hall. She loved its smell. Tonight for zenkai they were using little oil burners. The tatami felt warm, almost alive beneath her feet. The hall was filled to capacity. She was pleased with the sight. It was more encouraging than the usual handful of monks huddled half-freezing in the semi-gloom. The people gave her energy, and Roshi's words were fuel.

She stared at the shoji screen before her. "Mu, mu, mu." The patterns of the shoji began to dance in an odd way. Her eyes were unfocused though concentrated. The effort made the shoji seem to shine. Her breath came slower and slower. Mu, mu. She felt as if she were at the bottom of a clear pool. Sounds were muffled, words and sentences floating on the surface. She was at the very bottom, looking up a great, slow distance at the light. Mu, mu, mu. It came from the pit of her belly. A tangible peace was settling through her body, a vast stillness, a hollow, booming mu.

After zazen they had chanting. Usually she found it loud, even unpleasant, but this time she was very moved. She watched Hogen's pudgy little face. He was chanting with his whole heart. Although the incense, the words, and the costumes were still completely foreign to her, her eyes slid fondly across each ardent face. She felt she might cry.

Afterwards they had tea. Forty-five people knelt in lines behind their benches and one by one stood up to give a short self-introduction. Shonen translated for her. Someone asked if it was true that the foreign lady would really do *takuhatsu*. Shonen asked her.

"Tell me again what takuhatsu is," she whispered. "I've forgotten."

"Miss Annie," he whispered back, "you must learn this word. Takuhatsu is begging."

She was indignant. "Of course I'll go." Did he think because she was a woman or a foreigner that she wouldn't? But she began to wonder just what this begging could involve that her decision to do it produced such obvious awe in the assembly.

A handsome, elderly man signaled her to follow him, and they went with Shonen and two other men — a plumber and a skinny, awkward computer programmer — to a small bare room she hadn't seen before. Inevitably, they started smoking. They smiled and said their names, which she immediately forgot.

The elderly man made pleasant, inconsequential conversation about her family and her journey. She warmed to him at once. He spoke softly but firmly. When he flicked his ash, he'd rest a moment, watch it, and resume what he was saying. It gave an unhurried flow, almost melodic, to his manner. He exhaled a long, steady stream of smoke. "Miss Annie," he said, "do you know you are Buddha?"

"I beg your pardon?" she said.

"You are Buddha," he said.

"Do you mean some kind of reincarnation?" she said.

"No, I do not," he said.

"Well, Buddha died some twenty-five hundred years ago, didn't he?" She recalled Shonen mentioning that figure.

"No," he said, "the Buddha is alive and before my very eyes. Miss Annie, you are Buddha."

She was flattered but a bit embarrassed. "No, really," she said. "I can't even sit cross-legged properly."

"Plain Miss Annie even with weak legs is Buddha," he said. "You must know that. You must realize that in your every moment and every movement, you and Buddha are not different. You have nothing to seek. You are living Buddha. You have no need to search but you do not know that. You must take my word for it, but you will search in vain, search frustrated until you realize beyond any doubts or questions that you are Buddha completely and that you have never been anything but that."

Then he and the plumber told how they had reached enlightenment. The computer kid had not yet experienced kensho. They told other enlightenment stories, remembering this or that character, laughing. They spoke of the monk who was carrying a basin of hot water with great concentration. He bumped into a pole and came to an awakening. There was the one who was drinking his soup, saw a potato, and his world fell apart. He cried out in the silence of the meal. Another one stared at the sky all night, but believing it was only half an hour, met the dawn with tears. When Roshi came out of his room to wash, the monk was prostrating himself outside the door. He'd been there for an hour, weeping in gratitude. Many stories were not so dramatic. Most people were doing sesshin and got kensho in Roshi's room.

She went to her room extremely excited. Becoming enlightened needn't be a matter of decades in a mountain cave. It could be hers soon. He'd said that she'd never been anything but Buddha. The idea was intoxicating. The elderly man's voice was so authoritative, his manner compelling. That night when she fell asleep, her dreams were full of mu.

The next day Roshi suggested that she should buy thicker underwear before takuhatsu. He gave a monk named Bodhin money and asked him to accompany her to the village. She didn't particularly like Bodhin; he was the one who had corrected her leaf-sweeping. He was constantly picking on the new young monks, harshly pointing out their mistakes, making fools of them before the others. It seemed cruel when there were so many minute details to remember, none of which were taught systematically. Anyway, she and Bodhin were to go to the village together.

This was the first time she had left the monastery since she arrived. It crossed her mind to make a dash for it and escape now while she had the opportunity. She knew other monks had "leaped over the wall." Could she just disappear too?

It was a country village but bustling with life. The shops displayed their wares out front in colorful stalls. Everyone seemed to know everyone and in spite of the bitter weather chatted comfortably. Occasionally they bowed to Bodhin and Annie. Bodhin reverently returned the greetings. From the lampposts on every street hung bright plastic and tin decorations in the shape of colored snowflakes. In the afternoon sunlight they looked festive. Bodhin said that decorations always hung there, different ones depending on the season. She liked them. They were garish but gave every day an air of holiday. Some people stared at her curiously. One shopkeeper asked Bodhin if she was a boy or a girl.

Then they went into a shop where "Jingle Bells" was playing, and her heart missed a beat. The air had the crisp tingle of Christmas, but this was Japan, far from her father's hot punch and her mother's plum pudding. The next day would be Christmas Eve. She knew she must be strong. Mu, mu. The word had no appeal, couldn't distract her.

With twilight came the first snowflakes and gradually lights flickered on throughout the village. They walked back to the monastery slowly, silently.

They returned just in time for dinner. After the final clapper sounded, Annie was startled to see Mochian — the monk who had given her the bar of chocolate the day she became a priest — enter the room carrying a tray of soft drinks and a single bottle of champagne. The champagne was meant to be her Christmas celebration. Together the monks began singing "I'm Dreaming of a White Christmas." They all huddled around low benches, looking excited and blowing puffs of icy breath. Mochian opened the bottle. It was only the size of a beer bottle — just a sweet and swift sip for everyone. The tiny taste was merely tantalizing. She would have loved more.

Then the entertainment began. Mochian stood up slowly, breathed deeply, and, from the pit of his belly, poured forth his song. There was deep melancholy in it, as if the mountains were mourning beside a churning sea. It became wild, tempestuous. He seemed to sing with an emotion that was hardly human. When he had heaved the last strains from deep in his gut, the other monks all clapped uproariously, almost relieved that his suffering was over. Mochian smiled, knelt down at his place and poured the last drop of his champagne into Annie's empty cup. Her eyes were watering and she could scarcely tear them away from him long enough to ask Shonen, "What on earth was that about?"

"Frogs in a rice paddy at dawn," he said.

"What? It can't be! Are they all committing mass suicide or something?"

He looked at her, puzzled. "No, Miss Annie, no mass, no suicide, just frogs. I think Mochian-san likes frogs."

Hogen was next. He gently crooned "Silent Night." His face was cherubic. "Pleez, Miss Annie, not homeshikuness." But to her surprise she felt at home — a strange home, certainly, but with the peace of a real home. When it was her turn, she sang "God Rest Ye Merry, Gentlemen." She guessed they might be familiar with it, and, sure enough, they beamed in recognition. In this little Buddhist temple in the snowy mountains of Japan, the Christmas spirit was more genuine than any she had experienced in a long time.

NOELLE OXENHANDLER

Ah, But the Breezes . . .

FROM *Tricycle*

OFTEN A SPIRITUAL QUEST begins with the word *but.*

I have everything I need to make me happy, but I am not happy. . . .

For my neighbor, Sally, the quest began many years ago in a villa in southern France. It was a beautiful villa, covered with bougainvillea and facing the Mediterranean, and she was in the company of loving friends. "But I just couldn't be happy," she remembers. One restless, fitful night, she came across a book left behind by a previous guest. It was *The Autobiography of a Yogi,* and it led her to the practice that she has followed ever since.

As for Prince Siddhartha: his parents made sure that he had everything on earth to make him happy. He lived in a beautiful palace and roamed through lush gardens and enjoyed the company of loving friends and bountiful food and. . . .

Notice the *and*s? They were not enough the keep the *but* from his life.

The *but* of an old man, a sick man, a corpse. . . .

One day these sights pierced through the shield of *and*s that the King and Queen had made for their son. The minarets and the marble, the jasmine and honeysuckle, the silks and sweets, the laughter, music, and dancing: all these could not shield the prince from the *but* of suffering that he discovered outside the palace gate.

Outside: the word *but* derives from the Latin *ob,* meaning "out." Suffering is what we want to keep out, but somehow it always gets into our lives.

It doesn't always come in a strong dose. Sometimes it's subtle, homeopathic.

When I was fifteen, I fell in love with a boy I met when I twisted my ankle and my ski went flying over a cliff in the Haute-Savoie mountains in France. A handsome, dark-haired boy took off over the cliff and, nearly an hour later, handed me the ski that had plunged into a deep ravine. His name was Michel.

He attended a Jesuit boarding school in the nearby village, where he'd been sent for being unruly. When I visited him there, in his cell-like room, he read me the poems of his favorite poet, Rimbaud, the "enfant terrible." Then he showed me the secret stash of candy and cigarettes that he kept in a hollowed-out Bible. We went to the Mardi Gras celebration at his school that night, and he went as Lazarus, wrapped in a white sheet. That was Michel, always defying something: a sheer cliff, a school's rules, the idea of death. . . .

We met several times again that year when Michel was visiting his parents in Paris, which was where my family was spending the year. Shortly before our return to California, Michel's parents invited me to spend the following summer with them in their chalet in the High French Alps.

Now, between our handful of vivid moments from the past and the summer's wide open future, Michel and I had just enough raw matter to spin a dense web of fantasy. Back in California, I set my alarm clock an hour early on school nights so I'd have time to wake up and read his letters and to imagine, again and again, the scene of our reunion. *After a long journey, my train pulls up to the village station. Through the window I see a stone clock-tower, surrounded by white mountain peaks. And there he is. Waiting for me on the platform: handsome, dark-haired Michel. I step off the train, and we rush into each other's arms.*

At last the long school year came to an end, and I flew to Paris by myself and took the night-train that winds through the heart of France, from Paris all the way to Provence. Too excited to sleep on my narrow berth, I lay there in the dark, wrapped in my web of revery. At dawn's light, I looked out and saw meadows of wildflowers flying by, villages built of dark wood and stone, and brilliant white peaks in the distance. . . .

By late morning, the train arrived at the tiny village called Puy-St. Vincent. I stepped off the train and there he was, waiting for me: handsome, dark-haired Michel. We rushed toward each other, just as I had imagined. But in the moment of embracing him, I looked over his shoulder and saw a small pink plastic lobster, lying on the ground. Even in the bliss of being in his arms, I felt the shock of the alien thing, the thing that — in all those hours of daydreaming — I'd never once imagined.

It is thirty-four years since I stepped off the train in Puy-St. Vincent, and Michel died long ago in an avalanche on Mt. Everest. Yet there's a way that the moment of seeing the small pink lobster over his shoulder has happened again and again.

It's the moment of the *but*. The moment when something outside the pale of our own dreams, desires, expectations, intrudes. "But this wasn't in my plans! This is not what I had in mind!" Indeed, that summer in the Alps bore no resemblance to the summer I'd set my clock to dream of, morning after morning, in California. Unable to live up to the months of fantasy, my relationship with Michel quickly unraveled — and there I was, far from home, stuck for weeks in a house with a sullen boy who barely spoke to me. Looking back, it would be easy to see the lobster as a sinister omen. Yet from the first moment, I sensed it was a different kind of messenger. I didn't have words for it then, but somehow I knew that this was a small monster calling to me with life's big question. Can you include the outside, alien thing *in* the embrace?

To truly answer this question is to come up against the very edge of the human psyche. For from the very beginning, what we desire is *and*. The very opposite of *but*, the word *and* is linked to "in," and our life begins *in utero*. For the human infant, bliss is the *and* that comes as close as possible to that primal *in:* I am here *and* you are here *and* when I open my mouth your milk is *in* me *and* I am *in* your arms.

Alas, from the very beginning the *but* intrudes. Even the most attentive mother cannot fail to fail her infant at times: a hungry stomach aches, a wet diaper chafes, the bath water is too hot or too cold. . . . In the mouth of even the luckiest baby, sharp teeth soon intrude in the soft site of pleasure.

Yet our whole lives long, we go on wanting a version of the primal *and*. We fall in love, and we think we've found it again. My first two weeks in Puy-St. Vincent were blissful. Michel and I swam in deep, blue mountain lakes and hiked to where the world seemed nothing but glacier, rock, and clouds. Following the sound of a hundred small bells, we found the trail that led to the village shepherd: Bernard, a young man who spent his life alone with a hundred sheep. Back in the village, we had long, communal meals with his family and neighbors; we played volleyball in the evenings as the snowy mountains turned a flamboyant pink; we joined with other teenagers to help restore the crumbling Roman chapel, polishing old paintings with raw potato-halves and hearing each other's mock-confessions in the carved wooden booth. As a gift to Michel's family, I'd brought a beautiful white Mexican wedding hammock. Michel hung it up between two pine trees and we loved to lie in it, swinging out over the blue valley, murmuring to each other as we'd longed to during all those months of ink on paper. Whatever the words, in English or French, their import was this: You are here *and* I am here *and* you are *in* my arms *and* I am *in* your arms *and* this moment will go on *and* on *and* on.

In spite of my efforts to stay neutral, I got drawn into an escalating drama between Michel and his mother. She was terrified of his growing passion for scaling mountains, always higher and more inaccessible mountains. Deep down, she must have known where it would lead. I sympathized with her — and for this, Michel cut me off.

But this isn't what I wanted! This isn't how I thought it would be. . . .

Inevitably, we fall out of the hammock of bliss, the Garden of Eden. In some form or another, whether subtle or huge, the *but* arrives to thwart our desire.

Is this the end of the story?

No.

For there is another *but,* a *but* within the *but* of sorrow and disappointment. The poet Rilke asks us to fear neither suffering nor sadness:

> *The mountains are heavy, heavy the oceans,*
> *Ah, but the breezes, ah, but the spaces —*

Breezes . . . spaces . . . what is this *but* that can blow through our lives, softening the hard mountain of suffering, opening us to something beyond the contraction of sorrow?

One night in the village of Puy-St. Vincent, a painful dream jolted me out of sleep with the words, "I can't take this anymore!" Michel's iciness was unyielding, and I felt overcome with hurt and homesickness. I got out of bed and threw open the heavy wooden shutters. The black sky swirled with stars over the luminous white mountains. The scale of everything out there was so vast, and as I leaned into it, I felt something happening inside me. It was something very soft — like a breeze — yet forceful, and inside the walls of my chest, it pressed against something that wanted to shut down.

The feeling was painful, as though I might burst, yet it brought an exquisite relief. It helped me to discover a buoyancy in the heart of the heaviness, and I was able to stay through the summer. Michel remained sullen, but I made other friends, grew close to his family, and made my own bond with the mountains. When, on my last night, I stood outside his door and said, *"Bonsoir,* Michel," he threw open the door and asked me to forgive him.

Two years later, when I met a monk from Thailand who taught me how to meditate, I knew I'd found a link to that sustaining buoyancy. Though I was sitting in the basement of a college dormitory in Ohio, when I followed my breath I was opening those heavy wooden shutters again, inviting the breeze to come in, in. . . .

In Buddhism, the *but* of suffering — the old man, the sick man, the corpse — is met by the *but* of the path. "Existence is suffering," said the Buddha Gautama, "but there is a path to liberation." When we sit quietly in meditation, *but* after *but* presents itself. "But I don't want to feel this pain in my knees . . . this drowsiness . . . this restlessness . . . this anger . . . this grief . . . I can't bear to sit here anymore. I want *out!"*

Yet something remarkable happens when we go on sitting through all the *but*s, through all the thoughts, sensations, and emotions that we would so like to oust. Gradually they begin to feel less alien, less like *ob*-stacles in the way, rocks in the path. Our deepening awareness becomes a kind of dew, falling on everything equally, allowing everything to sparkle. Once, in the midst of a meditation retreat, a friend went for a walk in the woods and found to her amazement that the litter was beautiful. Rusty cans, a beer bottle lying on pine needles: everything was shining like a jewel. Once, after three months in a Zen monastery, I was taking a night flight home across the country when I became aware of a constriction in my chest: my fear of dying in a plane crash. With difficulty, I brought my attention to the fear, and then something began to happen, something that had the same huge energy as the airplane, plowing so forcefully into the night. The fear of flying disappeared and — like the lens of a kaleidoscope narrowing, then opening out again into a different configuration — a new fear appeared, then another, and another. Cancer, fire, the death of loved ones. . . . Then fear turned to grief: the heartbreak of Michel, my parents' divorce, lost friends. . . . Each fear, each grief arose in a vivid display of color and shape that, amazingly, had its own perfection, like one shimmering firework after another. Faced with the sheer power of this display, there was no room for fear or grief — only awe, and a sense of immense relief as each fear, each grief melted away.

This magnificent melting was not an experience that could be sustained in its intensity: the plane came back down to ground on the other side of the continent, and I too had to come back to ground. But the experience radically altered my sense of horizon, my understanding of what the human mind can encompass.

Notice the *but* there? It's a *but* with a double edge. At times, when confidence deserts us, when we contract with pain or fear or doubt, the past experience of that infinitely expanding horizon sustains us, encouraging us to rediscover it anew. "I can't quite see it now, but I know it's there." At other times, the past experience seems to indict us, to accuse us of having let the hard-won jewel slip through our fingers. "I had such a powerful experience of release, but now I'm bound again." This *but* can be the hardest passage of all. It's as though, having once belted out "Amazing Grace," we now have to sing it backwards: "For I was found, but now I'm lost; could see, but now I'm blind. . . ."

This is the *but* that the medieval mystic, Julien of Norwich, acknowledges in her description of the "rising" and "falling" of the spiritual life. "If there be anywhere on earth a lover of God who is always kept safe, I know nothing of it, for it was not shown to me. But this was shown: that in falling and rising again we are always kept in that same precious love."

And who was Julien of Norwich? The Queen of *and*. Her famous words, "all shall be well and all shall be well and all manner of thing shall be well," are spoken to those who have passed through the *but* — again and again and again. As Julien tells us, it's *and* that has the last word, ringing out like a bell in waves that encompass every sorrow. Yet without the *but*, we couldn't fully hear this sound. We'd be like those poor beautiful people in the deva realm who, having never experienced the least *ob*-struction, can never experience the joy of release. So it is that I propose the humble word *but* as our own seed-syllable, sacred mantra, secret of human happiness, breeze through the heart of suffering, conduit to the inexhaustible well of *and*.

R. R. RENO

Fighting the Noonday Devil

FROM *First Things*

FOR MOST OF THE MODERN ERA, Christian apologists have emphasized the role of pride as the primary barrier to faith. Take Milton, for example. At the outset of *Paradise Lost*, Satan rallies his fellow fallen angels with a speech of exculpation. Bidding farewell to the "happy Fields" now lost, Satan hails the "infernal world," promising his followers that they, with him, might make "Heav'n of Hell." What seems a disaster can be made a victory. Satan's reasoning is simple. "Here at least," he says, "we shall be free." "Here," he continues, "we may reign secure." The gain, then, is autonomy and self-possession. Thus, in famous words, Milton has Satan pronounce the purest formula of pride: "Better to reign in Hell, than to serve in Heav'n."

To a great extent, the standard story of modernity emphasizes exactly the self-confidence and self-assertion that Milton describes in *Paradise Lost*. The emerging powers of modern science gave the seventeenth and eighteenth century a keen sense of the real powers of the human intellect. Rebelling against servile obedience to dogmatic and clerical authority, progressive forces in Enlightenment culture championed free and open inquiry. The same sentiment, this standard story continues, characterizes modern moral and political thought. Against traditional moral ideals and social forms, modern thinkers have sought, and continue to seek, a pattern of life derived from and properly expressive of our humanity. Thus, Ralph Waldo Emerson shouts the battle cry of modernity: "Trust thyself." Against subservience to the ideals of another, Emerson writes, "Nothing is at last sacred but the integrity of your own mind." So central and important is this self-affirmation that Emerson reports that "if I am the Devil's child, I will then live from the Devil." Better to reign in the hell of self-affirmation than to subordinate the self to ideals or principles, no matter how heavenly.

This modern voice of rebellion against God's sovereignty is quite real. Yet, in the twilight of modernity, do people really attack the Christian tradition because they have vibrant Emersonian souls? Do the naysayers and critics of Christianity attract audiences of willful and self-assertive individualists who are eager to find leverage to free themselves from the constraining powers of dogma and priestcraft? Does secularism today stem from a deep self-trust and demonic pride?

The answer, I think, is no. Pride may go before the fall. However, after the fall, other spiritual temptations and difficulties predominate. In our times, whether we call the prevailing outlook late modern or postmodern, the vigor and ambition of the ideal of self-reliance has lost its luster. When the United States Army can adopt a fine Emersonian sentiment — "Be all you can be" — as a recruiting slogan, then surely what was once a fresh challenge has become a hopeless cliché. For this and other reasons, we need to turn our attention away from pride and look elsewhere for the deeper sources of resistance to the Christian message.

Looking elsewhere does not mean looking away from the Christian tradition. Christians have not always thought pride the deepest threat to faith. For the ancient spiritual writers of the monastic movement, spiritual apathy was far more dangerous than Milton's prideful Satan. Recalling the sixth verse of Psalm 91, the desert fathers wished to guard against "the sickness that lays waste at midday." Evagrius of Pontus, a fourth-century monk, is one of the earliest sources of information about the desert monastic movement, and he reports that gluttony, avarice, anger, and other vices threaten monastic life. Yet, of all these afflictions, he reports, "the demon of acedia — also called the noonday demon — is the one that causes the most serious trouble of all."

Acedia is a word of Greek origin that means, literally, "without care." In the Latin tradition of the seven deadly sins, it comes down to us as *tristitia* or *otiositas,* sadness or idleness. But citing synonyms and translations will not do. For the monastic tradition, acedia or sloth is a complex spiritual state that defies simple definition. It describes a lassitude and despair that overwhelms spiritual striving. Sloth is not mere idleness or laziness; it involves a *torpor animi,* a dullness of the soul that can stem from restlessness just as easily as from indolence. Bernard of Clairvaux speaks of a *sterilitas animae,* a sterility, dryness, and barrenness of his soul that makes the sweet honey of Psalm-singing seem tasteless and turns vigils into empty trials. Medieval English writers often speak of acedia as wanhope, a waning of confidence in the efficacy and importance of prayer. For Dante, on the fourth ledge of purgatory, those afflicted by acedia are described as suffering from *lento amore,* a slow love that cannot motivate and uplift, leaving the soul stagnant, unable to move under the heavy burden of sin.

Across these different descriptions, a common picture emerges. The noonday devil tempts us into a state of spiritual despair and sadness that drains us of our Christian hope. It makes the life of prayer and charity seem pointless and futile. In the heat of midday, as the monk tires and begins to feel that the commitment to desert solitude was a terrible miscalculation, the demon of acedia whispers despairing and exculpatory thoughts. "Did God intend for human beings to reach for the heavens?" "Does God really care whether we pray?" "Is it not unnatural to seek solitude and chastity?" According to another ancient writer in the Evagrian tradition, the noonday demon "stirs the monk also to long for different places in which he can find easily what is necessary for his life and can carry on a much less toilsome and more expedient profession. It is not on account of locality, the demon suggests, that one pleases God. He can be worshiped anywhere. . . . Thus the demon employs all his wiles so that the monk may leave his cell and flee to the race-course."

Are these temptations that afflict the monk as strange or alien as the unfamiliar Greek word, acedia? I think not. Let me update the whispering voice of sloth: "All things are sanctified by the Lord, and one could just as well worship on the golf course as in a sanctuary made by human hands." Or: "God is love, and love affirms; therefore, God accepts me just as I am. I need not exercise myself to change." Or: "We should not want to put God in a box, so the Christian tradition must be seen as a resource for our spiritual journeys, not as a mandatory itinerary. I can pick and choose according to my own spiritual needs."

In our day, these temptations seem far more dangerous than Em-

erson's "trust thyself." After all, how many people, believers or un-
believers, wish to reign anywhere, in heaven, hell, or even in their
own souls? Few, I imagine. Most of us just want to be left alone so
that we can get on with our lives. Most of us want to be safe. We
want to find a cocoon, a spiritually, psychologically, economically,
and physically gated community in which to live without danger
and disturbance. The carefree life, a life *a-cedia,* is our cultural
ideal. Pride may be the root of all evil, but in our day, the trunk,
branches, and leaves of evil are characterized by a belief that moral
responsibility, spiritual effort, and religious discipline are empty
burdens, ineffective and archaic demands that cannot lead us forward, inaccessible ideals that, even if we believe in them, are beyond our capacity.

Acedia, then, is a real threat, a deadly sin doing its deadly work in
the present age. Its presence can be detected rather clearly in two
features of our intellectual and moral culture. The first is the intellectual spirit of dispassion and coolness that grows out of the ideal
of "critical distance." This ideal often contributes to the *torpor animi*
that afflicts any who have entered into the habituating practices of
our universities. For many of our professors, the drama of education is to break the magic spell of immediacy. Just as the commonsense observation that the sun revolves around the earth is quite
false and must be corrected, so, we are told, we must step back
from the moral and social opinions we were taught as children.
Nothing that is given should be accepted. We must step back from
our initial assumptions and see them as being, at best, merely true
for us rather than being simply true.

In order to spur us toward critical thought, the dominant strategy of contemporary instruction is shock therapy. Anticipating the
method, the early modern essayist Montaigne described his desires
to "pile up here some ancient fashions that I have in my memory,
some like ours, others different, to the end that we may strengthen
and enlighten our judgment by reflection on the continual varia-
tion of human things." Montaigne is confident that by "piling up"
these examples, we will be forced to stop thinking parochially and
recognize that men and women have lived many different ways according to many different ideals and customs. We will be shocked
by the diversity, and for just this reason, we will be levered away
from an atavistic loyalty to our particular ways of viewing the world.

But the ancient fashions Montaigne catalogues are not simply diverse. He chooses very carefully, and in a way that also anticipates postmodern historiography and cultural study, his examples tend toward the prurient and base. Montaigne quotes ancient descriptions of how people wiped themselves after bowel movements, as well as peculiar post-coital practices. The shock, then, is redoubled, for not only do we see the diversity of cultures, but as Montaigne insinuates, we begin to worry that those beliefs and practices we think so decisive for human decency and moral rectitude will come to seem as silly and pointless as the ancient Roman expectation that men would pluck all the hairs off their chest, legs, and arms.

What Montaigne sought to achieve has become the very ideal of "critical thinking." He wants us to step back from our loyalty to the immediate and seemingly self-evident truths of our inherited way of life. He wants us to separate ourselves from our cultural context. To think responsibly about culture, morality, and religion, then, involves establishing critical distance. Just think about biblical criticism. In most cases, the basic strategy of instruction is to force pious students to step back from the immediacy of the canonical form of the text to see how what seems to be a doctrinally consistent and spiritually unified whole is, in fact, a text made up of heterogeneous sources and layers of editorial revision.

Or, more simply, consider the term "Hebrew Bible," which is now replacing "Old Testament." This terminological shift has many sources, including an anxiety about Christian supersessionism. However, among them is a pedagogical goal. We are not to engage these ancient writings as constituent elements of a unified witness to the crucified and risen Lord. Instead, we are to keep the prophetic power of the text at arm's length and allow the text to speak to us only as a witness to a now dead thing called "Ancient Israelite Religion." This pedagogical strategy distances us from living religious passions — passions that might overwhelm the cool judgment of the historical scholar in the present and that have no doubt led to religious violence in the past.

I do not wish to condemn the pedagogy of critical distance in toto. How can we undertake historical, social, and cultural inquiry without, in some way, breaking the magic charm of immediacy, without stepping back from our inherited context and preconceptions? Furthermore, in the Socratic tradition of Western thought, the leverage of objection and counterargument forces a moment of reflective hesitation that can heighten rather than diminish our ardor for the truth. My point, then, is not to criticize the critics. Rather, I want to draw attention to the spiritual consequences of critical distance, consequences that now prevail in spite of the best intentions of scholars and professors.

To learn that Muslims have many wives, that Hindus have many gods, and that Eskimos have many words for snow yields no insight other than the recognition of diversity. The effect is not to shift our loyalty from appearance to reality, as Plato portrayed the effect of the dialectic of Socrates. Nor does cultural study follow the pattern of modern science, where, for example, we move from the illusion of a moving sun that circles the earth to the accurate knowledge that the earth rotates on its axis. Quite the contrary. The now widespread effect of the modern critical project is to undermine our confidence that any moral or cultural system should properly command our full loyalty. For this reason, as John Henry Newman observed, critical thinking has "a tendency to blunt the practical energy of the mind. . . ." It loosens the bonds of commitment and distances us from the immediacy of truths we once thought unquestionable. Critical distance may free us from prejudice, but it can also undermine the hope that enduring truths might be found. It can engender a humility that sustains tolerance, but it can also so relax the passions of the intellect that our civility comes at the price of conviction.

The ways in which this leads to acedia are, I think, obvious. The very sentiments that the classical Christian authors feared are precisely the virtues modern educators seek to instill in their students. The *lento amore*, the slow love that Dante thinks must be purged from our souls, is the dispassionate heart that establishes critical distance and waits for compelling evidence. The *sterilitas animae* that so worries Bernard of Clairvaux describes quite well the ideal of a critical thinker who has purified himself of the corrupting parochialism that limits his larger, more universal vision. When someone prefaces a comment with the confession that he is speaking from a "white, male, upper-middle-class perspective," it reveals either a competition for the upper hand ("I am more critical than you are") or a despair of ever saying anything worthwhile.

*

Critical distance is not the only ideal of our time. We can never achieve an entirely carefree approach to life. Commitment energizes our culture even as critical inquiry encourages dispassionate analysis. Yet the very nobility of our commitments can create a distance that is as debilitating as critique. Since no actual society or movement lives up to that ideal, we can end up unengaged in fact and in action — pushing away evil rather than seeking the good. Controlled by what the old writers called *fastidium,* a fastidious conscience, we boil with outrage on the surface of our souls, while at a deeper level, we go slack. Thus, many so-called seekers do not seek at all; they wait for something worthy of their allegiance and the waiting becomes habitual and comfortable. Our society has far more of these "waiters" than "seekers."

This fastidiousness is evident in our cultural response to suffering, the second feature of our current intellectual and moral landscape that strikes me as emblematic. We recoil from cruelty, and this dominates our collective conscience as the *summum malum.* The taboos of traditional morality may evaporate as we cultivate critical distance, but no pure vacuum develops in their place. Instead, our sensitivity to suffering and our horror over cruelty increases. Just consider the case of my grandmother, who went to a public hanging at a county fair in Hannibal, Missouri, when she was a child. Today, we shudder at the thought. How, we ask ourselves, could our forebearers have been so insensitive to suffering and cruelty?

Once again, my point is not to criticize or support our present squeamishness. Most likely, we should be thankful that *something* of moral significance has filled the void created by critical consciousness. At least we cannot gaze upon torture and suffering with a dispassionate and carefree attitude. Nonetheless, we must recognize how contemporary moral sensibilities tempt us toward acedia. Our vague and general moral sentiments — "suffering is evil" — overwhelm our immediate duties and corrupt our ability to function within the complexities of ordinary moral relations. As Judith Shklar wrote, "To hate cruelty more than any other evil involves a radical rejection of both religious and political conventions. It dooms me to a life of skepticism, indecision, disgust, and often misanthropy."

Our misanthropy is swaddled in kindness, but it manifests the symptoms of acedia nonetheless. How many parents cannot muster the determination to discipline their children because they cannot bear inflicting the suffering it will require? How many educators have despaired of grading, not out of lassitude or neglect, but because they shrink from the thought of the hurt feelings of those who do poorly? The examples are but instances of a broad cultural trend. Demand and expectation are hurtful, and we turn away from zeal in order to soften the blows of discipline. Our general commitment to reduce suffering causes us to hesitate from inflicting the pain of shame. Thus, acedia, a languid disregard for moral and social standards, is now a virtue.

For this reason, I do not think our present culture of affirmation is based on an Emersonian conviction that each person is lit with genius. Rather, we hold our tongues and smile politely when people tell us of their divorces, abortions, infidelities, and transgressions because we do not want to make anyone feel bad. We indulge and we trim, because the thought of suffering paralyzes. Fixed on the horror of cruelty, the fastidious conscience is brought to inaction by the very passion of its commitment. Fearing evil — why add to the grief of divorce by condemning it? — we withdraw from action.

How can we bridge the distances demanded by critical thought? How can we overcome the fastidious conscience that cannot countenance the "no" of discipline? First, we need to guard against the tendency of modern theology to turn the afflictions of acedia into enticements toward virtue. Consider Paul Tillich's formulation of the "Protestant Principle." It is the negation of all positive, finite, and worldly forms of faith and practice. In this way, Tillich makes critical distance into a form of faith. "What makes Protestantism Protestant," he writes, "is the fact that it transcends its own religious and confessional character, that it cannot be identified wholly with any of its particular historical forms." The stepping back that marks critical thought is, then, the essence of true religion. "Protestantism," Tillich continues, "has a principle that stands beyond all its realizations." "It is not exhausted by any historical religion; it is not identical with the structure of the Reformation or of early Christianity or even with a religious form at all." Or still again, "The Protestant principle . . . contains the divine and human protest against any absolute claim made for a relative reality. . . ." Thus, Tillich draws a conclusion that is ubiquitous in modern progressive theologies: "Nobody can have the ultimate, nothing conditioned can possess the unconditional. And nobody can localize the divine that transcends space and time." Or to quote from a bumper sticker version of the same: my God is too big to fit into any one religion.

If Tillich's Protestant principle is true, then why in the world would anyone experience, let alone give in to, a burning desire to come to the Lord in baptism and worship? If nothing conditioned can possess the unconditioned, if the finite is not capable of the infinite, then who would not despair of the religious life? For you and I are finite, and being not capable of the infinite, we ought to just get on with our lives. Contrary to Tillich, we must stop pretending the distance and dispassion of modern intellectual life are covert forms of faithfulness. Critical thought may produce what St. Paul, in 2 Corinthians 7, calls worldly grief, the sorrow that any honest person must feel when he recognizes that sickness, disease, and death conquer finite flesh. But we must be crystal clear. Critical thought does not and cannot produce the godly grief that St. Paul commends. That comes from repentance and personal change, not critical insight.

This leads me to my second observation. In Dante's *Purgatorio,* the principle of sacramental penance holds sway. Vices are cured by their contrary, and thus the slow and tepid love of the slothful is purged by a frenzied fervor. So, in a picturesque scene, just as Dante and Virgil doze off on the ledge of *lento amore,* they are awakened by a crowd of penitents rushing by, shouting and weeping with overwrought passion. "Sharp fervor," says Virgil to those who run by, "makes up for negligence and delay which you perhaps used through lukewarmness in doing good." Here, we need to be careful not to moralize, for according to Dante, as for all premodern writers, the great work of charity is first and foremost the work of prayer. To the extent that we are brought to dispassion by critical thought, we must enter into the disciplines of daily prayer with all the greater fervor and commitment. The more we feel the torpor of critical distance, the more swiftly we must run toward the daily office, toward regular study of Scripture, toward the bread and the cup of the Eucharist. An intimacy with divine things is the proper way toward a passion for divine truth. We cannot enjoy that which we hold at a distance.

This insight also holds true for the intellectual life. Critical distance easily produces a *torpor animi.* But we must resist the temptation to forever look behind or above or below. At some point, we must train our minds on some aspect of study, whether Wordsworth's *Prelude* or a puzzling question in topology. We must allow ourselves to be romanced and ravished by the promise of truth. As St. Bonaventure observes in the prologue to the *Itinerarium mentis in Deum,* those who study must be "anointed with the oil of gladness" so that they might be inflamed with desire for wisdom. If we are to fight the noonday devil of acedia, then the *lento amore* of critical distance needs to be counteracted by forms of intellectual life that hasten toward an embrace of truth. Desire for truth needs to gain the upper hand over fear of error.

Evagrius Ponticus offers a different remedy for sloth. For him, the single great weapon against acedia is stability. This seems to contradict Dante's rushing throng, but it does not. The penitent are hurrying away from their negligence. Evagrius, however, is not concerned with how to restore the fallen, but how to prevent the monk from falling in the first place. He writes, "The time of temptation is not the time to leave one's cell, devising plausible pretexts. Rather, stand there firmly and be patient." When, a few centuries later, St. Benedict made stability the centerpiece of Western monasticism, he did so for the same reason. A great stratagem of the slothful is to hurry about from place to place to find a more congenial locale for their spiritual projects. The moment a postmodern seeker finds worship somewhat cold, off he goes to another church to try to find more "vitality," or even more likely, he logs onto Amazon.com and orders a book on Buddhist spirituality. We demand immediate results, and should we experience the dryness and tepidness that comes from distance and alienation, we respond by distancing ourselves still further.

This agitated search for something higher, something more transparent — "the pure gospel" — comes at a great cost. One can no more play games with separation and divorce in marriage and expect to enjoy the fruits of intimacy, than to do so in one's union with the body of Christ. One can no more serve Christ by loyalty to theological abstractions than serve human beings by loyalty to sentience. Only a focused love can overcome distance. After all, Dante's rushing crowds on the ledge of sloth are not going hither and yon. They are all going the same direction — toward Him in whom all will rest.

Knowing whether to follow Dante's advice and rush toward intimacy or to heed Evagrius and remain in stable loyalty cannot be reduced to a formula or principle. There are no intellectual solutions to spiritual problems. Like each of the seven deadly sins, acedia must be fought with spiritual discipline. Such discipline is profoundly alien to our culture, not because we have alternatives, but because we entertain the fantasy of life without spiritual demands. This fantasy is the most important legacy of modernity. For the great innovation of modern culture was the promise of progress without spiritual discipline. All we need to do is adopt the experimental method, calculate utility, institute the rule of law, establish democracy, trust the market. In each instance, scientific knowledge, the machinery of proper procedure, the invisible hand of a well-designed process, will carry us forward. If we will but believe in this promise, we are told, then we will be free to neglect our souls. For according to this modern dream, our virtues and vices are inconsequential matters of private taste and personal judgment. Thus, although our society is increasingly willing to use economic incentives and legal sanctions to influence behavior (welfare reform and laws against smoking are signal examples), we insist that all discipline must remain on the surfaces of life. Once economic and legal requirements are met, we insist upon our right to live as we wish.

This fantasy of life without spiritual demands demonstrates the depth of our captivity to acedia. Pride has no role here, for even when vicious, ambition shapes the soul. Our ideal, by contrast, is shapelessness. We want to be free . . . to be ourselves. Our ambition is a tautology empty of any will to shape or sharpen our lives. Even as we sculpt our bodies at the gym, we cultivate a languid spiritual disposition, one aptly described by Chaucer:

> *For ye be lyke the sweynte cate*
> *That wolde have fissh, but wostow what?*
> *He wolde nothing wete his clowes.*

In our sloth, we will not wet our feet in the frightening water of any spiritual discipline, Christian or otherwise. For fear of wounding

sensibilities, for fear of ethnocentric dogmatism, we abandon discipline, or we individualize discipline to the point that it is not discipline at all.

We must wet our claws. Neither Dante's urgent rush toward the
truth nor Evagrius's patient stability lead to an exhausted or desic-
cated existence. On the contrary, the spiritual disciplines they urge
serve the end of intimacy. Their strategies awaken and tether, ener-
gize and focus. They wish us to become persons with distinct outlines and deep purposes. Only as such persons can we be partners
in fellowship — with the truths we seek and with each other. One
can no more desire the blessings of marriage with indifference or a
wandering eye than seek a lasting truth with languid disregard or
lack of concentration. This holds true in our relation to God. We
must desire holiness to allow the burning coal to touch our lips,
and we must be attentive and focused to hear the still, small voice.
We should rush toward our Lord, for we can never become too intimate, and we should wait patiently with Him, for He always has
something more to give. To do so, we must place the pedagogy of
critical distance and the dictates of conscience within a larger vision of journey toward the truth, a journey in which the warm and
enduring embrace of love is to be cherished rather than mocked
or feared.

SARAH RUDEN

For the War Dead

FROM the *New Criterion*

Rapidly, darkly, all around,
The groves and fields are falling down.

We see it from the yard today:
The land, that's endless, ebbs away.

We did not dream this could be done.
Relentlessly we loved our son.

Take him along — we look to You.
What can be finished that You do?

It lies on stone — this woods, this hill.
It is as lasting as Your will.

But neither can this be undone:
The sear, our passion for our son.

OLIVER SACKS

The Mind's Eye:
What the Blind See

FROM *The New Yorker*

IN HIS LAST LETTER, Goethe wrote, "The Ancients said that the animals are taught through their organs; let me add to this, so are men, but they have the advantage of teaching their organs in return." He wrote this in 1832, a time when phrenology was at its height, and the brain was seen as a mosaic of "little organs" subserving everything from language to drawing ability to shyness. Each individual, it was believed, was given a fixed measure of this faculty or that, according to the luck of his birth. Though we no longer pay attention, as the phrenologists did, to the "bumps" on the head (each of which, supposedly, indicated a brain-mind organ beneath), neurology and neuroscience have stayed close to the idea of brain fixity and localization — the notion, in particular, that the highest part of the brain, the cerebral cortex, is effectively programmed from birth: this part to vision and visual processing, that part to hearing, that to touch, and so on.

This would seem to allow individuals little power of choice, of self-determination, let alone of adaptation, in the event of a neurological or perceptual mishap.

But to what extent are we — our experiences, our reactions — shaped, predetermined, by our brains, and to what extent do we shape our own brains? Does the mind run the brain or the brain the mind — or, rather, to what extent does one run the other? To what extent are we the authors, the creators, of our own experiences? The effects of a profound perceptual deprivation such as blindness can cast an unexpected light on this. To become blind, especially later in life, presents one with a huge, potentially overwhelming challenge: to find a new way of living, of ordering one's world, when the old way has been destroyed.

A dozen years ago, I was sent an extraordinary book called *Touching the Rock: An Experience of Blindness*. The author, John Hull, was a professor of religious education who had grown up in Australia and then moved to England. Hull had developed cataracts at the age of thirteen, and became completely blind in his left eye four years later. Vision in his right eye remained reasonable until he was thirty-five or so, and then started to deteriorate. There followed a decade of steadily failing vision, in which Hull needed stronger and stronger magnifying glasses, and had to write with thicker and thicker pens, until, in 1983, at the age of forty-eight, he became completely blind.

Touching the Rock is the journal he dictated in the three years that followed. It is full of piercing insights relating to Hull's life as a blind person, but most striking for me is Hull's description of how, in the years after his loss of sight, he experienced a gradual attenuation of visual imagery and memory, and finally a virtual extinction of them (except in dreams) — a state that he calls "deep blindness."

By this, Hull meant not only the loss of visual images and memories but a loss of the very idea of seeing, so that concepts like "here," "there," and "facing" seemed to lose meaning for him, and even the sense of objects having "appearances," visible characteristics, vanished. At this point, for example, he could no longer imagine how the numeral 3 looked, unless he traced it in the air with his hand. He could construct a "motor" image of a 3, but not a visual one.

Hull, though at first greatly distressed about the fading of visual memories and images — the fact that he could no longer conjure up the faces of his wife or children, or of familiar and loved landscapes and places — then came to accept it with remarkable equanimity; indeed, to regard it as a natural response to a nonvisual world. He seemed to regard this loss of visual imagery as a prerequisite for the full development, the heightening, of his other senses.

Two years after becoming completely blind, Hull had apparently become so nonvisual as to resemble someone who had been blind from birth. Hull's loss of visuality also reminded me of the sort of "cortical blindness" that can happen if the primary visual cortex is damaged, through a stroke or traumatic brain damage — although in Hull's case there was no direct damage to the visual cortex but, rather, a cutting off from any visual stimulation or input.

In a profoundly religious way, and in language sometimes reminiscent of that of St. John of the Cross, Hull enters into this state, surrenders himself, with a sort of acquiescence and joy. And such "deep" blindness he conceives as "an authentic and autonomous world, a place of its own. . . . Being a whole-body seer is to be in one of the concentrated human conditions."

Being a "whole-body seer," for Hull, means shifting his attention, his center of gravity, to the other senses, and he writes again and again of how these have assumed a new richness and power. Thus he speaks of how the sound of rain, never before accorded much attention, can now delineate a whole landscape for him, for its sound on the garden path is different from its sound as it drums on the lawn, or on the bushes in his garden, or on the fence dividing it from the road. "Rain," he writes, "has a way of bringing out the contours of everything; it throws a coloured blanket over previously invisible things; instead of an intermittent and thus fragmented world, the steadily falling rain creates continuity of acoustic experience . . . presents the fullness of an entire situation all at once . . . gives a sense of perspective and of the actual relationships of one part of the world to another."

With his new intensity of auditory experience (or attention), along with the sharpening of his other senses, Hull comes to feel a sense of intimacy with nature, an intensity of being-in-the-world, beyond anything he knew when he was sighted. Blindness now becomes for him "a dark, paradoxical gift." This is not just "compensation," he emphasizes, but a whole new order, a new mode of human being. With this he extricates himself from visual nostalgia, from the strain, or falsity, of trying to pass as "normal," and finds a new focus, a new freedom. His teaching at the university expands, becomes more fluent, his writing becomes stronger and deeper; he becomes intellectually and spiritually bolder, more confident. He feels he is on solid ground at last.

What Hull described seemed to me an astounding example of how an individual deprived of one form of perception could totally reshape himself to a new center, a new identity.

It is said that those who see normally as infants but then become blind within the first two years of life retain no memories of seeing, have no visual imagery and no visual elements in their dreams (and, in this way, are comparable to those born blind). It is similar with those who lose hearing before the age of two: they have no sense of having "lost" the world of sound, nor any sense of "silence," as hearing people sometimes imagine. For those who lose sight so early, the very concepts of "sight" or "blindness" soon cease to have meaning, and there is no sense of losing the world of vision, only of living fully in a world constructed by the other senses.

But it seemed extraordinary to me that such an annihilation of visual memory as Hull describes could happen equally to an adult, with decades, an entire lifetime, of rich and richly categorized visual experience to call upon. And yet I could not doubt the authenticity of Hull's account, which he relates with the most scrupulous care and lucidity.

Important studies of adaptation in the brain were begun in the 1970s by, among others, Helen Neville, a cognitive neuroscientist now working in Oregon. She showed that in prelingually deaf people (that is, those who had been born deaf or become deaf before the age of two or so) the auditory parts of the brain had not degenerated or atrophied. These had remained active and functional, but with an activity and a function that were new: they had been transformed, "reallocated," in Neville's term, for processing visual language. Comparable studies in those born blind, or early blinded, show that the visual areas of the cortex, similarly, may be reallocated in function, and used to process sound and touch.

With the reallocation of the visual cortex to touch and other senses, these can take on a hyperacuity that perhaps no sighted person can imagine. Bernard Morin, the blind mathematician who in the 1960s had shown how a sphere could be turned inside out, felt that his achievement required a special sort of spatial perception and imagination. And a similar sort of spatial giftedness has been central to the work of Geerat Vermeij, a blind biologist who has been able to delineate many new species of mollusk based on tiny variations in the shapes and contours of their shells.

Faced with such findings and reports, neurologists began to concede that there might be a certain flexibility or plasticity in the brain, at least in the early years of life. But when this critical period was over, it was assumed, the brain became inflexible, and no further changes of a radical type could occur. The experiences that Hull so carefully recounts give the lie to this. It is clear that his perceptions, his brain, did finally change, in a fundamental way. Indeed, Alvaro Pascual-Leone and his colleagues in Boston have recently shown that, even in adult, sighted volunteers, as little as five days of being blindfolded produces marked shifts to nonvisual forms of behavior and cognition, and they have demonstrated the physiological changes in the brain that go along with this. And only last month, Italian researchers published a study showing that sighted volunteers kept in the dark for as little as ninety *minutes* may show a striking enhancement of tactile-spatial sensitivity.

The brain, clearly, is capable of changing even in adulthood, and I assumed that Hull's experience was typical of acquired blindness — the response, sooner or later, of everyone who becomes blind, even in adult life.

So when I came to publish an essay on Hull's book in 1991, I was taken aback to receive a number of letters from blind people, letters that were often somewhat puzzled, and occasionally indignant, in tone. Many of my correspondents, it seemed, could not identify with Hull's experience, and said that they themselves, even decades after losing their sight, had never lost their visual images or memories. One correspondent, who had lost her sight at fifteen, wrote, "Even though I am totally blind . . . I consider myself a very visual person. I still 'see' objects in front of me. As I am typing now I can see my hands on the keyboard. . . . I don't feel comfortable in a new environment until I have a mental picture of its appearance. I need a mental map for my independent moving, too."

Had I been wrong, or at least one-sided, in accepting Hull's experience as a typical response to blindness? Had I been guilty of emphasizing one mode of response too strongly, oblivious to the possibilities of radically different responses?

This feeling came to a head in 1996, when I received a letter from an Australian psychologist named Zoltan Torey. Torey wrote to me not about blindness but about a book he had written on the brain-mind problem and the nature of consciousness. (The book was published by Oxford University Press as *The Crucible of Consciousness* in 1999.) In his letter Torey also spoke of how he had been blinded in an accident at the age of twenty-one while working at a chemical factory, and how, although "advised to switch from a visual to an auditory mode of adjustment," he had moved in the opposite direction and resolved to develop instead his "inner eye," his powers of visual imagery, to their greatest possible extent.

In this, it seemed, he had been extremely successful, developing a remarkable power of generating, holding, and manipulating images in his mind, so much so that he had been able to construct an imagined visual world that seemed almost as real and intense to him as the perceptual one he had lost — and, indeed, sometimes more real, more intense, a sort of controlled dream or hallucination. This imagery, moreover, enabled him to do things that might have seemed scarcely possible for a blind man. "I replaced the entire roof guttering of my multi-gabled home single-handed," he wrote, "and solely on the strength of the accurate and well-focused manipulation of my now totally pliable and responsive mental space." (Torey later expanded on this episode, mentioning the great alarm of his neighbors at seeing a blind man, alone, on the roof of his house — and, even more terrifying to them, at night, in pitch darkness.)

And it enabled him to think in ways that had not been available to him before, to envisage solutions, models, designs, to project himself to the inside of machines and other systems, and, finally, to grasp by visual thought and simulation (complemented by all the data of neuroscience) the complexities of that ultimate system, the human brain-mind.

When I wrote back to Torey, I suggested that he consider writing another book, a more personal one, exploring how his life had been affected by blindness and how he had responded to this in the most improbable and seemingly paradoxical of ways. *Out of Darkness* is the memoir he has now written, and in it Torey describes his early memories with great visual intensity and humor. Scenes are remembered or reconstructed in brief, poetic glimpses of his childhood and youth in Hungary before the Second World War: the sky-blue buses of Budapest, the egg-yellow trams, the lighting of gas lamps, the funicular on the Buda side. He describes a carefree and privileged youth, roaming with his father in the wooded mountains above the Danube, playing games and pranks at school, growing up in a highly intellectual environment of writers, actors, professionals of every sort. Torey's father was the head of a large motion-picture studio and would often give his son scripts to read. "This," Torey writes, "gave me the opportunity to visualize stories, plots and characters, to work my imagination — a skill that was to become a lifeline and source of strength in the years ahead."

All of this came to a brutal end with the Nazi occupation, the siege of Buda, and then the Soviet occupation. Torey, now an adolescent, found himself passionately drawn to the big questions — the mystery of the universe, of life, and above all the mystery of consciousness, of the mind. In 1948, nineteen years old and feeling that he needed to immerse himself in biology, engineering, neuroscience, and psychology, but knowing that there was no chance of study, of an intellectual life, in Soviet Hungary, Torey made his escape and eventually found his way to Australia, where, penniless and without connections, he did various manual jobs. In June 1951, loosening the plug in a vat of acid at the chemical factory where he worked, he had the accident that bisected his life.

"The last thing I saw with complete clarity was a glint of light in the flood of acid that was to engulf my face and change my life. It was a nanosecond of sparkle, framed by the black circle of the drumface less than a foot away. This as the final scene, the slender thread that ties me to my visual past."

When it became clear that his corneas had been hopelessly damaged and that he would have to live his life as a blind man, he was advised to rebuild his representation of the world on the basis of hearing and touch and to "forget about sight and visualizing altogether." But this was something that Torey could not or would not do. He had emphasized, in his first letter to me, the importance of a most critical choice at this juncture: "I immediately resolved to find out how far a partially sense-deprived brain could go to rebuild a life." Put this way, it sounds abstract, like an experiment. But in his book one senses the tremendous feelings underlying his resolution — the horror of darkness, "the empty darkness," as Torey often calls it, "the grey fog that was engulfing me," and the passionate desire to hold on to light and sight, to maintain, if only in memory and imagination, a vivid and living visual world. The very title of his book says all this, and the note of defiance is sounded from the start.

Hull, who did not use his potential for imagery in a deliberate way, lost it in two or three years and became unable to remember which way round a 3 went; Torey, on the other hand, soon became able to multiply four-figure numbers by each other, as on a blackboard, visualizing the whole operation in his mind, "painting" the suboperations in different colors.

Well aware that the imagination (or the brain), unrestrained by the usual perceptual input, may run away with itself in a wildly associative or self-serving way — as may happen in deliria, hallucinations, or dreams — Torey maintained a cautious and "scientific" attitude to his own visual imagery, taking pains to check the accuracy of his images by every means available. "I learned," he writes, "to hold the image in a tentative way, conferring credibility and status on it only when some information would tip the balance in its favor." Indeed, he soon gained enough confidence in the reliability of his visual imagery to stake his life upon it, as when he undertook roof repairs by himself. And this confidence extended to other, purely mental projects. He became able "to imagine, to visualize, for example, the inside of a differential gearbox in action as if from inside its casing. I was able to watch the cogs bite, lock and revolve, distributing the spin as required. I began to play around with this internal view in connection with mechanical and technical problems, visualizing how subcomponents relate in the atom, or in the living cell." This power of imagery was crucial, Torey thought, in enabling him to arrive at a solution of the brain-mind problem by visualizing the brain "as a perpetual juggling act of interacting routines."

In a famous study of creativity, the French mathematician Jacques Hadamard asked many scientists and mathematicians, including Einstein, about their thought processes. Einstein replied, "The physical entities which seem to serve as elements in thought are . . . more or less clear images which can be 'voluntarily' reproduced and combined. [Some are] of visual and some of muscular type. Conventional words or other signs have to be sought for laboriously only in a secondary stage." Torey cites this and adds, "Nor was Einstein unique in this respect. Hadamard found that almost all scientists work this way, and this was also the way my project evolved."

*

Soon after receiving Torey's manuscript, I received the proofs of
yet another memoir by a blind person: Sabriye Tenberken's *My
Path Leads to Tibet*. While Hull and Torey are thinkers, preoccupied
in their different ways by inwardness, states of brain and mind,
Tenberken is a doer; she has travelled, often alone, all over Tibet,
where for centuries blind people have been treated as less than human and denied education, work, respect, or a role in the community. Virtually single-handed, Tenberken has transformed their situation over the past half-dozen years, devising a form of Tibetan
Braille, establishing schools for the blind, and integrating the graduates of these schools into their communities.

Tenberken herself had impaired vision almost from birth but
was able to make out faces and landscapes until she was twelve. As a
child in Germany, she had a particular predilection for colors and
loved painting, and when she was no longer able to decipher
shapes and forms, she could still use colors to identify objects.
Tenberken has, indeed, an intense synesthesia. "As far back as I can
remember," she writes, "numbers and words have instantly trig-
gered colors in me. . . . The number 4, for example, [is] gold. 5 is
light green. 9 is vermillion. . . . Days of the week as well as months
have their colors, too. I have them arranged in geometrical forma-
tions, in circular sectors, a little like a pie. When I need to recall on
which day a particular event happened, the first thing that pops up
on my inner screen is the day's color, then its position in the pie."
Her synesthesia has persisted and been intensified, it seems, by her
blindness.

Though she has been totally blind for twenty years now, Tenberken continues to use all her other senses, along with verbal descriptions, visual memories, and a strong pictorial and synesthetic sensibility, to construct "pictures" of landscapes and rooms,
of environments and scenes — pictures so lively and detailed as
to astonish her listeners. These images may sometimes be wildly
or comically different from reality, as she relates in one incident
when she and a companion drove to Nam Co, the great salt lake
in Tibet. Turning eagerly toward the lake, Tenberken saw in her
mind's eye "a beach of crystallized salt shimmering like snow under an evening sun, at the edge of a vast body of turquoise water. . . . And down below, on the deep green mountain flanks, a few
nomads were watching their yaks grazing." But it then turns out

that she has been facing in the wrong direction, not "looking" at the lake at all, and that she has been "staring" at rocks and a gray landscape. These disparities don't faze her in the least — she is happy to have so vivid a visual imagination. Hers is essentially an artistic imagination, which can be impressionistic, romantic, not veridical at all, where Torey's imagination is that of an engineer and has to be factual, accurate down to the last detail.

I had now read three memoirs, strikingly different in their depictions of the visual experience of blinded people: Hull, with his acquiescent descent into imageless "deep blindness;" Torey, with his "compulsive visualization" and meticulous construction of an internal visual world; and Tenberken, with her impulsive, almost novelistic, visual freedom, along with her remarkable and specific gift of synesthesia. Was there any such thing, I now wondered, as a "typical" blind experience?

I recently met two other people blinded in adult life who shared their experiences with me.

Dennis Shulman, a clinical psychologist and psychoanalyst who lectures on Biblical topics, is an affable, stocky, bearded man in his fifties who gradually lost his sight in his teens, becoming completely blind by the time he entered college. He immediately confirmed that his experience was unlike Hull's: "I still live in a visual world after thirty-five years of blindness. I have very vivid visual memories and images. My wife, whom I have never seen — I think of her visually. My kids, too. I see myself visually — but it is as I last saw myself, when I was thirteen, though I try hard to update the image. I often give public lectures, and my notes are in Braille; but when I go over them in my mind, I see the Braille notes visually — they are visual images, not tactile."

Arlene Gordon, a charming woman in her seventies, a former social worker, said that things were very similar for her: "If I move my arms back and forth in front of my eyes, I see them, even though I have been blind for more than thirty years." It seemed that moving her arms was immediately translated for her into a visual image. Listening to talking books, she added, made her eyes tire if she listened too long; she seemed to herself to be reading at such times, the sound of the spoken words being transformed to lines of print on a vividly visualized book in front of her. This involved a sort of cognitive exertion (similar perhaps to translating one language into another), and sooner or later this would give her an eye ache.

I was reminded of Amy, a colleague who had been deafened by scarlet fever at the age of nine but who was so adept a lipreader that I often forgot she was deaf. Once, when I absent-mindedly turned away from her as I was speaking, she said sharply, "I can no longer hear you."

"You mean you can no longer see me," I said.

"*You* may call it seeing," she answered, "but I experience it as hearing."

Amy, though totally deaf, still constructed the sound of speech in her mind. Both Dennis and Arlene, similarly, spoke not only of a heightening of visual imagery and imagination since losing their eyesight, but also of what seemed to be a much readier transference of information from verbal description — or from their own sense of touch, movement, hearing, or smell — into a visual form. On the whole, their experiences seemed quite similar to Torey's, even though they had not systematically exercised their powers of visual imagery in the way that he had, or consciously tried to make an entire virtual world of sight.

There is increasing evidence from neuroscience for the extraordinarily rich interconnectedness and interactions of the sensory areas of the brain, and the difficulty, therefore, of saying that anything is purely visual or purely auditory, or purely anything. This is evident in the very titles of some recent papers — Pascual-Leone and his colleagues at Harvard now write of "The Metamodal Organization of the Brain," and Shinsuke Shimojo and his group at Caltech, who are also exploring intersensory perceptual phenomena, recently published a paper called "What You See Is What You Hear" and stress that sensory modalities can never be considered in isolation. The world of the blind, of the blinded, it seems, can be especially rich in such in-between states — the intersensory, the metamodal — states for which we have no common language.

Arlene, like Dennis, still identifies herself in many ways as a visual person. "I have a very strong sense of color," she said. "I pick out my own clothes. I think, Oh, that will go with this or that, once I have been told the colors." Indeed, she was dressed very smartly and took obvious pride in her appearance.

"I love travelling," she continued. "I 'saw' Venice when I was there." She explained how her travelling companions would describe places, and she would then construct a visual image from these details, her reading, and her own visual memories. "Sighted people enjoy travelling with me," she said. "I ask them questions, then they look and see things they wouldn't otherwise. Too often people with sight don't see anything! It's a reciprocal process — we enrich each other's worlds."

If we are sighted, we build our own images, using our eyes, our visual information, so instantly and seamlessly that it seems to us we are experiencing "reality" itself. One may need to see people who are color-blind or motion-blind, those who have lost certain visual capacities from cerebral injury, to realize the enormous act of analysis and synthesis, the dozens of subsystems involved in the subjectively simple act of seeing. But can a visual image be built using *nonvisual* information — information conveyed by the other senses, by memory, or by verbal description?

There have, of course, been many blind poets and writers, from Homer on. Most of these were born with normal vision and lost their sight in boyhood or adulthood (like Milton). I loved reading Prescott's *Conquest of Mexico* and *Conquest of Peru* as a boy and feel that I first saw these lands through his intensely visual, almost hallucinogenic descriptions, and I was amazed to discover, years later, that Prescott not only had never visited Mexico or Peru, but had been virtually blind since the age of eighteen. Did he, like Torey, compensate for his blindness by developing such powers of visual imagery that he could experience a "virtual reality" of sight? Or were his brilliant visual descriptions in a sense simulated, made possible by the evocative and pictorial powers of language? To what extent can language, a picturing in words, provide a substitute for actual seeing and for the visual, pictorial imagination? Blind children, it has often been noted, tend to be precocious verbally, and may develop such fluency in the verbal description of faces and places as to leave others (and perhaps themselves) uncertain as to whether they are actually blind. Helen Keller's writing, to give a famous example, startles one with its brilliantly visual quality.

When I asked Dennis and Arlene whether they had read John Hull's book, Arlene said, "I was stunned when I read it. His experiences are so unlike mine." Perhaps, she added, Hull had "renounced" his inner vision. Dennis agreed, but said, "We are only two individuals. You are going to have to talk to dozens of people. . . . But in the meanwhile you should read Jacques Lusseyran's memoir."

Lusseyran was a French Resistance fighter whose memoir, *And There Was Light,* deals mostly with his experiences fighting the Nazis and later with the time he spent in Buchenwald, but includes many beautiful descriptions of his early adaptations to blindness. He was blinded in an accident when he was not quite eight years old, an age that he came to feel was "ideal" for such an eventuality, for, while he already had a rich visual experience to call on, "the habits of a boy of eight are not yet formed, either in body or in mind. His body is infinitely supple." And suppleness, agility, indeed came to characterize his response to blindness.

Many of his initial responses were of loss, both of imagery and of interests:

> A very short time after I went blind I forgot the faces of my mother and father and the faces of most of the people I loved. . . . I stopped caring whether people were dark or fair, with blue eyes or green. I felt that sighted people spent too much time observing these empty things. . . . I no longer even thought about them. People no longer seemed to possess them. Sometimes in my mind men and women appeared without heads or fingers.

This is similar to Hull, who writes, "Increasingly, I am no longer even trying to imagine what people look like. . . . I am finding it more and more difficult to realize that people look like anything, to put any meaning into the idea that they have an appearance."

But then, while relinquishing the actual visual world and many of its values and categories, Lusseyran starts to construct and to use an imaginary visual world more like Torey's.

This started as a sensation of light, a formless, flooding, streaming radiance. Neurological terms are bound to sound reductive in this almost mystical context. Yet one might venture to interpret this as a "release" phenomenon, a spontaneous, almost eruptive arousal of the visual cortex, now deprived of its normal visual input. This is a phenomenon analogous, perhaps, to tinnitus or phantom limbs, though endowed here, by a devout and precociously imaginative little boy, with some element of the supernal. But then, it becomes clear, he does find himself in possession of great powers of visual imagery and not just a formless luminosity.

The visual cortex, the inner eye, having now been activated, Lusseyran's mind constructed a "screen" upon which whatever he thought or desired was projected and, if need be, manipulated, as on a computer screen. "This screen was not like a blackboard, rectangular or square, which so quickly reaches the edge of its frame," he writes. "My screen was always as big as I needed it to be. Because it was nowhere in space, it was everywhere at the same time. . . . Names, figures, and objects in general did not appear on my screen without shape, nor just in black and white, but in all the colors of the rainbow. Nothing entered my mind without being bathed in a certain amount of light. . . . In a few months my personal world had turned into a painter's studio."

Great powers of visualization were crucial to the young Lusseyran, even in something as nonvisual (one would think) as learning Braille (he visualizes the Braille dots, as Dennis does), and in his brilliant successes at school. They were no less crucial in the real, outside world. He describes walks with his sighted friend Jean and how, as they were climbing together up the side of a hill above the Seine Valley, he could say:

> "Just look! This time we're on top. . . . You'll see the whole bend of the river, unless the sun gets in your eyes!" Jean was startled, opened his eyes wide and cried: "You're right." This little scene was often repeated between us, in a thousand forms.

"Every time someone mentioned an event," Lusseyran relates, "the event immediately projected itself in its place on the screen, which was a kind of inner canvas. . . . Comparing my world with his, [Jean] found that his held fewer pictures and not nearly as many colors. This made him almost angry. 'When it comes to that,' he used to say, 'which one of us two is blind?'"

It was his supernormal powers of visualization and visual manipulation — visualizing people's position and movement, the topography of any space, visualizing strategies for defense and attack — coupled with his charismatic personality (and seemingly infallible "nose" or "ear" for detecting falsehood, possible traitors), which later made Lusseyran an icon in the French Resistance.

Dennis, earlier, had spoken of how the heightening of his other senses had increased his sensitivity to moods in other people and to the most delicate nuances in their speech and self-presentation. He could now recognize many of his patients by smell, he said, and he could often pick up states of tension or anxiety which they might not even be aware of. He felt that he had become far more sensitive to others' emotional states since losing his sight, for he was no longer taken in by visual appearances, which most people learn to camouflage. Voices and smells, by contrast, he felt, could reveal people's depths. He had come to think of most sighted people, he joked, as "visually dependent."

In a subsequent essay, Lusseyran inveighs against the "despotism," the "idol worship," of sight, and sees the "task" of blindness as reminding us of our other, deeper modes of perception and their mutuality. "A blind person has a better sense of feeling, of taste, of touch," he writes, and speaks of these as "the gifts of the blind." And all of these, Lusseyran feels, blend into a single, fundamental sense, a deep attentiveness, a slow, almost prehensile attention, a sensuous, intimate being at one with the world which sight, with its quick, flicking, facile quality, continually distracts us from. This is very close to Hull's concept of "deep blindness" as infinitely more than mere compensation but a unique form of perception, a precious and special mode of being.

What happens when the visual cortex is no longer limited, or constrained, by any visual input? The simple answer is that, isolated from the outside, the visual cortex becomes hypersensitive to internal stimuli of all sorts: its own autonomous activity; signals from other brain areas — auditory, tactile, and verbal areas; and the thoughts and emotions of the blinded individual. Sometimes, as sight deteriorates, hallucinations occur — of geometrical patterns, or occasionally of silent, moving figures or scenes that appear and disappear spontaneously, without any relation to the contents of consciousness or intention or context.

Something perhaps akin to this is described by Hull as occurring almost convulsively as he was losing the last of his sight. "About a year after I was registered blind," he writes, "I began to have such strong images of what people's faces looked like that they were almost like hallucinations."

These imperious images were so engrossing as to preempt consciousness: "Sometimes," Hull adds, "I would become so absorbed in gazing upon these images, which seemed to come and go without any intention on my part, that I would entirely lose the thread of what was being said to me. I would come back with a shock . . . and I would feel as if I had dropped off to sleep for a few minutes in front of the wireless." Though related to the context of speaking with people, these visions came and went in their own way, without any reference to his intentions, conjured up not by him but by his brain.

The fact that Hull is the only one of the four authors to describe this sort of release phenomenon is perhaps an indication that his visual cortex was starting to escape from his control. One has to wonder whether this signalled its impending demise, at least as an organ of useful visual imagery and memory. Why this should have occurred with him, and how common such a course is, is something one can only speculate on.

Torey, unlike Hull, clearly played a very active role in building up his visual imagery, took control of it the moment the bandages were taken off, and never apparently experienced, or allowed, the sort of involuntary imagery Hull describes. Perhaps this was because he was already very much at home with visual imagery and used to manipulating it in his own way. We know that Torey was quite visually inclined before his accident and skilled from boyhood in creating visual narratives based on the film scripts his father gave him. We have no such information about Hull, for his journal entries start only when he has become blind.

For Lusseyran and Tenberken, there is an added physiological factor: both were attracted to painting, in love with colors, and strongly synesthetic — prone to visualizing numbers, letters, words, music, etc. as shapes and colors — before becoming blind. They already had an overconnectedness, a "cross talk," between the visual cortex and other parts of the brain primarily concerned with language, sound, and music. Given such a neurological situation (synesthesia is congenital, often familial), the persistence of visual imagery and synesthesia, or its heightening, might be almost inevitable in the event of blindness.

Torey required months of intense cognitive discipline dedicated to improving his visual imagery, making it more tenacious, more stable, more malleable, whereas Lusseyran seemed to do this almost effortlessly from the start. Perhaps this was aided by the fact that Lusseyran was not yet eight when blinded (while Torey was twenty-one), and his brain was, accordingly, more plastic, more able to adapt to a new and drastic contingency.

But adaptability does not end with youth. It is clear that Arlene, becoming blind in her forties, was able to adapt in quite radical ways, too, developing not exactly synesthesia but something more flexible and useful: the ability to "see" her hands moving before her, to "see" the words of books read to her, to construct detailed visual images from verbal descriptions. Did she adapt, or did her brain do so? One has a sense that Torey's adaptation was largely shaped by conscious motive, will, and purpose; that Lusseyran's was shaped by overwhelming physiological disposition; and that Arlene's lies somewhere in between. Hull's, meanwhile, remains enigmatic.

There has been much recent work on the neural bases of visual imagery — this can be investigated by brain imaging of various types (PET scanning, functional MRIs, etc.) — and it is now generally accepted that visual imagery activates the cortex in a similar way, and with almost the same intensity, as visual perception itself. And yet studies on the effects of blindness on the human cortex have shown that functional changes may start to occur in a few days and can become profound as the days stretch into months or years.

Torey, who is well aware of all this research, attributes Hull's loss of visual imagery and memory to the fact that he did not struggle to maintain it, to heighten and systematize and use it, as Torey himself did. (Indeed, Torey expresses horror at what he regards as Hull's passivity, at his letting himself slide into deep blindness.) Perhaps Torey was able to stave off an otherwise inevitable loss of neuronal function in the visual cortex; but perhaps, again, such neural degeneration is quite variable, irrespective of whether or not there is conscious visualization. And, of course, Hull had been losing vision gradually for many years, whereas for Torey blindness was instantaneous and total. It would be of great interest to know the results of brain imaging in the two men, and indeed to look at a large number of people with acquired blindness, to see what correlations, what predictions could be made.

*

But what if their differences reflect an underlying predisposition independent of blindness? What of visual imagery in the sighted?

I first became conscious that there could be huge variations in visual imagery and visual memory when I was fourteen or so. My mother was a surgeon and comparative anatomist, and I had brought her a lizard's skeleton from school. She gazed at this intently for a minute, turning it round in her hands, then put it down and without looking at it again did a number of drawings of it, rotating it mentally by thirty degrees each time, so that she produced a series, the last drawing exactly the same as the first. I could not imagine how she had done this, and when she said that she could "see" the skeleton in her mind just as clearly and vividly as if she were looking at it, and that she simply rotated the image through a twelfth of a circle each time, I felt bewildered, and very stupid. I could hardly see anything with my mind's eye — at most, faint, evanescent images over which I had no control.

I did have vivid images as I was falling asleep, and in dreams, and once when I had a high fever — but otherwise I saw nothing, or almost nothing, when I tried to visualize, and had great difficulty picturing anybody or anything. Coincidentally or not, I could not draw for toffee.

My mother had hoped I would follow in her footsteps and become a surgeon, but when she realized how lacking in visual powers I was (and how clumsy, lacking in mechanical skill, too), she resigned herself to the idea that I would have to specialize in something else.

I was, however, to get a vivid idea of what mental imagery could be like when, during the 1960s, I had a period of experimenting with large doses of amphetamines. These can produce striking perceptual changes, including dramatic enhancements of visual imagery and memory (as well as heightenings of the other senses, as I describe in "The Dog Beneath the Skin," a story in *The Man Who Mistook His Wife for a Hat*). For a period of two weeks or so, I found that I could do the most accurate anatomical drawings. I had only to look at a picture or an anatomical specimen, and its image would remain both vivid and stable, and I could easily hold it in my mind for hours. I could mentally project the image onto the paper before me — it was as clear and distinct as if projected by a camera lucida — and trace its outlines with a pencil. My drawings were not elegant, but they were, everyone agreed, very detailed and accurate and could bear comparison with some of the drawings in our neuroanatomy textbook. This heightening of imagery attached to everything — I had only to think of a face, a place, a picture, a paragraph in a book to see it vividly in my mind. But when the amphetamine-induced state faded, after a couple of weeks I could no longer visualize, no longer project images, no longer draw — nor have I been able to do so in the decades since.

A few months ago, at a medical conference in Boston, I spoke of Torey's and Hull's experiences of blindness, and of how "enabled" Torey seemed to be by the powers of visualization he had developed, and how "disabled" Hull was — in some ways, at least — by the loss of his powers of visual imagery and memory. After my talk, a man in the audience came up to me and asked how well, in my estimation, *sighted* people could function if they had no visual imagery. He went on to say that he had no visual imagery whatever, at least none that he could deliberately evoke, and that no one in his family had any, either. Indeed, he had assumed this was the case with everyone until he came to participate in some psychological tests at Harvard and realized that he apparently lacked a mental power that all the other students, in varying degrees, had.

"And what do you do?" I asked him, wondering what this poor man *could* do.

"I am a surgeon," he replied. "A vascular surgeon. An anatomist, too. And I design solar panels."

But how, I asked him, did he recognize what he was seeing?

"It's not a problem," he answered. "I guess there must be representations or models in the brain that get matched up with what I am seeing and doing. But they are not conscious. I cannot evoke them."

This seemed to be at odds with my mother's experience — she, clearly, did have extremely vivid and readily manipulable visual imagery, though (it now seemed) this may have been a bonus, a luxury, and not a prerequisite for her career as a surgeon.

Is this also the case with Torey? Is his greatly developed visual imagery, though clearly a source of much pleasure, not as indispensable as he takes it to be? Might he, in fact, have done everything he did, from carpentry to roof repair to making a model of the mind, without any conscious imagery at all? He himself raises this question.

The role of mental imagery in thinking was explored by Francis Galton, Darwin's irrepressible cousin, who wrote on subjects as various as fingerprints, eugenics, dog whistles, criminality, twins, visionaries, psychometric measures, and hereditary genius. His inquiry into visual imagery took the form of a questionnaire, with such questions as "Can you recall with distinctness the features of all near relations and many other persons? Can you at will cause your mental image . . . to sit, stand, or turn slowly around? Can you . . . see it with enough distinctness to enable you to sketch it leisurely (supposing yourself able to draw)?" The vascular surgeon would have been hopeless on such tests — indeed, it was questions such as these which had floored him when he was a student at Harvard. And yet, finally, how much had it mattered?

As to the significance of such imagery, Galton is ambiguous and guarded. He suggests, in one breath, that "scientific men, as a class, have feeble powers of visual representation" and, in another, that "a vivid visualizing faculty is of much importance in connection with the higher processes of generalized thoughts." He feels that "it is undoubtedly the fact that mechanicians, engineers and architects usually possess the faculty of seeing mental images with remarkable clearness and precision," but goes on to say, "I am, however, bound to say, that the missing faculty seems to be replaced so serviceably by other modes of conception . . . that men who declare themselves entirely deficient in the power of seeing mental pictures can nevertheless give lifelike descriptions of what they have seen, and can otherwise express themselves as if they were gifted with a vivid visual imagination. They can also become painters of the rank of Royal Academicians." I have a cousin, a professional architect, who maintains that he cannot visualize anything whatever. "How do you think?" I once asked him. He shook his head and said, "I don't know." Do any of us, finally, know how we think?

When I talk to people, blind or sighted, or when I try to think of my own internal representations, I find myself uncertain whether words, symbols, and images of various types are the primary tools of thought or whether there are forms of thought antecedent to all of these, forms of thought essentially amodal. Psychologists have sometimes spoken of "interlingua" or "mentalese," which they conceive to be the brain's own language, and Lev Vygotsky, the great Russian psychologist, used to speak of "thinking in pure meanings." I cannot decide whether this is nonsense or profound truth — it is this sort of reef I end up on when I think about thinking.

Galton's seemingly contradictory statements about imagery — is it antithetical to abstract thinking, or integral to it? — may stem from his failure to distinguish between fundamentally different levels of imagery. Simple visual imagery such as he describes may suffice for the design of a screw, an engine, or a surgical operation, and it may be relatively easy to model these essentially reproductive forms of imagery or to simulate them by constructing video games or virtual realities of various sorts. Such powers may be invaluable, but there is something passive and mechanical and impersonal about them, which makes them utterly different from the higher and more personal powers of the imagination, where there is a continual struggle for concepts and form and meaning, a calling upon all the powers of the self. Imagination dissolves and transforms, unifies and creates, while drawing upon the "lower" powers of memory and association. It is by such imagination, such "vision," that we create or construct our individual worlds.

At this level, one can no longer say of one's mental landscapes what is visual, what is auditory, what is image, what is language, what is intellectual, what is emotional — they are all fused together and imbued with our own individual perspectives and values. Such a unified vision shines out from Hull's memoir no less than from Torey's, despite the fact that one has become "non-visual" and the other "hypervisual." What seems at first to be so decisive a difference between the two men is not, finally, a radical one, so far as personal development and sensibility go. Even though the paths they have followed might seem irreconcilable, both men have "used" blindness (if one can employ such a term for processes which are deeply mysterious and far below, or above, the level of consciousness and voluntary control) to release their own creative capacities and emotional selves, and both have achieved a rich and full realization of their own individual worlds.

SALLIE TISDALE

The Birth

FROM *Portland Magazine*

BELLE PRESSES HER HEAD against the wide bars near where I sit, between a hay bale and a stepladder. My smell is uncommon here; her questing trunk slithers toward me like a snake sliding out of a basket. The tip hangs in the air snuffling, a few feet from my lap. She fixes me with a flecked, amber eye, resting like a stone in a pool of wrinkles, blinking slowly.

There is a sign on the wall beside me, in faded yellow letters: DANGER DANGER — the word repeated, to drive the point home.

She exhales in a great whoosh at my feet, to let me know my place in things, and the hay on the floor spins away in the wind of her breath.

This is not my first time inside the elephant barn at the Oregon Zoo; when I wrote a long story about their efforts to protect and propagate the endangered Asian elephants, I got to know most of the keepers, and the elephants as well. Still, I'm a stranger here, snuck in tonight by friendly hands for a special event. The keepers, a few in coveralls and boots and most in pressed uniforms now soiled with sweat and dirt, enjoy sharing their hard, anonymous work. Mike, the veterinarian, wanders in and out, looking for something to do.

Belle is the old woman; she looks old, her hips sunk like a dowager's shoulders. She is Sunshine's grandmother; Pet is Sunshine's mother. Pet was an orphan, taken in her childhood in Thailand to be sold as a token to the Americans. Here they are made into a family, bound together. Pet is in labor; coming toward the delivery of the twenty-fifth calf to be born here after almost two years of pregnancy. In the big coal room, they stay close together, often touching, always in reach. When our voices die away for a moment, I can hear a rumbling stomach, churning carrots and hay. Belle rocks slowly against the wall, rubbing her crinkled rump with the sound of crumbling tissue, all the while flipping the end of her trunk back and forth against its own length, so that it slaps itself, whap, whap, whap. They move like hills walking, like tectonic plates shifting, oceans pulling moons. Their power is potent and occult; they never seem to hurry. Sunshine presses her broad forehead against the iron bars, which are as thick as my arms. She has two dull, short tushes, nerveless teeth almost mistaken for small tusks. Her wide, flat ear is a giant fan of skin, speckled pink, flickering, enormous gingko leaves. One ear has a little tear in its edge, like ripped paper. She is a teenager; she acts like a teenager, slipping her restive trunk out into the water trough beside the bars. She is a bit of a rascal, a rule-breaker. Her trunk climbs seemingly of its own accord through the trough and out, reaching for me. Her inquiring nostrils blossom and flicker, a foot away. Jim strolls over and leans on the wall beside her. He swats her trunk fondly, and she walks the tip up and down his arm while he massages it.

A spasm of labor rolls along Pet's side, a shifting, asymmetrical bulge. She lifts a leg, swinging a foot. The soft curve of her mountainous body is marred by the muscular contractions, the fetus rolling in its tight bed. I watch with a careful nonchalance, taking notes, trying to hide my pleasure at being allowed inside tonight, where I am not really supposed to be. I'm afraid that if I half begin to show my thrilled appreciation, it will suddenly be time to go. I want to be part of the casual, abbreviated conversations, the insider lingo, the easy motions of working men who've worked together a long time. But they are all as full of tension as I am, their jokes a mask for a barely suppressed excitement.

There's not really a good reason for us to be here. There's not much anyone can do to hurry the process along or solve any problems that might arise. Elephants are so outside the size of things, their biology still unknown in many ways, that we are rather helpless here. Pet has had several babies already, and they know what to do; they practically choreograph the event.

Sunshine steps up behind Pet and sticks her trunk inside the pendulous lips of her pink vagina. They stand still a moment, in repose, a moment of pure and intimate biology. One of the blessings of being near animals is their confidence in their own nature, their freedom from the bewildering questions of identity that plague human beings. They are incapable of being embarrassed by this event; to do so would be outside nature, and only humans try to function outside nature. Sunshine inhales Pet's scent, and with a slow and infinite grace, swings her trunk out, under, and up in a particular inverted curve — an arc known as the flehmen. She presses the quivering tip against her palate, where there are two small oval openings leading to a gland called the vomeronasal organ. I am not blessed with this organ, and neither are you. There she reads pheromones and hormones, a succinct report on the labor and the baby to come. Then she yawns, dangling her vast lower lip, and lets the pink loaf of her tongue hang out.

Elephants are earth, loam, soil; they are doughy and firm; they are "the nearest thing on earth / to a cloud," in Heathcote Williams's words. They are at ease doing what animals do, except for how we've messed everything up. Nothing can ever again be as it once was.

People are restless; elephants are restless. The air is thick with dust from the stacked bales of timothy hay, and over that is an unrepeatable perfume I know as the smell of the barn — a little urine and manure, the sweet hay, and especially the savor of the animals themselves — a ripe smell, mature and pleasant. Outside the glass wall in the viewing area are layers of people, ignored by the elephants who are long used to people there. The visitors lean on the window with a yearning I recognize, a kind of murmuring hunger for something none of us can quite name. Pet raises her tail for a moment and I can hear a collective "Aaah!" from the crowd, a moment of hope to be present at this rare birth, to have that bit of luck and enter, just like that, a totem magic.

Bang! Bang! Wood slamming on metal, a crashing door, a gigantic whoosh like a miniature storm passing. This is the father, Hugo, a tall, scary circus elephant who joined the herd a few years ago. He is temperamental, dangerous; he knows tricks. Today he is demanding to know why no one is paying him his due. Bang! And he crashes his dissatisfied head against the bars.

The three cows ignore Hugo's outburst, and instead eat mouthfuls of hay one after the other in an easy, swinging rhythm — tossing it into their huge mouths and, like old women covering themselves with shawls, lightly onto their backs to coat themselves with straw and greenish pollen.

Pet urinates in a great splash on the cement floor, as much liquid as a tub of water emptied and thundering across the floor and foaming like a tide. Then she stands stiff and still, squeezing her sides, rear legs planted and tail stiff. Belle slowly slides her trunk along one of Pet's swollen human-shaped breasts, which point toward the floor and are swollen tight, slowly leaking fluid.

The regular keepers, unable to sit around any longer, come to the bars for a visit. Charlie brings Belle a chocolate chip cookie, a tiny bite in the delicate grip of her trunk. She downs it rapidly and asks for another, and then another. Jay playfully tosses apples to them, to "the girls," and one after another is caught and disappears into big, dark mouths. Now the three elephants are leaning on the bars in a row, heads together, their three trunks rooting through the keepers' khaki uniform pockets, pushing into their dirty hands, all six ochre eyes watching. Suddenly they start rocking back and forth as though on cue, trunks swinging like the Andrew Sisters snapping their fingers in time. I lean against a wall, caught by this collision of the strange and the ordinary, the familiar and the unknown. The impossibly unknown, impossible to understand — impossible not to convince yourself that you understand.

People come and go, new faces, greetings, farewells. Someone brings sandwiches, a thermos of coffee is passed around. The keepers take turns with their regular chores, with the rest of the herd. The big hydraulic door in the back slides open, and one of the bull elephants passes by, trotting. I hear the distant plop of straw-thickened stool, and Roger and Jim enter the cage to sweep it away, very small men in a forest of gray flesh.

Pet turns around, presents her huge, ovaline rear to my view, and I can see the knuckling of the labor like a thundercloud rolling across her back. A big plug of mucus, ivory-colored, thick, hangs stickily from her vulva. She flicks her trunk at it, annoyed, until it drops to the floor. Sunshine strokes Pet's vulva a moment, then returns to the food.

*

I never tire of watching them — never. They are elegant, strapping, healthy, unafraid. Bristly black hair sticks up through the hay-snow on their backs. Their faces seem to me to be Egyptian faces, defined and sculpted into spare planes. Their almond eyes are like whale eyes, calm and deep, set into skulls full of domes and bubbles, great billowy vaults of brain and air-balanced upwellings of bone to protect big, whorled minds. Jay leans on the wall and Pet plants a sudden wet kiss on his cheek. Snort. Snuff. A series of blips, a rumble, silence. Then, outside the yard, a single, long, trumpeting cry. Belle lifts a leg and holds it there, as though she were waiting to try on shoes, or step up stairs, or have a pedicure.

The sky is turning white in the early evening, milky through the high cathedral windows. Jim, tall and thin, comes over to visit with Belle; she thrusts her trunk at him and he whacks her as though she were a freshly waxed car, and then gives her another apple.

The overhead lights come on. The zoo is about to close and I'm waiting to be thrown out, when the curator comes in. But he only says hello and asks me if I have ideas for the baby's name. He is glad, nervous.

"I don't suppose you know the Thai word for twenty-five," he asks, watching the cows. This baby will be the twenty-fifth one born here — the first in years, a rare and celebrated event.

"I hope it's a girl," he adds. The herd needs a girl — all the world's herds, all of elephants, need a girl, a fertile, healthy girl. Elephant births were, in a strange way, almost routine here for a few magical years. But it couldn't last, and now each one is profound — apocalyptic. We people, who can't contain ourselves, have hunted and harried elephants to the ground; they run before the nets like hares before the hounds. Except for people, elephants have no natural predators, but one is enough. Each calf is a beauty, a pearl, a prize.

A sudden squeal, and the keepers who have been half-dozing on chairs and hay bales look up with interest. This is how elephants sing near calves — a long squeal colliding with a squeak, a mew, then whirring, rumbling, beeping in a stew of noise. Yet the elephants appear not to have moved at all. They aren't posturing or seeming to do anything. It is simply an invisible room of sound filling every corner from several directions, bouncing around the high cement walls. It stops as suddenly as it began. In a few minutes people drop their heads again and lift their legs back up onto chairs.

The elephant has always had a place among humans, always been a source of story pregnant with meaning. The elephant has been considered an egg — from which was born the Earth — and a rain cloud, bound to the Earth. Elephants were assumed to have once had wings; are still thought to worship the moon. They were — they are — sacred beasts, rotund angels. Not little cherubs, not baby angels, but the massive and demanding angel of the Old Testament — beings full of jealousies, duty, and reluctant love.

I imagine the bars gone, the cement floor as grass, the walls as leafy trees. I imagine Belle coming at me, a stranger in her territory, blowing her authority in my face. Even here, they are barely contained. The air is filled with their unapologetic scent. A herd of elephants on the move, wrote Frank Buck, "is regarded as an elemental force that is not to be disputed. The thing to do is to get out of the way as when a storm comes."

Are they vast, emotional angels — or more like demigods, the half-holy divine offspring, not quite perfect but filled with power? Or are they a kind of elfin fold, giant pixies, like the imps and trolls of tales but stranded in a shrunken place. An elephant can pick up a dime off the floor with a slight twist of the lip. They can use doorknobs. They are flibbertigibbets, sprites as big as hills.

In fact, I have sometimes thought of them as the tragic descendants of aliens — I imagine a roaming galactic species, large and wise and full of strong feelings, trapped here by some cosmic accident a long time ago and since devolved from their technology to a simple life of peace, food, sex, and family. They are certainly humanoid, oddly enough; perhaps in the lost reaches of the past, we had an unknown common ancestor. Humans are aliens, too, after all, trapped on this difficult planet. We would be wise not to disdain what seem to be their lesser ways.

Eyes like stones in a pond, where I sit out of harm's way. Out of love's way, stung by acute envy for the men who lean casually against the walls, quick to alarm but warmed by a peculiar trust. The love between two species is not like the love within one.

Whap, whap. Belle slaps her trunk. Night has taken hold; the lingering volunteers are shooed out against their will. A security guard leans on the doorway to the main viewing room, watching the cows with the same fascination as everyone he sent away had done.

Bets beckons silently and leads me up a hidden spiral stairway beside the bars to an aerie looking down on the cage. Everything is coated with layers of cobwebs and dust, years of it, fine and sticky and musty, draped over the pipes in veils and over lights, boxes, forgotten tools, lidded white pails.

There is one yellow globe on above the cows, and all the other lights are turned off now. People are quiet, keeping to themselves, settling in for a vigil.

Bets and I, moving as quietly as we can, watch from the aerie. The cows seem smaller and more contained up here; but I can also see the complex, stealthy shifts of relation between them, their constant touching. Then Pet walks into a far corner, her back to the room, and her vulva swells outward. We can see the perineum bulging, a shiny curve. Then she relaxes again. We throw a towel over the railing's netted cobwebs and lean cautiously over.

"She knows we're up here," Bets whispers, nodding her head toward big Belle, who gazes up into the darkness for a moment. She could reach us if she tried.

Bets is silently exultant, reaching for her camcorder again and again to capture the nuances of labor, never before recorded. How Sunshine tastes Pet's mucus again and again. The way Belle so slowly leaves the hay and walks over to stroke Pet every now and then. Suddenly the cement wall on which we lean begins to vibrate and the air fills with a thudding, seismic shiver; a boom so distant and deep that it seems to come from underground. I question Bets with my eyes, and she confirms — it is only Packy, the patriarch and Sunshine's father, ramming his great skull against the wall. He is the largest Asian bull in captivity; when he complains, the whole barn dances to it.

Later, when I'm in my chair again, Mike comes to lean silently on the wall, urging Pet on. He whispers to her, simple exhortations, cheers, like a parent watching soccer. He is her doctor, after all. Belle checks his pocket and tries to grab his coffee cup; he whacks her trunk with it and she kisses his ear. All this is happening above me, where I sit; Belle turns from Mike's pockets to look down at me a moment, with royal disdain.

They move together into the far corner, tapping each other, huddled. Below Pet's flicking tail a bulge rises, and she squeals, ponderously shifting her weight this way and that; then there is only the rustle of skin on skin, a distant fan, the occasional, muffled thud of a bull banging on the wall.

Her legs are streaked with creamy, sticky mucus. This is the time; this must be the time. We hold our breath. Then she turns around, quite relaxed, and to the keepers' general disgust begins to eat hay, working her fat cheeks in and out like a bellows.

Finally, Jim climbs to the top of the bales, twenty feet above the room, and goes to sleep. Jay pulls two chairs together and curls up. Mike stretches out under a blanket on a bed of straw. I nod off in my chair and jerk awake, watching the shadowed motion of the cows through tired eyes. All at once, Sunshine folds her front legs beneath her, rolls onto her side, and falls asleep. I turn my head into my own shoulder and smell my hair, thick with scents of dust, hay, and the ineluctable perfume of elephant.

Suddenly I wake up, shaking, lost, wild. Pet is flapping her ears wildly, squeaking; she craps and pees and lapses back into silence. The big echoing barn is black, all shadow, except for the sulfurous light of their room. Am I sleeping or awake? Is this a fragment of dream, am I suspended between worlds? I seem to float in a small pool of yellow light, a bubble floating in darkness through the drift of tiny particles. Far away I see the black silhouettes of ponderous bodies swaying, bodies ten feet high.

This is when I should tell you about the birth itself. But I wasn't there; no one was there. Pet's labor stopped; she closed it down. Even when we all finally fell asleep, she held tight to this calf. I left in the middle of the night; the next morning, everyone left, left her completely alone, and then she delivered. She was attended by Belle and Sunshine, the soothing midwives. We had usurped every other moment, including conception; this one was kept apart.

The baby died. It was a boy, all wrong — eyes too flat, skull misshapen, one leg deformed, an oddly angled spine. He couldn't stand, a misbegotten product of too few genes. Mike moved him away from Pet, so she wouldn't grow too attached, and milked her melony breasts himself, squeezing out the milk by drops, by hand, and fed the calf through a tube for a day.

"It's just one of those things," he said to me, after he'd put the calf to death.

Just one of those things.

One day while resting, God fell asleep and dreamed of a fantastic creature — strong and delicate at once, powerful enough to hold up the world, graceful enough to move silently through the jungle. God woke up laughing and decided to make the elephant.

The elephant held up the world. Now the elephants, God's most amazing dream, are dying. And I fear the world, bereft, will sink of its own weight, out of sight.

MIROSLAV VOLF

God's Delight

FROM *Christian Century*

I HAVE ALWAYS BEEN fascinated by the phrase "The Lord make his face shine upon you." God's blessing, God's protection, God's peace, God's grace — all part of that same benediction — are great goods, and if I had to choose between them and God's shining face, I might well opt for them. But God's shining face outdoes them all. For God's blessing, protection, peace, and grace concern things that we possess, do, and suffer, while God's shining face concerns our very being. It stands for God's sheer delight that we exist and live before him. Yet I rarely "see" God's face shining upon me, and given that I am an inveterate sinner, it is not easy to know exactly why God's face should shine on me.

I know what I am missing. Our second son, Aaron, is a sweet little boy who loves to cuddle, to the point of hugging hardwood floors if his parents are not conveniently around. When I pick him up, he buries his head into my shoulder and holds tight around my neck. Then he suddenly lifts his head and looks me straight in the eyes, his face beaming with delight, and says, "Tata" (Croatian for "daddy"), for no other reason than that I am with him.

Aaron delights in me because he does not remember my transgressions against him and does not know in advance what will happen. But could we imagine God as a child, in blissful forgetfulness of what was and naïve ignorance of what is to come? What would happen to Aaron's shining face if, when he looked me in the eyes, he could remember a big daddy hand pulling him away from the joy of scattering plant dirt all over our oriental rugs? What if he could, somewhere in the future, catch a glimpse of daddy's mighty frustration descending upon him for no reason other than that he happened to be there? Unlike Aaron, God knows past, present, and future, and his gaze penetrates below surfaces to the dark chambers of our deceitful hearts. We are all sinners. How then can God delight in us?

Am I forgetting that God is love? No, I am not. God loves all prodigal daughters and sons, notwithstanding their ever present sin against God and neighbors. But is this love that delights? It is the kind of love committed to the well-being of the beloved, love that suffers pain at the beloved's journey into the far country, love that wants the beloved to return as a true lover. Would it not be wrong for God to delight even in the wrongdoer? Is not distance between us and God — even terror of God — appropriate as long as we remain prodigals? Is this not what the prophet Isaiah felt when he exclaimed, "Woe is me! I am lost, for I am a man of unclean lips . . . yet my eyes have seen the King, the Lord of hosts!"?

Why is it that we think that God should delight in us when we act — and in an important sense also are — contrary to God as the source of all goodness, truth, and beauty? Is not longing for God's shining face just an echo of the infantile desire to be affirmed no matter what — a desire so pervasive in our culture that we cannot imagine how anyone could disapprove of something we do and still love us? Should we not rather live content with God's frowning face, knowing well that God's condemnation of sin is a form God's love must take if the sinner is to be redeemed? Should we not grow up, face the truth about ourselves, learn to live with God's disapproval, and find comfort in God's love out of which this disapproval is born? God's shining face would then be a promise for the world to come, where God would have nothing to disapprove of and one would rest in God's eternal delight.

But that can be only partly right. The priestly benediction is given for the here and now, not for the then and there. It speaks of a God who can make God's face shine on people in the midst of the darkness of their sin. But how can that be? How can God's face shine on a sinful creature? Miracle of miracles, it turns out that God is not completely unlike my son in the moment when his face shines upon mine. What does the forgiving God do with our sins? Here is what the scripture says: God covers them, God disperses them like mist, God puts them behind his back, God hides them,

God forgets them. As Søren Kierkegaard puts it: "The one who loves forgives in this way: he forgives, he forgets, he blots out the sin, in love he turns toward the one he forgives; but when he turns toward him, he of course cannot see what is lying behind his back."

Difficulties abound. Is it possible for the all-knowing God not to see certain things? How can God both see so as to condemn sin, and not see so as to delight in the forgiven one? Can God switch off realms of knowledge at will? These are tough philosophical and theological questions with no easy answers. This is no place to enter the debate, but I can make one general suggestion. If you have a notion of God that precludes the shining of God's face on a sinner, you should give up that notion of God in favor of God's shining face. Provided, of course, that you want to worship the God of Abraham.

A blessing for those who agree and disagree with me about God's forgetting: "The Lord make his face shine upon you, and be gracious to you; the Lord lift up his countenance upon you, and give you peace."

C. K. WILLIAMS

Doves

FROM *The New Yorker*

So much crap in my head,
so many rubbishy facts,
so many half-baked
theories and opinions,
so many public figures
I care nothing about
but who stick like pitch;
so much political swill.

So much crap, yet
so much I don't know
and would dearly like to:
I recognize nearly none
of the birdsongs of dawn —
all I'm sure of is
the maddeningly vapid *who,*
who-who of the doves.

And I don't know half
the names of flowers
and trees, and still less
of humankind's myths,
the benevolent ones,
from the days before ours;
water-plashed wastes,
radiant intercessions.

So few poems entire,
such a meager handful
of precise recollections of paintings:
detritus instead, junk,
numbers I should long ago
have erased, inane
"information" I'll doubtlessly
take with me to the grave.

So much crap, and yet,
now, morning, that first
sapphire dome of glow,
the glow! The first sounds
of being awake, *the sounds!* —
a wind whispering, but even
trucks clanking past,
even the idiot doves.

And within me, along
with the garbage, faces, faces
and voices, so many
lives woven into mine,
such improbable quantities
of memory; so much already
forgotten, lost, pruned away —
yet the doves, the doves!

PAUL J. WILLIS

Spokane: A Triptych

FROM *Image*

I Should Have Talked

IN HIS BOOK *Desert Solitaire,* Edward Abbey refers offhandedly to American evangelicalism as a form of mental illness. I am hoping he is wrong. And it seems to me that Abbey himself, in his many barbs directed at his childhood faith, cannot quite turn his eyes away from it. In this, I think, he is like Mark Twain — both of them Christ-haunted in twisted and peculiar ways. If there is a mental illness of faith, there may also be a mental illness of lost faith.

But Abbey's comment invites agreement, even from evangelicals. At the very least, evangelicalism seems to encourage strange forms of delusional, masochistic behavior. This literally came home to me some years ago, during the time my wife and I were still in school, when a sadly afflicted man spent the night with us in Spokane. Sharon and I picked him up on a grimy winter afternoon at the bus station. He had come from Pullman, eighty miles south. His wife, Jill, an acquaintance of Sharon's, had asked if Jerry could stay overnight before flying out to Toronto. I had met Jerry the month before, just before we had moved north to Spokane. He had been witnessing door-to-door with booklets from the Seventh-day Adventist Church, and had knocked on our door as well. One look at his weak eyes and childlike face and I knew he was a little off. Sharon told me she didn't know all the details, but Jill had told her that Jerry was now mentally ill and hadn't held a job for the last two years. They lived on unemployment.

Jerry stepped off the bus carrying a bulging suitcase with broken clasps; it was held together with knotted twine. He spoke softly, ending almost every sentence with *you know.* "I appreciate this, you know." We drove to our apartment, where he sat on the couch and said little. "That's what I do most, you know," he said during dinner. "Just sit on the couch. Don't seem to have the energy." While helping me wash the dishes, he confided that he planned to enter the ministry. It was hard to know how to reply.

When we finished the dishes, he said, "I'd like to join you in your family worship later this evening, you know."

"Well," I replied, "we were just planning to study tonight, actually."

"We have family worship every night," he said. "We sing some familiar choruses and the kids say their memory verses, you know. Jamie, he can usually say his, but Jay can usually only recognize his verse. Jay's just two, you know. You and Sharon could just pick out some familiar choruses for later on this evening, you know."

As I think about it now, I realize how little it would have cost us to read some scripture and sing some songs with Jerry that night. I'd like to think that today I would have done so. But on that night, out of pure stubbornness, I suppose, not to mention several poems I had to read for my seminar in the pastoral, I ignored his request. At some level, I felt a kind of creeping revulsion. The idea of family worship felt tainted by his mental illness.

When Jerry saw that Sharon and I were intent on our schoolwork, he left to go witnessing in the neighborhood. I cringed as the door closed behind him. What had we unleashed on our block? Earlier in the evening he had told me about a man on the bus with whom he had shared the gospel. "I offered him the booklet and he took it," he said with a hopeful look.

Over Christmas Jerry had been in the hospital for tests. He had spent several hours lying in a room with a tube all the way down his throat. Next to him had been a man about to go into surgery. A month later Jerry heard fourth-hand about a man who had died at the hospital. Jerry was sure it was the man he had lain next to for those few hours.

"I should have talked to him," he said. "I've learned my lesson now — I should have talked to him."

"How could you have talked to him with a tube down your throat?" I asked.

"I should have talked to him," Jerry said.

When Jerry got back from witnessing, he returned a call from his wife. "I love you, honey," he said, and then laughed a three-beat, quiet, crazy, embarrassed laugh: "Hee-hee-hee." A minute later he said, "I love you, honey. Hee-hee-hee." He said it exactly the same way.

Then Jerry went out to run for exercise. He wore his winter coat, checked slacks, and leather street shoes. He wouldn't borrow my tennis shoes and sweat pants. Soon enough he came back and took a shower and padded around in his pajamas. Just before going to bed, he settled down for a little while and read a book called *The Christian Father*. The next day he would fly to Canada to stay with his parents for a month. I hoped that when I drove him to the airport in the morning we could have some kind of friendly talk. I think I felt ashamed of myself for not warming up to him.

In the morning, however, the streets were thick with fresh snow. Getting Jerry to the airport was suddenly going to be a challenge. As best I could I put on our ancient chains. We drove through fishtailing traffic on the interstate, my arms rigid, and a loose set of links on the left rear tire mercilessly flogged the fender. The whole way there, I didn't say a word.

Just this morning, twenty years later, I happened to have break-fast with a couple who have taken care of five mentally handi-capped adults in their home for the last fifteen years. What man-ner of love is this? I thought. Other friends have done this kind of thing as well — even an English professor friend — and my wife has worked off and on in group homes for the retarded. And of course there is the famous example of Henri Nouwen, the Catholic theologian who devoted the last years of his life to serving the men-tally disabled. Perhaps it is true that evangelicalism in its more ex-treme forms offers a ready means of expression for the unhinged among us. But perhaps it is more true that the mentally ill offer to us the plainest picture of ourselves, our deepest longing for a love we hope both to know and to share. If so, I hope I get another try.

And You Visited Me

When I showed up for my two o'clock tutorial with Dr. Jordan, I found he was gone. A note on the door said he was ill. So I went across the street to the university library to ask his wife, a librarian, how he was doing. Not well, she said, and gave me the name of a hospital near Spokane, eighty or ninety miles away. I knew he was not a healthy man, but she wasn't very clear about the details of his illness. Would he like a visitor? Since I lived in Spokane, it would not be difficult for me to see him. His wife said a visit might be just the thing. But she didn't look me in the eye.

So three days later, after I had returned home from my weekly stint of tutorials and seminars, I drove out to the named hospital. It rested on the north shore of a quiet lake among ponderosas, spreading lawns, and mossy granite outcroppings. I parked the car and walked past a brown-brick wing behind a row of cedar trees. At the visitor registration desk, I gave my name and asked to see Rath Jordan.

The receptionist looked through her papers and said, "I'm sorry, but there is no Rath Jordan here."

I asked her to check again.

"No, sorry. No one by that name."

"There must be some mistake," I said.

"No mistake," she said less pleasantly.

But I didn't leave, and eventually she left her desk and disappeared into another room behind her.

When I had proposed a tutorial in the short story in January, Dr. Jordan had responded to me with a similarly abrupt *no*. He was too busy trying to complete a freshman introduction to literature text for Random House, which, he informed me, two other professors in the department had dropped in his lap because they were too damn lazy to keep up their end of the work. "In two years, neither of them ever wrote a single word." He said *a single word* with slowed, staccato emphasis.

Furthermore, he was too ill to do a study with me. His pancreas and adrenal glands did not function properly, and as a result his body chemistry was precarious. Periodically he would lose all "higher cognitive function." As it was, his mind did not work properly until noon. So there would be no tutorial. That was clear.

Could he recommend other professors, key readings? He went down the list of names carefully: "Too limited in his reading; no real penetration of thought; more of a writer than a critic." No, he couldn't fully recommend anyone. Then he pulled out one book, another, and another, warmed to his most favorite of subjects, waxed eloquent, gained in his face a glow of passion. I excused myself to turn in a paper and then returned. He looked up like a boy who has just decided to play hooky.

"Let's do it," he said.

And so we met for an hour and a half, every Tuesday afternoon. By March we had read Chekhov, Crane, Verga, Fitzgerald. Chekhov was his love.

"'The Lady with the Pet Dog,'" he liked to say, "was Chekhov's way of telling Tolstoy how life really worked. You can't impose a smug moral order the way Tolstoy does in *Anna Karenina.*"

"Yes," I liked to reply, "but what if Chekhov has subtracted something that Tolstoy did not impose, but merely recognized as inherent?"

After a long wait, the receptionist returned from the back room with surprising evidence of the existence of Rath Jordan. She gave me directions to his ward, where I met him in an old, dirty hallway. He was fully clothed, thin, and pale, and shook my hand warmly. Odd-looking people sauntered about, also dressed in street clothes. They wore strange gazes and expressions. It very belatedly dawned on me what kind of hospital this was. Dr. Jordan ushered me into a dusty lounge, and we sat down on some grimy rubber furniture in playschool blues and greens and yellows. An AM radio blared, and several men played billiards on a battered table.

"Sorry I missed my appointment on Tuesday," he said, "but my body chemistry went completely topsy-turvy. When that happens, I become unavoidably suicidal."

I started inside, but tried not to show it.

"I've just been released from seventy-two hours of intensive observation — along with some pretty hardcore people. I talked to a guy this morning who wired a shotgun under a store manager's throat. He connected the trigger to his own hand with an electrical cord. When the police gunned him down, he automatically set off the shotgun."

I wondered why he was telling me this. Was it to show that he himself was not so deranged as that — or to show that we all were?

"We line up for medication here," he said. "Just like in the *Cuckoo's Nest.* I feel like I'm in that movie sometimes."

I had brought a volume of Fitzgerald, just in case he wanted to talk literature. He did — very badly. We arranged for a small, dingy coffee room to ourselves. It had one tall, narrow window of many small panes; I wondered if the lattice work was an iron grill. We managed a discussion about one Fitzgerald story, "The Diamond as Big as the Ritz," and then he wandered onto the turf of other writers. Clearly, he enjoyed talking. Every once in a while I would interject an observation apropos of the subject he had happened upon. He would stop and say, "Yes, I hadn't thought of that. Very good!" I suppose that this return to the role of caretaker felt reassuring to him. The spell was broken only once, by an attendant with a paper cup of water and a pair of pills. He took them obediently.

Soon afterward our time ended. He put his hand to his head and said, "You'd better leave. I'm getting tired. I can handle being intellectually tired — that's one thing. Or being physically tired — that's almost pleasant. It's being emotionally wiped out that gets me."

He asked if I could come back every other day — he'd have to be here two weeks. "We'd get a lot done that way," he said. Then he apologized for not having reviewed the stories. He wasn't allowed any books.

"I'll let you borrow this one," I offered.

"Okay," he said. "I think I can keep it locked up safe."

Before I left he took me by the arm and said how good it was that I had come. He held my gaze, and his eyes were weak and watery. "If anyone asks about me," he said less certainly, "tell them I'm getting much better and hope to be back soon."

Amo, Amas, Amat

In those student years that we lived in Spokane, Sharon and I eventually moved to a blond-brick apartment house just west of downtown. Just across the hall from us lived an elderly couple from Plentywood, Montana. Henry Raaen was a Norwegian bachelor farmer until the age of forty-nine, when he married Minnie, a schoolteacher. She had played the organ at the Lutheran church where he had sung in the choir. They celebrated their fiftieth anniversary the summer after we met them. Then Mr. Raaen turned one hundred, and Mrs. Raaen a spry eighty-seven.

One evening they invited us over for dessert, and by request I brought along my textbook for the Latin I was starting to learn.

Mrs. Raaen had been a passionate teacher of Latin, and she often complained, or gloated rather, that young people these days were no longer interested in the Latin tongue. When I handed her my text, she found a line in the preface that she read to us with sad glee: "It is notorious that every year increasing numbers of students enter college without Latin."

She turned the pages slowly, looking up to tell us about a former teacher of her acquaintance who could not speak of the death of Julius Caesar without breaking into tears. "Sometimes," said Mrs. Raaen, "I lie awake at night reviewing my conjugations."

Then she got to the first set of verbs in the book. "Oh, yes," she said approvingly. Then, "Henry, do you remember the first conjugation?"

Up to this point, Henry had held a rigid silence. Part-blind, part-deaf, chock-full of arthritis, he sat erect in a red sweater and tie. Even the tops of his ears held deep, pale wrinkles. I wondered how his hundred-year-old mind worked.

He answered his wife like a cannon shot: *"Amo-amas-amat-amamus-amatis-amant!"*

Mrs. Raaen paged through the text for another five minutes, fondly absorbed. "Yes," she said, "I recognize most of the words on every page. But it would be too hard to get it all back. Too hard now to get it all back." Her face and voice were sadly resigned.

"May I make a motion," croaked Mr. Raaen, "that we put the Latin aside and proceed with dessert?"

Mrs. Raaen agreed, but then she happened upon the vocabulary index in the back and the keyed exercises that go with every lesson. Dessert did not come for some time.

A few weeks later we invited the Raaens to our apartment to listen to *A Prairie Home Companion* on the radio. We thought they would be the perfect audience. For two hours they sat with us politely in our living room, the volume turned up very high, while Garrison Keillor said droll things about Lutherans and Norwegian bachelor farmers. Mr. and Mrs. Raaen gave the program their complete and stolid attention. They never laughed. They never smiled. When Garrison Keillor at last said, "Good night, everybody. Good night, now," Henry and Minnie rose to their feet with a kind of puzzled dignity and thanked us for having them. Then they left. *Exeunt ambo.*

We later moved just upstairs from them, and from time to time we would hear a crash from below, indicating that Mr. Raaen had fallen off the toilet or out of bed. I would hurry downstairs and restore Mr. Raaen to something like tranquility, and life would go on. Occasionally an ambulance would come to the door, an occasion that Mrs. Raaen always met with sureness and solemnity. She would follow the stretcher out the door with head held high, arm in arm with the paramedic. This was it, she was thinking. After all these years, the final act, and she would march out like royalty. The fact that she got to repeat this performance several times in no way lessened the effect. She only improved with practice.

A few weeks before Mr. Raaen turned one hundred and three, just before Christmas, Sharon gave birth to our first child, a baby boy. Soon after we had brought him home, we took Jonathan down to the Raaens's apartment and into their bedroom, where Mr. Raaen lay cadaverously beneath the covers. With some effort he propped himself up and stretched out a hand of blessing upon the head of our little son. I have forgotten to say that Mr. Raaen was a giant man, well over six feet in length, with huge, horny, spreading hands. Could Simeon in the Temple, when he met with the holy infant, have looked or acted any other way?

Then Mr. Raaen held out a five-dollar bill that he had hidden in the blankets. "From the oldest man in the building to the youngest!" he shouted.

That next year, of course, he died.

> *Nunc dimittis servum tuum Domine,*
> *Secundum verbum tuum in pace.*
>
> Lord, now let your servant depart,
> According to your word, in peace.

The Visiting

FROM *The New Yorker*

I suffer from insomnia, from loneliness I sleep;
in the midst of the talk and the laughter
all at once you are there —

Hour of waking up and writhing
with humiliation, or
of wishes answered before

one was aware of what they were.
And let me ask you this: the dead,
where *aren't* they?

Hour when the ones who can't rest
go to bed, and the ones
who can't wake go to work —

Dark blue morning glory
I reach to touch, there is another world
and it is this world.

Then the light streamed in yellow
and blue through long windows, and blood
turned to wine in my veins.

Tears of wine
rode down my cheek.
It's happening, I thought,

though it had never happened
before. I squeezed
my eyes closed, gazing into

a darkness all of light. The more
you tried to hold it back, the more
sweetly and irresistibly it arrived.

Contributors

Rick Bass is the author of twenty books of fiction and nonfiction, most recently *Caribou Rising,* and the forthcoming novel *The Diezmo* (Houghton Mifflin). He lives in northwest Montana's Yaak Valley, where he is active with a number of local and regional environmental organizations working to protect the last roadless areas in the Kootenai National Forest.

Dan Bellm is the author of two books of poetry, *One Hand on the Wheel* and *Buried Treasure,* winner of the annual Poetry Center Prize from Cleveland University Press. He is at work on a third collection, a poem sequence related to the Jewish practice of studying weekly portions of the Torah in an annual cycle. He lives in San Francisco.

Scott Cairns is the author of several collections of poems, including *Philokalia, Recovered Body, Figures for the Ghost,* and others. He is at work on a new collection entitled *Slow Pilgrim.*

Robin Cody is the author of *Ricochet River* and *Voyage of a Summer Sun,* winner of the Oregon Book Award for literary nonfiction. He taught English at The American School in Paris and was dean of admissions at Reed College. He drives a special ed school bus in Portland, Oregon.

Robert Coles is the James Agee Professor of social ethics at Harvard University. He is the author of *The Children of Crisis* series (in five volumes) and of biographies of Erik H. Erickson, Dorothy Day, and Walker Percy. He is also a professor of psychiatry and medical humanities at Harvard Medical School. He was trained in child psychology and psychoanalysis.

Robert Cording is professor of English at Holy Cross College and the author of four collections of poems: *Against Consolation, Heavy Grace, What*

Binds Us to This World, and *Life-list,* which won the Ohio State University Press/Journal award. He has received fellowships from the National Endowment of the Arts, twice from the Connecticut Commission of the Arts, and from Bread Loaf. He lives in Woodstock, Connecticut, with his wife and three children.

Lindsey Crittenden is the author of an award-winning volume of short stories, *The View from Below.* Her essays and short fiction have appeared in several national and regional magazines. She has recently completed a novel and is at work on a memoir about prayer. She teaches writing in San Francisco and Berkeley.

Mark Doty is the author of several books of poetry, most recently *Source,* and two memoirs, *Heaven's Coast* and *Firebird.* A Guggenheim, Ingram-Merrill, and White Fellow, he has also received the National Book Critics Circle Award and the PEN/Martha Albrand Prize for nonfiction. He teaches at the University of Houston and divides his time between Houston, Texas, and Provincetown, Massachusetts.

David James Duncan is a father, flyfisher, practitioner of what he calls "direct, small-scale compassion/activism," and the author of *The River Why, The Brothers K,* and *My Story As Told by Water.* His work has won a Lannan Fellowship, the 2001 Western States Book Award, a National Book Award nomination, and — with Wendell Berry, for their book *Citizen's Dissent* — the American Library Association's 2003 Eli Oboler Award for the Preservation of Intellectual Freedom.

Joseph Epstein is the author of sixteen books. He is currently working on a study of friendship and on an intellectual portrait of Alexis de Tocqueville.

James Fredericks is a priest of the Archdiocese of San Francisco and a member of the Department of Theological Studies of Loyola Marymount University. He is the author of *Faith Among Faiths: Christian Theology and the Non-Christian Religions* and *Buddhists and Christians: Through Comparative Theology to a New Solidarity.*

Peter Friederici is the author of *The Suburban Wild* and other books. He lives in Flagstaff, Arizona, where he writes about nature and the environment and edits a public radio show called *Earth Notes.* He is at work on books about the Sonoran Desert and ecological restoration.

David Gelernter is a contributing editor at the *Weekly Standard,* a board member of the National Endowment for the Arts, and a professor of computer science at Yale University. He studied religion and the Bible at Yale and the Talmud at R. Shlomo Riskin's Lincoln Square Yeshiva. He has written about the Bible and Judaic philosophy for *Orim, Conservative Judaism, Sh'ma, Commentary,* and elsewhere.

Natalie Goldberg is the author, most recently, of *The Great Failure: A Bartender, a Monk, and My Unlikely Path to Truth.* She has written nine other books, including *Writing Down the Bones, Wild Mind, Thunder and Lightning,* and *Top of My Lungs.* She teaches writing workshops and retreats as well as zen practice at the Mabel Dodge Luhan House in Taos, New Mexico.

Allen Hoey has published two full-length collections of poems, *A Fire in the Cold House of Being* and *What Persists,* and has placed essays and poems in many journals. He currently teaches composition, literature, and Buddhism at Bucks County Community College, outside Philadelphia.

Andrew Hudgins has published numerous books of poetry, including *Ecstatic in the Poison, Babylon in a Jar, The Glass Hammer, The Never-Ending, After the Lost War,* and *Saints and Strangers.* He is also the author of a collection of literary essays, *The Grass Anvil.* He has received the Poets Prize and has been a finalist for the Pulitzer Prize and the National Book Award.

Pico Iyer is the author of many books on the romance between cultures, including *Video Night in Kathmandu, The Lady and the Monk, The Global Soul,* and a Sufi romance, *Abandon.* His most recent book, *Sun After Dark,* is about the pursuit of conscience and clarity in some of the poorest countries of the world.

Philip Levine's many books include *Breath; So Ask: Essays, Conversations, and Interviews; The Bread of Time: Toward an Autobiography; The Mercy; The Simple Truth* (Pulitzer Prize for poetry, 1995); and *What Work Is* (National Book Award for poetry, 1991).

B. K. Loren is the author of *The Way of the River* as well as numerous works of fiction and nonfiction that have appeared in periodicals including *Parabola, Orion,* and *Utne.* She has been the recipient of several national writing fellowships and awards, including the Roberts-Rhinehart National Fellowship.

Thomas Lynch is the author of *The Undertaking: Life Studies from the Dismal Trade,* which was a finalist for the National Book Award, and *Bodies in Motion and at Rest.* He lives in Milford, Michigan, where for the past thirty years he has been a funeral director.

Bill McKibben is a freelance journalist, essayist, and the author of several books. His groundbreaking *The End of Nature* has been published in sixteen languages. McKibben lives in upstate New York, where he is a lay leader and Sunday school teacher. His most recent book, *Enough*, is about the moral ramifications of biological engineering.

W. S. Merwin's books include *The Pupil, The River Sound,* and *The Folding Cliffs.* He was awarded the Pulitzer Prize for poetry in 1971.

Jack Miles is the author of several books, including *Christ: A Crisis in the Life of God* and *God: A Biography,* which won the Pulitzer Prize for biography in 1996. His writings have appeared in numerous anthologies and national publications, including the *Atlantic Monthly,* the *New York Times,* the *Boston Globe,* the *Washington Post,* and the *Los Angeles Times,* where he served for ten years as literary editor and as a member of the newspaper's editorial board. He is currently a MacArthur Fellow.

Patricia Monaghan is the author of several books of nonfiction, including *The Red-Haired Girl from the Bog: The Landscape of Celtic Myth and Spirit,* as well as three books of poetry, most recently the physics-inspired *Dancing with Chaos.* She teaches science and literature at DePaul University.

Seyyed Hossein Nasr is the author of over fifty books, including *The Heart of Islam, Man and Nature, Religion and the Order of Nature,* and *Knowledge and the Sacred.* He is University Professor of Islamic Studies at George Washington University.

Kathleen Norris's books include *The Virgin of Bennington, Amazing Grace, The Cloister Walk,* and *Dakota.*

Maura O'Halloran is the author of *Pure Heart, Enlightened Mind.* In 1982, she received dharma transmission at the Kannonji Temple in Japan. She died in a bus accident in Thailand six months later.

Noelle Oxenhandler's most recent book is *The Eros of Parenthood.* Her essays have appeared in many national and literary magazines, including *The New Yorker, The New York Times Magazine, Vogue, Tricycle,* and *Parabola.* She lives in northern California with her daughter.

R. R. Reno's recent publications include *Redemptive Change: Atonement and the Christian Cure of the Soul* and *In the Ruins of the Church: Sustaining Faith in an Age of Diminished Christianity.* He is the general editor for a new series of theological commentaries on the Bible, *Theological Exegesis of the Bible,* and teaches theology at Creighton University in Omaha, Nebraska.

Sarah Ruden is an investigative journalist, translator, writer, and editor for local businesses and charities in South Africa. Her latest book is a translation of an ancient Greek comedy by Aristophanes, *Lysistrata.*

Oliver Sacks is the author of numerous books, including *Oaxaca Journal, Uncle Tungsten, An Anthropologist on Mars, The Island of the Colorblind,* and *The Man Who Mistook His Wife for a Hat.*

Sallie Tisdale's most recent book is *The Best Thing I Ever Tasted: The Secret of Food,* a finalist for the James Beard award. She is currently working on a book about the lives of female Zen ancestors from India, China, and Japan. She works part-time as a nurse on a cancer ward and is a lay teacher at Dharma Rain Zen Center in Portland, Oregon.

Miroslav Volf's books include *Exclusion and Embrace* and *After Our Likeness.* He is the director of the Yale Center for Faith and Culture and Henry B. Wright Professor of Theology at Yale University Divinity School.

C. K. Williams is the author of many books, including *The Singing, Repair* (Pulitzer Prize for poetry), and the memoir *Misgivings: My Mother, My Father, Myself.*

Paul J. Willis is a professor of English at Westmont College in Santa Barbara, California. His essays have appeared in *Books & Culture, River Teeth,* and elsewhere. His most recent chapbook of poetry is *The Deep and Secret Color of Ice.*

Franz Wright was awarded the 2004 Pulitzer Prize for Poetry for his collection *Walking to Martha's Vineyard.* Previous collections include *The Beforelife* and *Ill Lit: Selected and New Poems.*

Philip Zaleski is the editor of the *Best American Spiritual Writing* series. His other books include two with his wife, Carol Zaleski: *The Book of Heaven* and the forthcoming *The Language of Paradise* (Houghton Mifflin). His writings have appeared in many national publications, including the *New York Times,* the *Boston Globe,* and the *Los Angeles Times.* He is a senior editor at *Parabola* and a research associate at Smith College.

Notable Spiritual Writing of 2003

Selected by Philip Zaleski

Christopher Bamford
  "Badilaya," *Parabola,* Spring
Stephen M. Barr
  "Retelling the Story of Science," *First Things,* March
Rick Bass
  "Landscape and Imagination," *The Kenyon Review,* Summer
Ben Birnbaum
  "Morning Watch, *Image,* Spring
Joseph Bruchac
  "The Hawk in the Prison," *Parabola,* Summer

Robert Cording
  "Lord God Bird," *Orion,* January/February

Andre Dubus
  "Pity People," *Portland Magazine,* Summer

Paul Kane
  "Inner Landscapes as Sacred Landscapes," *The Kenyon Review,* Summer/Fall

Richard Lehnert
  "Essay on Compassion," *The Sun,* July

Rodger Martin
  "Prayer, Christmas Eve, for Recovery of My Dog," *Christianity and Literature,*
  Summer
Dan Masterson
  "Tunnel of Cloistered Refuge," *The Georgia Review,* Spring
Gilbert Meilander
  "Why Remember?" *First Things,* August/September

STANLEY MOSS
"To My Friend Born Blind," *The New Yorker,* February 3

JOHN O'GRADY
"Darkness Notable," *Quest,* September/October

DAVIDE RONDONI
"Good Friday," *Image,* Fall
VINCENT ROSSI
"Uncreated Peace," *Sophia,* Summer

LUCI SHAW
"Negligible," *Christian Century,* August 9
LEWIS B. SMEDES
"What's God Up To?" *Christian Century,* May 3

WENDY WRIGHT
"Little Things," *Weavings,* January/February

PHILIP YANCEY
"Holy Sex," *Christianity Today,* October

THE B·E·S·T AMERICAN SERIES®

THE BEST AMERICAN SHORT STORIES® 2004

Lorrie Moore, guest editor, Katrina Kenison, series editor. "Story for story, readers can't beat *The Best American Short Stories* series" (*Chicago Tribune*). This year's most beloved short fiction anthology is edited by the critically acclaimed author Lorrie Moore and includes stories by Annie Proulx, Sherman Alexie, Paula Fox, Thomas McGuane, and Alice Munro, among others.

0-618-19735-4 PA $14.00 / 0-618-19734-6 CL $27.50
0-618-30046-5 CASS $26.00 / 0-618-29965-3 CD $30.00

THE BEST AMERICAN ESSAYS® 2004

Louis Menand, guest editor, Robert Atwan, series editor. Since 1986, *The Best American Essays* series has gathered the best nonfiction writing of the year and established itself as the best anthology of its kind. Edited by Louis Menand, author of *The Metaphysical Club* and staff writer for *The New Yorker,* this year's volume features writing by Kathryn Chetkovich, Jonathan Franzen, Kyoko Mori, Cynthia Zarin, and others.

0-618-35709-2 PA $14.00 / 0-618-35706-8 CL $27.50

THE BEST AMERICAN MYSTERY STORIES™ 2004

Nelson DeMille, guest editor, Otto Penzler, series editor. This perennially popular anthology is a favorite of mystery buffs and general readers alike. This year's volume is edited by the best-selling suspense author Nelson DeMille and offers pieces by Stephen King, Joyce Carol Oates, Jonathon King, Jeff Abbott, Scott Wolven, and others.

0-618-32967-6 PA $14.00 / 0-618-32968-4 CL $27.50 / 0-618-49742-0 CD $30.00

THE BEST AMERICAN SPORTS WRITING™ 2004

Richard Ben Cramer, guest editor, Glenn Stout, series editor. This series has garnered wide acclaim for its stellar sports writing and topnotch editors. Now Richard Ben Cramer, the Pulitzer Prize–winning journalist and author of the best-selling *Joe DiMaggio*, continues that tradition with pieces by Ira Berkow, Susan Orlean, William Nack, Charles P. Pierce, Rick Telander, and others.

0-618-25139-1 PA $14.00 / 0-618-25134-0 CL $27.50

THE BEST AMERICAN TRAVEL WRITING 2004

Pico Iyer, guest editor, Jason Wilson, series editor. *The Best American Travel Writing 2004* is edited by Pico Iyer, the author of *Video Night in Kathmandu* and *Sun After*

THE B·E·S·T AMERICAN SERIES®

Dark. Giving new life to armchair travel this year are Roger Angell, Joan Didion, John McPhee, Adam Gopnik, and many others.

0-618-34126-9 PA $14.00 / 0-618-34125-0 CL $27.50

THE BEST AMERICAN SCIENCE AND NATURE WRITING 2004

Steven Pinker, guest editor, Tim Folger, series editor. This year's edition promises to be another "eclectic, provocative collection" (*Entertainment Weekly*). Edited by Steven Pinker, author of *The Blank Slate* and *The Language Instinct,* it features work by Gregg Easterbrook, Atul Gawande, Peggy Orenstein, Jonathan Rauch, Chet Raymo, Nicholas Wade, and others.

0-618-24698-3 PA $14.00 / 0-618-24697-5 CL $27.50

THE BEST AMERICAN RECIPES 2004–2005

Edited by Fran McCullough and Molly Stevens. "Give this book to any cook who is looking for the newest, latest recipes and the stories behind them" (*Chicago Tribune*). Offering the very best of what America is cooking, as well as the latest trends, timesaving tips, and techniques, this year's edition includes a foreword by the renowned chef Bobby Flay.

0-618-45506-X CL $26.00

THE BEST AMERICAN NONREQUIRED READING 2004

Edited by Dave Eggers, Introduction by Viggo Mortensen. Edited by the best-selling author Dave Eggers, this genre-busting volume draws the finest, most interesting, and least expected fiction, nonfiction, humor, alternative comics, and more from publications large, small, and on-line. This year's collection features writing by David Sedaris, Daniel Alarcón, David Mamet, Thom Jones, and others.

0-618-34123-4 PA $14.00 / 0-618-34122-6 CL $27.50 / 0-618-49743-9 CD $26.00

THE BEST AMERICAN SPIRITUAL WRITING 2004

Edited by Philip Zaleski, Introduction by Jack Miles. The latest addition to the acclaimed Best American series, *The Best American Spiritual Writing 2004* brings the year's finest writing about faith and spirituality to all readers. With an introduction by the best-selling author Jack Miles, this year's volume represents a wide range of perspectives and features pieces by Robert Coles, Bill McKibben, Oliver Sacks, Pico Iyer, and many others.

0-618-44303-7 PA $14.00 / 0-618-44302-9 CL $27.50

HOUGHTON MIFFLIN COMPANY www.houghtonmifflinbooks.com